DRUG WARS

While the shockingly high prices of prescription drugs continue to dominate the news, the strategies used by pharmaceutical companies to prevent generic competition are poorly understood, even by the lawmakers responsible for regulating them. In this groundbreaking work, Robin Feldman and Evan Frondorf illuminate the inner workings of the pharmaceutical market and show how drug companies twist health policy to achieve goals contrary to the public interest. In highly engaging prose, they offer specific examples of how generic competition has been stifled for years, with costs climbing into the billions and everyday consumers paying the price. *Drug Wars* is a guide to the current landscape, a road map for reform, and a warning of what's to come. It should be read by policy makers, academics, patients, and anyone else concerned with the soaring costs of prescription drugs.

Robin Feldman is an award-winning teacher and scholar who has published more than forty articles and books. Feldman has been cited by the White House, members of Congress, and numerous federal agencies, and she has testified before committees of the U.S. House and Senate, as well as the California legislature. In 2016, Feldman was named one of the Women Leaders in Law & Technology, the only academic to receive the honor.

Evan Frondorf's legal work with Professor Feldman has been published in journals at Harvard and Stanford, including papers on patent demands and generic pharmaceuticals. He studied economics at Yale and graduated Phi Beta Kappa and magna cum laude, and he was named a Rhodes Scholar finalist in 2015. He is also the current sportswriter for the *Yale Alumni Magazine*. At Yale, he was heavily involved in sports broadcasting and served as a deputy sports editor at the *Yale Daily News*.

Drug Wars

HOW BIG PHARMA RAISES PRICES AND KEEPS GENERICS OFF THE MARKET

ROBIN FELDMAN

University of California Hastings College of the Law

EVAN FRONDORF

University of California Hastings College of the Law

CAMBRIDGE
UNIVERSITY PRESS

CAMBRIDGE
UNIVERSITY PRESS

One Liberty Plaza, 20th Floor, New York, NY 10006, USA

Cambridge University Press is part of the University of Cambridge.

It furthers the University's mission by disseminating knowledge in the pursuit of education, learning, and research at the highest international levels of excellence.

www.cambridge.org
Information on this title: www.cambridge.org/9781107168480
DOI: 10.1017/9781316717424

First published 2017

Printed in the United States of America by Sheridan Books, Inc.

A *catalogue record for this publication is available from the British Library.*

Library of Congress Cataloging-in-Publication Data
Names: Feldman, Robin, author. | Frondorf, Evan, author.
Title: Drug wars: how big pharma raises prices and keeps generics off the market / Robin Feldman, Evan Frondorf.
Description: New York, NY: Cambridge University Press, 2017. | Includes bibliographical references and index.
Identifiers: LCCN 2017004139 | ISBN 9781107168480 (hardback)
Subjects: | MESH: Drug Costs | Drugs, Generic – supply & distribution | Patents as Topic | Drug Industry – economics | Drug Industry – legislation & jurisprudence | Economic Competition – legislation & jurisprudence | United States
Classification: LCC RA401.A3 | NLM QV 736 AA1 | DDC 338.4/76151–dc23
LC record available at https://lccn.loc.gov/2017004139

ISBN 978-1-107-16848-0 Hardback

*This book is dedicated to my husband, Boris Feldman,
in our thirtieth year of marriage, and to our
children, Natalie, Talya, Eli, Sam, and Adam. – Robin*

To my supportive family and friends, wherever I go. – Evan

Contents

Table and Figures

Acknowledgments

Portions of this book are based on two articles and are included here with the permission of both journals. Those articles are Robin Feldman & Evan Frondorf, *Drug Wars: A New Generation of Generic Pharmaceutical Delay*, 53 HARV. J. ON LEGIS. 499 (2016), reprinted with the permission of the Trustees of Harvard University, and Robin Feldman, Evan Frondorf, Andrew K. Cordova, & Connie Wang, *Empirical Evidence of Drug Pricing Games – A Citizen's Pathway Gone Astray*, (forthcoming 2017 in the Stanford Technology Law Review) reprinted with the permission of Stanford Technology Law Review.

We wish to express our thanks to Drew Amerson, Alice Armitage, Matt Avery, Michael Carrier, Scott Hemphill, Cheryl Johnson, Kurt Karst, Mark Lemley, Joe Lukens, and Daryl Wander for their comments, suggestions, and clarifications. We are grateful beyond measure to Grace Bradshaw, Jonathan Cohen, Isil Selen Denemec, Gabriella Gallego, John Gray, Arya Moshiri, Betty Chang Rowe, Naira Simmons, Omar Vaquero, and Connie Wang for their insights and research, and, above all, to Andrew Cordova for research design and coordination of the research. Rosie Buchanan was instrumental in guiding us through the coding process for our empirical work, and John Gray's data insights were critical to the analysis. Nanette McGuinness provided incomparable proofreading, and Sarah K. Delson created the fabulous cover design. While the book was in process, Evan Frondorf completed his position at the University of California Hastings College of the Law, began a full-time position at Stripe, and thus, had to bow out of the final stages of the book production. His contributions to the book were immeasurable.

In accordance with the protocols outlined in the Harvard Journal of Law & Technology Open Letter on Ethical Norms,[1] all of the data is publicly available

---

[1] Robin Feldman, Mark A. Lemley, Jonathan, S. Masur, Arti K. Rai, *Open Letter on Ethical Norms in Intellectual Property Scholarship*, 29 HARVARD J.L. & TECH. 339 (2016) (signed by dozens of professors).

for future use by other academics on SSRN.com. In further accord with the Open Letter, donation information for the University of California Hastings Institute for Innovation Law, which Robin Feldman directs, can be found at http://innovation .uchastings.edu/about/funding/funding-for-academic-year-2015–2016/. No private or corporate donor accounts for more than 10 percent of the institute's budget.

Prologue

Big Scandals, Higher Prices

A PHARMA UNDER FIRE

Each January, the J. P. Morgan Healthcare Conference rolls into San Francisco, towing along hundreds of pharmaceutical and biotech companies and nearly 10,000 attendees looking to hear about the latest developments in one of the world's hottest industries. Suits hobnob with scientists, financial journalists breathlessly cover the proceedings, and, controversially, companies throw cocktail parties with women hired to attend and improve diversity numbers.[1] Deal making generally takes place behind closed hotel room doors at the glamorous Westin St. Francis in the heart of San Francisco's Financial District, but crowds still turn out for investor presentations and occasionally heated Q&As asking, "What drugs are in the pipeline?" or "How are clinical trials coming along?"

In January 2016, the mood was far less rosy. After years of hypergrowth in biotechnology and health care, stocks experienced a precipitous drop in the second half of 2015.[2] By the beginning of the annual conference, the NASDAQ's Biotechnology Index had lost more than 25 percent of its value in six months.[3] *Bloomberg* reported that biotech stocks experienced their worst trading day for a J. P. Morgan conference opening day since the beginning of 2001's gathering.[4] Statistical indicators of unease were certainly present. The number of initial public offerings (IPOs) had

---

[1] Sasha Damouni, Doni Bloomfield, & Caroline Chen, *At Biotech Party, Gender Diversity Means Cocktail Waitresses*, BLOOMBERG (Jan. 13, 2016), www.bloomberg.com/news/articles/2016-01-13/at-biotech-party-gender-diversity-means-cocktail-waitresses.

[2] NASDAQ Biotechnology Index, GOOGLE FINANCE, www.google.com/finance?q=INDEXNASDAQ %3ANBI&ei=TQHCV5CVE82N2AaopojYCw (click "Historical prices" and view prices from July 2015 to January 2016). The index peaked at an all-time high, 4,165.87, on July 20, 2015, before falling to 3,052.56 on January 11, 2016, the day the conference opened. That fall is equivalent to a 26.7% drop.

[3] *Ibid.*

[4] Drew Armstrong, Caroline Chen, & Sasha Damouni, *Worst Start to Health Conference Since 2001 Has Investors Glum*, BLOOMBERG (Jan. 11, 2016), www.bloomberg.com/news/articles/2016-01-11/worst-start-to-health-conference-since-2001-has-investors-glum.

fallen dramatically in the last year. Instead of raising money through IPOs, large pharmaceutical and biotech firms were looking to boost their cash flow through mergers and acquisitions, with deals totaling $220 billion in 2014 compared to just $65 billion in 2007.[5]

Yet perhaps the most salient problem at the 2016 conference was the public outcry over rising pharmaceutical prices. List prices for branded medications had climbed more than 12 percent in 2015 and more than 14 percent the previous year, with overall spending on medication up 8.5 percent.[6] Even with insurance, these cost increases have the power to affect the health and well-being of patients directly. According to the Kaiser Family Foundation, almost one-quarter of people said their family chose not to fill at least one prescription in the last year, with numbers rising for those in poor or fair health.[7] A similar survey from Kaiser found that people believe the government's top two health care priorities should be related to the price of medication.[8]

This rising concern was exacerbated by a number of national public scandals over dramatic, sudden price increases for existing drugs. Outside the Westin in San Francisco, a cadre of protesters railed against Gilead Science's pricing of Sovaldi, a breakthrough cure for hepatitis C that Gilead had priced at $84,000 for the three-month course of treatment.[9] Signs read, "Gilead = Greed" and "Don't Be Greedy! Treat the Needy!"[10]

In that respect, perhaps the biggest story at the J. P. Morgan Healthcare Conference was about who *wasn't* in attendance. And with that, we arrive at the story of Martin Shkreli – yes, that guy. The "Pharma Bro," who at the age of thirty-two became a global poster child for the excesses of Big Pharma, had long walked the hallways of the Westin in his time running hedge funds and pharmaceutical companies. When he led the hedge fund MSMB Capital Management in 2010, Shkreli entered the

---

[5] Robert Weisman, *Drug Price Policies, China May Slow Biotech Bull Market*, Boston Globe (Jan. 10, 2016), www.bostonglobe.com/business/2016/01/10/biotech-bull-market-may-slow/PzzRRSFujEkiDntFt MT5IP/story.html.

[6] Press Release, IMS Health, IMS Health Study: U.S. Drug Spending Growth Reaches 8.5 Percent in 2015 (Apr. 14, 2016), www.imshealth.com/en/about-us/news/ims-health-study-us-drug-spending-growth-reaches-8.5-percent-in-2015; Katie Thomas, *Drug Prices Keep Rising Despite Intense Criticism*, N.Y. Times (Apr. 26, 2016), www.nytimes.com/2016/04/27/business/drug-prices-keep-rising-despite-intense-criticism.html?_r=0.

[7] Bianca DiJulio, Jamie Firth, & Mollyann Brodie, *Kaiser Health Tracking Poll: August 2015*, Kaiser Family Foundation (Aug. 20, 2015), http://kff.org/health-costs/poll-finding/kaiser-health-tracking-poll-august-2015/.

[8] Bianca DiJulio, Jamie Firth, & Mollyann Brodie, *Kaiser Health Tracking Poll: April 2015*, Kaiser Family Foundation (Apr. 21, 2015), http://kff.org/health-costs/poll-finding/kaiser-health-tracking-poll-april-2015/.

[9] Rebecca Robbins, *Drug Makers Dismiss Outrage over High Prices as 'Abomination,'* STAT (Jan. 12, 2016), www.statnews.com/2016/01/12/public-outrage-drug-prices/.

[10] *Ibid.*

annals of the conference's history by peppering a pharma founder with questions during a public session. The founder's company, MannKind, was applying for FDA approval of an inhaled insulin product; Shkreli, as part of his hedge fund strategy, was shorting the company's stock.[11]

That kind of behavior – in addition to brash missives on Twitter,[12] wunderkind status on the annual Forbes 30 under 30 list, all-day live streaming of his computer screen and office activities, and, more recently, his multimillion dollar purchase of the only copy of a new Wu-Tang Clan album, only to fight publicly later with the artists over the purchase – got Shkreli attention in biotech circles.[13]

Yet pharma's bad boy wasn't in California in January 2016, having just starred in the industry's biggest public relations disaster in years. In September 2015, Shkreli's latest company, Turing Pharmaceuticals, became the subject of intense scrutiny after raising the price of a drug by almost 5,500 percent overnight.[14] Turing had bought the rights to Daraprim, an antimalarial drug also used for treatment of infections common in HIV-positive patients, for $55 million. The company then immediately raised the price of the drug from $13.50 a tablet to $750 a tablet.[15] A one-month course of the drug became $20,000, up from just $400 before the increase. The magnitude of the price increase for a potentially lifesaving drug led to immediate public outrage, particularly because the drug was originally approved in 1953 and had been off-patent for decades. In the midst of a heated 2016 presidential primary season, candidates including Hillary Clinton, Bernie Sanders, and Donald Trump denounced Shkreli's actions, and Daraprim soon became the most dramatic example of exorbitant price increases. Drug pricing had once again become a political issue and a core part of campaign messaging. Shkreli eventually promised, and then quickly walked back, a price decrease.

Shkreli was not alone in his tactics; the media's newfound villain just took the blunt of the criticism. Other companies, such as Valeant Pharmaceuticals, also

[11] Arlene Weintraub, *Gadfly Pharma Investor Shkreli Starts Anew after Ousting from Retrophin*, FORBES (Feb. 27, 2015), www.forbes.com/sites/arleneweintraub/2015/02/27/gadfly-pharma-investor-shkreli-starts-anew-after-ousting-from-retrophin/#5303e3e5359d; Allie Conti, *Why Is Martin Shkreli Still Talking?* VICE (Jan. 27, 2016), www.vice.com/read/why-is-martin-shkreli-still-talking.

[12] Examples of interesting Twitter behavior: Martin Shkreli (@MartinShkreli), TWITTER (Jun. 10, 2016, 7:48 PM), https://twitter.com/MartinShkreli/status/741431768247640064; Martin Shkreli (@Martin Shkreli), TWITTER (Jun. 10, 2016, 7:47 PM), https://twitter.com/MartinShkreli/status/741431597761736704.

[13] Devin Leonard & Annmarie Hordern, *Who Bought the Most Expensive Album Ever Made?* BLOOMBERG BUSINESSWEEK (Dec. 9, 2015), www.bloomberg.com/features/2015-martin-shkreli-wu-tang-clan-album/.

[14] Andrew Pollack, *Drug Goes from $13.50 a Tablet to $750, Overnight*, N.Y. TIMES (Sept. 20, 2015), www.nytimes.com/2015/09/21/business/a-huge-overnight-increase-in-a-drugs-price-raises-protests.html. The price of the drug was as low as $1 in 2010, before a series of acquisitions. *Ibid.*

[15] *Ibid.*

came under fire in the fall of 2015. In one example, Valeant sold a drug called Duexis that simply combined the active ingredient in Motrin with the active ingredient in Pepcid, but charged $1,500 for the privilege of a monthly prescription.[16] Prescribing the two drugs separately would cost no more than $40, but Valeant had increased the price of its combination drug by about 1,000 percent in the four years since the drug was introduced.[17] Notably, Valeant also pushed its main competition out of the market. According to the *New York Times*, Valeant acquired Vimovo – a simple combination of naproxen (Aleve) and esomeprazole (Nexium) – and then immediately raised the price to make it equal to that of Valeant's drug.[18] Around the same time as these stories broke, federal prosecutors announced an investigation of Valeant, for reasons discussed later in this book.

Criminal investigations were numerous that fall, with the most notable being the arrest of Shkreli early in the morning of December 17, 2015. Federal authorities charged Shkreli with multiple counts of securities fraud and conspiracy, reaching back to his tenure at MCMB Capital and Retrophin, a previous pharmaceutical company.[19] Allegedly, Shkreli had taken money from Retrophin to pay back investors who lost money at MCMB.[20] (The FBI also made sure to inform the public that the Wu-Tang Clan album had not been seized – sorry, Clan fans.)[21] Shkreli resigned from Turing the next day, and then made a famous appearance testifying in front of the House Committee on Oversight and Government Reform in February 2016. With charges pending against him, Skhreli answered every question, no matter how trivial, with a knowing smirk and the same response: "On the advice of counsel, I invoke my Fifth Amendment privilege against self-incrimination and respectfully decline to answer your question."[22] The spectacle lasted no more than ten minutes.

While Shkreli smirked his way through his congressional hearing, attendees at the 2016 J. P. Morgan Conference were far more worried. Big Pharma and its perceived excesses were back in the spotlight, and attention was shifting to a core pharma revenue strategy – simply raising prices. Price increases had occurred across the board, on everything from gallstone treatments to, stunningly, the drug used for

---

[16]   Andrew Pollack, *Drug Makers Sidestep Barriers on Pricing*, N.Y. TIMES (Oct. 19, 2015), www.nytimes .com/2015/10/20/business/drug-makers-sidestep-barriers-on-pricing.html?smid=pl-share&_r=0.

[17]   *Ibid.*

[18]   *Ibid.*

[19]   Stephanie Clifford & Matthew Goldstein, *Shkreli Indictment Portrays Small-Time Fraud*, N.Y. TIMES (Dec. 17, 2015), http://nyti.ms/1mbrPVh.

[20]   Additional charges were made in June 2016. Dan Mangan, *'Pharma Bro' Martin Shkreli Pleads Guilty to New Charges*, CNBC (Jun. 6, 2016), www.nbcnews.com/business/business-news/pharma-bro-martin-shkreli-pleads-not-guily-new-charge-n586676.

[21]   FBI New York (@NewYorkFBI), TWITTER (Dec. 17, 2015, 3:12 PM), https://twitter.com/NewYorkFBI/ status/677597263540191232.

[22]   U.S. House Committee on Oversight and Government Reform, *Developments in the Prescription Drug Market: Oversight*, YOUTUBE (Feb. 4, 2016), www.youtube.com/watch?v=BPPerZLjp4M.

physician-assisted suicide.[23] A shocking *Wall Street Journal* piece revealed that between 2010 and 2014, U.S. prices for the thirty best-selling drugs rose four times faster than prescription volume, and eight times faster than inflation.[24] Put another way, 80 percent of the growth in profits of the twenty largest drug companies in 2015 resulted from price increases.[25] Put still *another* way, customers of CVS Health spent 12.7 percent more on drugs in 2015 than in the previous year, and more than 80 percent of that additional spending was the result of price increases.[26] U.S. President Barack Obama even got into the academic mix, publishing a paper in the *Journal of the American Medical Association* that, in part, called attention to rising spending on prescription medication.[27] And in the days before his 2017 inauguration, the next U.S. president, Donald Trump, sharply criticized the pharmaceutical industry. "We have to . . . create new bidding procedures for the drug industry because they're getting away with murder. . . . Pharma, pharma has a lot of lobbies and a lot of lobbyists and a lot of power."[28]

The brunt of the pain is felt by U.S. citizens – one drug that costs less than $400 a year in some countries has a list price around $300,000 in the United States.[29] The rest of the world, however, has not been immune to the plague of skyrocketing prices, and some governments have taken dramatic action. In a popular story, the *New York Times* reported on an unprecedented deal the Egyptian government struck with Gilead, in which Gilead provides its $84,000 hepatitis C treatment, Sovaldi, to the Egyptian government for $900, in exchange for strict distribution requirements to prevent black market sales, particularly to countries where the price

---

[23] Examples: Ed Silverman, *Mylan Raised Prices for Some Drugs by Huge Amounts*, STAT (Jun. 10, 2016), www.statnews.com/pharmalot/2016/06/10/mylan-drug-prices-increase/ (describing the price increase for gallstone medication); April Dembosky, *Drug Company Jacks Up Cost Of Aid-In-Dying Medication*, NPR (Mar. 23, 2016), www.npr.org/sections/health-shots/2016/03/23/471595323/drug-company-jacks-up-cost-of-aid-in-dying-medication (discussing price increases for physician-assisted suicide medication).

[24] Joseph Walker, *For Prescription Drug Makers, Price Increases Drive Revenue*, WALL ST. J. (Oct. 5, 2015), www.wsj.com/articles/for-prescription-drug-makers-price-increases-drive-revenue-1444096750. The *Wall Street Journal*'s coverage of pharmaceutical price increases was later a finalist for a Pulitzer Prize. *2016 Pulitzer Prizes*, The Pulitzer Prizes – Columbia University, www.pulitzer.org/prize-winners-by-year/2016.

[25] Walker, *For Prescription Drug Makers, Price Increases Drive Revenue*, *supra* note 24.

[26] *Ibid.*

[27] Barack Obama, *United States Health Care Reform: Progress to Date and Next Steps*, J. AM. MED. ASS'N E1, E5 (Jul. 11, 2016), http://jama.jamanetwork.com/article.aspx?articleid=2533698&utm_campaign=articlePDF&utm_medium=articlePDFlink&utm_source=articlePDF&utm_content=jama.2016.9797.

[28] *Donald Trump's News Conference: Full Transcript and Video*, N.Y. TIMES (Jan. 11, 2017), https://www.nytimes.com/2017/01/11/us/politics/trump-press-conference-transcript.html?_r=0.

[29] Bethany McLean, *The Valeant Meltdown and Wall Street's Major Drug Problem*, VANITY FAIR (Jun. 5, 2016), www.vanityfair.com/news/2016/06/the-valeant-meltdown-and-wall-streets-major-drug-problem.

is dramatically higher.[30] Egypt then provides the medication free to its citizens, a country so ravaged by hepatitis that it spends one-third of its national health budget on the disease.[31] Similarly, in 2016, Colombia's health minister forced Novartis to lower the price of its Gleevec leukemia treatment, a medication that costs $15,000 per year in Colombia, where the average annual income is approximately $8,000.[32]

With this information about global pricing scandals out in the open, everyone at the conference buzzed about pharmaceutical pricing. Presenters dismissed concerns and talked strategically about price increases. At the Borgia Room in the Westin St. Francis, Biogen's CEO answered questions about why the price of its multiple sclerosis therapies had only risen 3.9 percent in the previous year. (One of these multiple sclerosis medications, Avonex, had experienced a 93 percent price increase between 2000 and 2014, rising to more than $60,000 annually.)[33] Biogen's CEO responded: "We're trying not to put a target on our foreheads … [Don't want] to wave the red flag in front of the bull, whatever you want to call it." Later: "It's unlikely there will be any official government action on drug pricing this year. … Right now, it's possible to take a price increase. But it's wise to be prudent."

A member of Sanofi's executive committee was more blunt: "Everybody has to make money. Should it be surprising? We do serve different stakeholders."[34] Expressing similar frustration on an earnings call, the CEO of Alnylam decried the scrutiny as "political demagoguery," but admitted that companies would now need to "think about their growth based on productivity not based on artificial price increases."[35] During its J. P. Morgan conference presentation, AbbVie revealed projections that its operating margin would increase to 50 percent by 2020 compared to a 36 percent margin in 2014.[36] That improvement would occur as part of a $17 billion revenue increase in the same time frame, with only $4 billion of that increase

[30] Donald G. McNeil Jr., *Curing Hepatitis C, in an Experiment the Size of Egypt*, N.Y. Times (Dec. 15, 2015), www.nytimes.com/2015/12/16/health/hepatitis-c-treatment-egypt.html?smid=pl-share.

[31] *Ibid.*

[32] Ed Silverman, *Colombia Plans to Unilaterally Lower the Cost of a Novartis Cancer Drug*, STAT (Jun. 9, 2016), www.statnews.com/pharmalot/2016/06/09/colombia-novartis-gleevec/; Ed Silverman, *Novartis, Colombia Face Off Over Cancer Drug Cost*, STAT (Jun. 14, 2016), www.statnews.com/pharmalot/2016/06/14/novartis-colombia-drug-costs/.

[33] Ed Silverman, *Multiple Sclerosis Drug Prices Rose at an 'Alarming' Rate: Study*, Wall St. J. (Apr. 24, 2015), http://blogs.wsj.com/pharmalot/2015/04/24/multiple-sclerosis-drug-prices-rose-at-an-alarming-rate-study/.

[34] Ed Silverman, *Sanofi on Rx Pricing: 'Everyone Has to Make Money,'* STAT (Jan. 13, 2016), https://embed.scribblelive.com/Embed/v7.aspx?Ibid=1755036&Page=4&overlay=false.

[35] Lee Fang, *Pharma Executives Worry about Presidential Candidates Demanding Reform*, Intercept (Feb. 2, 2016), https://theintercept.com/2016/02/02/goldman-sachs-pharma/.

[36] Presentation, AbbVie, 2016 J. P. Morgan Healthcare Conference (Jan. 13, 2016), www.abbvieinvestor.com/phoenix.zhtml?c=251551&p=irol-presentations. One should note that operating margin is not directly equivalent to profit margin, as it does not include fixed costs such as research and development.

attributable to newly introduced drugs from the development pipeline.[37] On the basis of current trends, most of the remaining $13 billion would be generated by price increases, not increased sales volume.

Of course, Shkreli and other pharmaceutical executives would tell a different story about high prices. New treatments have immense value in improving quality of life, extending life spans, and eliminating the need for invasive medical procedures to be used instead.[38] The hefty price for some of these pharmaceuticals reflects the value they offer to patients.

There is certainly some truth to these statements, as well as an obvious counter-argument: Why would prices of existing drugs, some of which have been available for decades, increase when constantly improving medical care would suggest that their relative value should decrease or remain stagnant? The routine price bumps suggest that pharmaceutical companies are taking advantage of price inelasticity and minimal competition to push pricing to its limit.

All of this begs the question: How *do* these price increases go unchallenged? Shouldn't other drug makers step in to provide competition in the marketplace? That is where generic drugs enter the picture. Always looming in the back of the minds of pharma executives is the threat of generic competition. Nothing has more power to shift the all-important bottom line. A United Therapeutics executive at the J. P. Morgan event referred to a generic launch as a generic intrusion.

In a way, generics are quite an intrusion. Brand-name drug companies, who enjoy a monopoly in the market for a drug until generic entry, face a nearly instantaneous plummet in market share and price. Within a year of entry by the first generic, a brand-name drug generally loses an average of 80–90 percent of its market share.[39] As multiple generic competitors enter the market, the price of most drugs eventually falls to 15–20 percent of the original brand-name cost.[40]

For companies that rely on just one or two patent-protected drugs for the majority of their revenues, generic competition can be a rude awakening. Considering that generic entry often coincides with the expiration of a brand-name company's patents

---

[37] *Ibid.*

[38] Victoria Colliver, *Biotech Execs Talk "Value" in Backlash against High Drug Prices*, S.F. Chron. (Jun. 9, 2016), www.sfchronicle.com/business/article/Biotech-execs-talk-value-in-backlash-7974134. php; Rebecca Robbins, *With Tens of Millions on Hand, Drug Makers Fight State Efforts to Force Down Prices*, STAT (Jun. 9, 2016), www.statnews.com/2016/06/09/drug-companies-fight-back/.

[39] *See ibid.; see also* Henry G. Grabowski *et al.*, *Evolving Brand-Name and Generic Drug Competition May Warrant a Revision of the Hatch-Waxman Act*, 30 Health Aff. 2157, 2163, exhibit 4 (2011). In fact, for the period between 2004 and 2008, Grabowski *et al.* found that the average drug with more than $1 billion in annual sales had more than ten generic competitors one year after first generic entry. *See ibid.* at 2160 exhibit 1.

[40] *See Facts about Generic Drugs*, U.S. Food & Drug Admin., www.fda.gov/Drugs/ResourcesForYou/ Consumers/BuyingUsingMedicineSafely/UnderstandingGenericDrugs/ucm167991.htm (last updated June 28, 2016).

or FDA exclusivities, it is no surprise that looming generic competition is often referred to as the "patent cliff." Channeling his best eulogist, Shkreli once tweeted about the brand-name view of the patent cliff:

> Every time a drug goes generic, I grieve. Let us not mourn the dearly departed, instead celebrate the profits and new assets it has brought us. – @MartinShkreli, April 10, 2012, 7:46 A.M.[41]

Hold your sympathy for drug makers, however – this humbling event of patent expiration is supposed to happen! As citizens, in fact, we actually bestow limited-time rights on drug companies in the form of patents. Society gives companies the opportunity to make billions, and with good reason. The hope is that the promise of that opportunity will incentivize companies to innovate in ways that will benefit all of us. Patents are not the type of inalienable rights to life and liberty one might think. Nor are patents the same as core rights in our homes and land.[42] Rather, patents are time-limited government grants that exist for a specific purpose only: that is, to incentivize innovation for the benefit of society.[43]

In the pharmaceutical space, the prevailing explanation for strong patent rights is the following: given the astronomical cost of drug research and development, patents provide a necessary period for pharmaceutical companies to recoup their costs and profit from their invention. In return, society benefits from new treatments, and we hope some of the earnings are returned to future research and development. Celebrate the profits, celebrate the assets, and then return to research!

Pharmaceuticals have long served as a prototypical example, sharing the pedestal with blockbuster movies, for the continuing benefits of intellectual property, because of their high initial fixed costs along with the multiple research failures and dead ends that occur on the way to producing one medication that receives market approval.[44] (Researchers disagree vehemently about the costs of getting a medication to market, but most research puts the expense somewhere in the high hundreds of millions or even billions of dollars.)[45] In designing those rights, society strives to strike the proper

---

[41] Martin Shkreli (@MartinShkreli), Twitter (Apr. 10, 2012, 7:46 AM), https://twitter.com/MartinShkreli/status/189695905790832640.

[42] For an explanation of why patents are not core property rights, *see* Robin Feldman, *Federalism, First Amendment and Patents: The Fraud Fallacy*, 18 Colum. Sci. & Tech. L. Rev. 30, 71–72 (2015).

[43] U.S. Const., art. I, § 8, cl. 8 ("The Congress shall have power … To promote the Progress of Science and useful Arts, by securing for limited Times to Authors and Inventors the exclusive Right to their respective Writings and Discoveries").

[44] *See* Mark Lemley, *IP in a World without Scarcity*, 90 N.Y.U. L. Rev. 460, 464–65 (2015), www.nyulawreview.org/sites/default/files/pdf/NYULawReview-90-2-Lemley.pdf, for a fascinating discussion of this issue.

[45] *See* Steve Morgan *et al.*, *The Cost of Drug Development: A Systematic Review*, 100 Health Policy 4 (2011), www.ncbi.nlm.nih.gov/pubmed/21256615 (discovering estimates of drug development cost ranging from $161 million to $1.8 billion); *see also* Aaron E. Carroll, *$2.6 Billion to*

balance, giving pharmaceutical companies the opportunity to recoup investment without blocking the incentive for others to innovate further in the future.

That balance means all good things must come to an end – maybe. When a drug's patents or exclusivities expire or are found invalid, in theory, anyone who can obtain FDA approval becomes eligible to sell the medication, and thus generic competition begins. The expectation is that the brand-name pharma company, having likely enjoyed more than a decade of unimpeded sales, heads back to the lab bench, ready to discover new treatments with improved therapeutic benefits for patients. R&D activity, however, is expensive and difficult – mergers, acquisitions, and obstruction are cheaper and simpler. As a result, it has become far too easy to spend time and resources exhausting legal and regulatory options, pushing the patent cliff as far away as possible.

The temptation to avoid the impact of the patent cliff can be overpowering when even a few months of additional monopoly profits can be worth hundreds of millions of dollars or more.[46] For example, Gilead's previously mentioned hepatitis C drug, Sovaldi, earned $7.9 billion in sales in 2014, making it the top-earning drug in the United States. Three additional months of sales at that rate would be worth $1.98 billion. Similarly, Pfizer's Nexium took in $5.9 billion in revenue in the same year – three additional months would be worth $1.48 billion.

These enormous and precariously fleeting revenue streams encourage companies to expend tremendous energy blocking generic entry by any means possible, with companies using ever more clever and complicated strategies. As a result, many pharmaceutical firms may no longer compete solely on the basis of innovation, but rather on their ability to manipulate policy mechanisms and pathways to extend monopoly and duopoly terms. The lure of the easy way out means that many companies fail to follow the advice of their colleague Mr. Shkreli and instead prolong the generic mourning period.

Of course, this behavior undermines the goals of intellectual property and can provide less than optimal innovation and pricing effects. As an example, let us return to Mr. Shkreli and his actions at Turing. While Daraprim was already off-patent at the time Turing purchased distribution rights for the drug, Shkreli's company used a modified version of an emerging generic delay strategy to keep all competition off the market, allowing the eye-popping price increase to occur.

Develop a Drug? New Estimate Makes Questionable Assumptions, N.Y. TIMES (Nov. 18, 2014), www.nytimes.com/2014/11/19/upshot/calculating-the-real-costs-of-developing-a-new-drug.html (describing the conflict in determining how much it costs to develop a drug).

[46] Lacie Glover, *Here Are the Top-Selling Drugs in the US*, TIME (June 26, 2015), http://time.com/money/ 3938166/top-selling-drugs-sovaldi-abilify-humira/?xid=soc_socialflow_twitter_money. Fifty-five drugs earned more than $1 billion in revenue in 2013. *U.S. Pharmaceutical Sales – 2013*, DRUGS, www.drugs .com/stats/top100/2013/sales (last updated Feb. 2014).

Specifically, when Turing acquired the rights to Daraprim, it maintained a restricted distribution system originally put in place by Impax, the previous owner.[47] In fact, Turing requested that a restricted distribution system be established before the sale occurred. As we will discuss later, restricted or controlled distribution systems are mandated by the FDA as part of safety protocols when a drug presents special concerns regarding safety, administration, or storage. Yet Impax (and later, Turing) instituted its restricted distribution system without the FDA and for no apparent safety reason at all, making the drug only available through Walgreen's Specialty Pharmacy.[48] Along with creating access problems for hospitals,[49] the move in part may have been designed to make it difficult for generics to gain access to the samples needed to gain approval for a generic version of the drug.[50]

Comments from Turing executives support this implication. In response to the Daraprim pricing controversy and the potential for generic competition, the director of patient access at Turing said the following: "Most likely I would block that purchase [by a generic]. We spent a lot of money for this drug. We would like to do our best to avoid generic competition. It's inevitable. They seem to figure out a way [to make generics], no matter what. But I'm certainly not going to make it easier for them."[51] The comments suggest a concerted effort to block generic competition, and a failure to accept the intent of the generic drug system. Although Turing executives may have spoken more directly than others, actions in many corners of the pharmaceutical industry reflect a similar mind-set. Turing's actions, specifically the use of restricted distribution to block competition, are now under investigation by the New York attorney general, and U.S. lawmakers have also called on the FTC to look into the Turing business model.[52]

As other academics have detailed, the Daraprim system was not the first time a Shkreli-led company implemented a restricted distribution system.[53] Notably,

---

[47] Michael Carrier & Aaron Kesselheim, *The Daraprim Price Hike and a Role for Antitrust*, HEALTH AFF. BLOG (Oct. 21, 2015), http://healthaffairs.org/blog/2015/10/21/the-daraprim-price-hike-and-a-role-for-antitrust/.

[48] *Ibid.*

[49] Letter from Stephen B. Calderwood, President, Infectious Diseases Soc'y of Am., and Adaora Adimora, Chair, HIV Medicine Ass'n, to Tom Evegan, Head of Managed Markets, Turing Pharm., and Kevin Bernier, Nat'l Dir. of All. Dev. & Pub. Affairs, Turing Pharm. (Sept. 8, 2015), www.hivma.org/uploadedFiles/HIVMA/HomePageContent/PyrimethamineLetterFINAL.pdf.

[50] Michael A. Carrier, Nicole L. Levidow, & Aaron S. Kesselheim, *Using Antitrust Law to Challenge Turing's Daraprim Price Increase*, 31 BERKELEY TECH. L.J. (2016), http://ssrn.com/abstract=2724604.

[51] Ed Silverman, *How Martin Shkreli Prevents Generic Versions of His Pricey Pill*, STAT (Oct. 5, 2015), http://pharmalot.com/how-martin-shkreli-prevents-generic-versions-of-his-pricey-pill/.

[52] Andrew Pollack, *New York Attorney General Examining Whether Turing Restricted Drug Access*, N.Y. TIMES (Oct. 12, 2015), www.nytimes.com/2015/10/13/business/new-york-attorney-general-examining-if-turing-restricted-drug-access.html.

[53] *See* Carrier, Levidow, & Kesselheim, *Using Antitrust Law, supra* note 50, at *20–21.

Shkreli's previous company, Retrophin, bought the rights to a rare kidney-disorder drug called Thiola. Retrophin increased the price of the drug 2000 percent from $1.50 to $30 a pill, but it also created a still-active closed distribution system known as "Thiola Total Care."[54] This system requires a patient and the patient's doctor to *fax* enrollment forms to Retrophin, which then manages direct shipments not through an online system but only over the phone.[55] Notably, although it may be a technical error, the enrollment form on the Total Care Hub Web site automatically fills in the bubble for "dispense as written," which would prevent a pharmacist from substituting a generic form of the drug for Thiola.[56] Documents that Turing turned over to Congress in advance of the infamous February 2016 hearing revealed that, internally, it was known that "exclusivity (closed distribution) creates a barrier and pricing power."[57]

That is what this book is about: the schemes, strategies, and tactics – not competition, not R&D – that pharmaceutical companies use to keep prices high and generic drugs off the market, denying consumers billions in cost savings and health benefits every year. It is about more than price, revenue, and profit. These issues of regulation may be prosaically dry on paper but they are enormously important in effect. Astounding technological advances in medicine dominate the headlines and rightfully draw our attention. Legal and regulatory environments, however, play a huge role in how well these advances actually serve the public. Policy choices on issues as esoteric as how similar a generic drug's fed-state bioavailability must be to its branded equivalent's bioavailability can have just as large an impact on the quality of health. Hidden among these technical details are strategies for sky-high pricing. All consumers suffer, and for the less fortunate, the lack of generic competition can force patients to make a decision between refilling prescriptions and making rent.

From our perch at the UC Hastings Institute for Innovation Law, less than a mile from the esteemed Westin St. Francis, we have researched the strategies and tactics that have appeared over the years. These tactics range from downright illegal collusive settlement agreements between brand-name companies and generics, to complex webs of deals, to the profoundly absurd (a dispute over the *type* of orange juice used to test the safety of a generic), to truly puzzling patents (like one for an

---

[54] *Ibid.*

[55] *Thiola Total Care Hub*, Thiola, www.thiola.com/hub.

[56] *Patient Enrollment Form for Thiola Total Care Hub*, Thiola, www.thiola.com/assets/pdf/THI010V2 .pdf.

[57] *See* Carrier, Levidow, & Kesselheim, *Using Antitrust Law, supra* note 50, at *21 (citing Memorandum from Democratic Staff to Democratic Members of the Full H. Comm. on Oversight and Gov't Reform Regarding Documents Obtained by Comm. from Turing Pharm. 3 (Feb. 2, 2016), http:// democrats.oversight.house.gov/sites/democrats.oversight.house.gov/files/documents/Memo%20 on%20Turing%20Documents.pdf).

ineffective capsule that dissolves before it reaches the drug's absorption site), to a single new sentence on a drug label claiming that the medication is better absorbed when taken with food, with the last scenario potentially preventing consumers from enjoying up to $3 billion in cost savings.

During this era of heated discussion of pharmaceutical pricing policy, it is critical to detail the behind-the-scenes mechanisms contributing to rising pharmaceutical costs. In the legal arena, it is also a time of immense litigation and conversation about the legality of certain delay tactics, with cases even reaching the U.S. Supreme Court. These policy discussions heighten the importance of revealing the complex webs that have been woven.

Further, as completely new types of drugs emerge, far different from the old-school pills and capsules we are accustomed to using, it is important to ensure that a robust competitive market of brand-name and generic medication exists, and that existing regulation is not being used to manipulate these markets. This book is not an exhaustive look into how pricing decisions are made, how pharmaceutical companies decide what drugs to develop or produce, or other issues related to drug costs including insurance policies, potential overprescription, and misuse. Each of those issues could fill its own tome. Instead, we focus on the mix of antitrust, regulatory abuse, intellectual property law, and clever marketing that encompasses the world of generic pharmaceutical delay and obstruction. Before we begin, however, we provide an overview of the unique landscape of pharmaceutical economics and a brief primer of how generic entry and distribution are currently regulated.

With that, we will never mention the Westin St. Francis or the 33rd Annual J. P. Morgan Healthcare Conference in stunning San Francisco again. Promise. We reserve the right, however, to return to Mr. Shkreli. Sorry.

B A NOTE BEFORE WE BEGIN

Despite the excesses and concerns we detail in this book, pharmaceuticals have contributed immensely to improved health and quality of life across the world. Many treatments are now an essential part of everyday life. Every year, we see new cures developed through private invention. Despite pricing controversies, Sovaldi is essentially a miracle cure for hepatitis C. Research and development *are* expensive, and intellectual property systems are essential for incentivizing spending and innovation.

The concern, of course, is that pharmaceutical companies are shifting away from innovative activity, choosing instead to manipulate legal and regulatory pathways that sustain existing sources of monopoly revenue. This activity fails to improve medicine and health care, while subverting the intent of the patent system and the balance society has chosen between private incentives and the public good. It also blocks creative, new innovators from entering the market. A similar problem is at hand when pharmaceutical companies choose to introduce new versions of drugs or introduce drugs in already clogged market segments. Both of these actions generally fail to advance public health, keep prices high for consumers for long-existing treatments, and can be anticompetitive. Society needs new clinical trials – not new lawsuits, new mergers, or new extended-release, individually packaged antacids.

Granted, one cannot fully blame companies for engaging in behavior that is strongly in their economic self-interests when regulation is unclear or riddled with loopholes. If society wishes its interests to prevail, then the legal system must bring the incentives of the players into proper alignment with the goals of society, by creating either sufficient incentives or sufficient disincentives. We cannot expect the rats in the maze to run in the direction society wishes if the cheese is located at the other end. And, as the generic system in the United States currently operates, the cheese is poorly located. In this book, we will discuss concerns with current regulation and suggest avenues for reform.

C THE STRANGE ECONOMICS OF PHARMACEUTICALS

Drugs can save lives, improve our well-being, and help us maintain healthy lifestyles. But why do we (and our insurers) pay so much for them? Why are such large price increases possible? Better yet, when we receive a prescription, why don't we know how much it *really* costs, or whether we'll get a brand name drug or its generic? The answers lie in the complicated market structure for pharmaceuticals, where patients require drugs, doctors prescribe what they believe is the most effective medication, pharmacists fill these prescriptions, and an insurer picks up most of the tab. There is a decoupling of who makes drug choices and who pays for them – a classic informational problem of markets and economics.

In fact, the pharmaceutical market does not operate much like a standard market at all. In a perfect world, consumers deciding which drug to purchase would have complete information for the decision-making process. They would know about all the drugs available to treat their particular illness or condition; the efficacy, side effects, and risks of those drugs; the possible competitors and alternatives; and, finally, the price of the medication. Producers would have the same information, and Adam Smith's famous invisible hand would work to bring the market to an equilibrium of supply and demand. "Perfect competition" would occur when there are enough producers and consumers in the market that price is eventually set at the marginal cost of producing the medication.

Using those definitions, the pharmaceutical market, unsurprisingly, is not particularly well-functioning. The problem starts with the initial fixed costs of development even to get one drug to market, which means that sales at marginal cost are nowhere near large enough to recoup the initial investment. If all drugs were instantly priced at the pennies on the dollar they cost to produce, we would not have any pharmaceuticals. Enter the patent system, which artificially creates opportunities for monopolies and duopolies over a certain period of time in exchange for disclosing the invention to the public.

These patent-created markets without competition set the stage for prices far above marginal cost. In other markets, such as the market for paper towels, people may look for near-substitutes instead of paying for the monopoly good. You'll live with the standard roll when the extra-absorbent, organic, double roll is four times as expensive. But some pharmaceuticals exist in a market or class of their own. Patients aren't going to give up their antidepressant for another drug when the efficacy is lower or unknown. The only true substitute is a bioequivalent generic.

Even in a monopoly market, however, price shouldn't be unbounded. The niche market for extra-absorbent, double roll, paper towels isn't a necessity when other classes of paper towel are available, and thus some price sensitivity exists. If demand falls for the special paper towels, the price should also fall, which would increase demand and allow our bespoke paper towel manufacturer to maximize its profits. Here, pharmaceutical buyers (everyone) still can't catch a break. Many drugs are necessities for the patients who use them, especially those for rare disorders. The price is quite *inelastic*, meaning that demand is not responsive to price – people will pay whatever they need to secure the good. That might explain the Daraprim price increase: the drug serves to treat rare parasitic infections, and patients are unlikely to forgo treatment.[58]

Although some drugs may have no worthy substitute, many do. Numerous antibiotics can be prescribed for basic infections; an incredible number of topical rash creams are available, not to mention painkillers. Some of these drugs have generic equivalents; some do not. Here, the lack of perfect information comes into play.

The choice of a prescription is a classic principal–agent model,[59] in which patients are the "principals" that allow doctors, the "agents," to make prescription choices on their behalf. The decoupling of who writes the prescription and who ends up paying for the medication raises an agency problem in which the doctor has little incentive to keep costs low, especially when the doctor's primary criterion behind a medication choice is efficacy. The doctor's role is to prescribe the medication believed to be the best fit, and there is little reason for the doctor to choose something that is 99 percent as effective, even if the price is dramatically lower.

[58] Pollack, *Drug Goes from $13.50 a Tablet to $750, Overnight, supra* note 14.
[59] The theory has long been part of economics and other fields, so it has no one particular origin, but the best-known economic paper tackling a description of the issue is: Stephen A. Ross, *The Economic Theory of Agency: The Principal's Problem*, 63 Am. Econ. Rev. 134 (1973), https://assets.aeaweb.org/ assets/production/journals/aer/top20/63.2.134-139.pdf.

Our doctors sound a little callous there, don't they? Why wouldn't they think at all about price? It's not malicious – doctors are involved in their own principal–agent relationship. They are not experts on drug prices, product hopping, and shifts in the pharmaceutical market – they have exquisitely imperfect information themselves. Instead, much of their new information about new drugs comes from promotional visits and information from branded manufacturers. Thus, some of their own agency regarding prescribing decisions is restricted by the stream of information they receive from drug manufacturers.

Further, doctors are bombarded by requests from patients who are subject to direct-to-consumer (DTC) advertising for medication on television, on the Internet, and in print media. The United States and New Zealand are the only two countries in the world that permit direct-to-consumer advertising,[60] and this advertising has been shown to increase the number of patient requests or inquiries about specific drugs dramatically.[61] Thus, it could be argued that patients actually have more agency over their prescription decisions in the United States than in other countries. However, these advertisements are generally only for new brand-name drugs, and they present information to a populace that is ill equipped to make informed decisions about whether the product is actually well-suited for them.[62]

At the next step, pharmacists act as an agent, filling the medication for the patient, although their control is generally limited to what is permitted by generic substitution laws. Quite a bit of substitution takes place at this step, however, since doctors often write prescriptions with the more well-known brand name, assuming that a generic will be prescribed if available. (Of course, advertising may mean a doctor may be more likely to prescribe a new brand-name drug that does not have a generic substitute.)

Other players include insurance companies and their associated "pharmaceutical benefit managers" (PBMs), who manage drug purchases for hospitals and insurers. Insurers will often institute differential co-pays for their policyholders depending on the type of drug that is prescribed. In turn, drugs can move up and down the co-pay

---

[60] *Keeping Watch over Direct-to-Consumer Ads*, U.S. FOOD & DRUG ADMIN., www.fda.gov/ForConsumers/ConsumerUpdates/ucm107170.htm (last updated June 14, 2016). One of the authors recently made a trip to New Zealand and spent an inordinate amount of time scouring for evidence of direct-to-consumer pharmaceutical advertising, flipping through magazines at gas stations and carefully viewing television commercials. Other than your everyday public health campaigns, he found nothing, and left the country sorely disappointed.

[61] Kathryn Aiken, John Swasy, & Amie Braman, *Patient and Physician Attitudes and Behaviors Associated With DTC Promotion of Prescription Drugs – Summary of FDA Survey Research Results*, U.S. FOOD & DRUG ADMIN. 26 (2004), http://www.fda.gov/downloads/Drugs/ScienceResearch/ResearchAreas/DrugMarketingAdvertisingandCommunicationsResearch/UCM152860.pdf

[62] We will return to DTC advertising later in the context of "product hopping" strategies used to extend the life of a drug.

price list, or "formulary," depending on deals the PBM has made with the pharmaceutical company or their distributor. In some cases, insurers and PBMs may refuse to cover certain drugs when a worthy, cheaper substitute is available (or as part of a strategy to convince a manufacturer to lower prices).[63] Yet even this standard pharmacy model is being challenged by so-called specialty pharmacies that stock a limited selection of drugs. We noted this practice earlier in the context of Daraprim, and will discuss it further in Chapter 4. By only allowing prescriptions for particular drugs to be filled at particular pharmacies, the potential for generic substitution, prescription changes, or insurer interference can be reduced dramatically for the brand-name company trying to hold on to its market position.

In general, PBM discounts and deals are so prevalent that few insurers actually pay the "list" price for a drug. Some commentators have compared the system to the maximum hotel room rate that hoteliers are required to post in a room – it is there and it represents some sort of theoretical maximum, but no one has actually ever paid that rate unless the Super Bowl or Beyoncé or both are in town.[64] Thus, no one really knows what a drug will cost for any given person – certainly not the doctor prescribing the drug or the patient paying for it!

Some pharmaceutical manufacturers have argued that these discounts from the "list price" should allay concerns about rising prices. If those high prices are never actually being passed on to insurers or consumers, perhaps the price is more of a negotiating tactic than an actual concern for the market. Recent *Bloomberg* data show, however, that postrebate price increases for many drugs still come in substantially above inflation.[65] Even after factoring in average discounts of 37 percent in 2015 for the drugs studied, list prices still increased anywhere from 22 percent to a whopping 442 percent from 2009 to 2015.[66]

At the end of the road, we finally meet our patient, who pays the pharmacist whatever the co-pay is for the prescription – which is the balance after insurance coverage is factored in. The uninsured often will face the list price of the drug, meaning they end up the worst of anyone in this complicated web. The insured, however, are not immune to sticker stock. Even with Medicare coverage, for example, yearly co-pay prices for expensive rheumatoid arthritis and cancer specialty medications can range from $4,000 to nearly $12,000 – staggering numbers that are prohibitive for many covered patients.[67]

---

[63] Carolyn Y. Johnson, *Secret Rebates, Coupons, and Exclusions: How the Battle over High Drug Prices Is Really Being Fought*, Wash. Post (May 12, 2016), www.washingtonpost.com/news/wonk/wp/2016/05/12/the-drug-price-arms-race-that-leaves-patients-caught-in-the-middle/.

[64] Thomas, *Drug Prices Keep Rising Despite Intense Criticism, supra* note 6.

[65] Robert Langreth, Michael Keller, & Christopher Cannon, *Decoding Big Pharma's Secret Drug Pricing Practices*, Bloomberg (Jun. 29, 2016), www.bloomberg.com/graphics/2016-drug-prices/.

[66] *Ibid.*

[67] Joseph Walker, *Patients Struggle with High Drug Prices*, Wall St. J. (Dec. 31, 2015), www.wsj.com/articles/patients-struggle-with-high-drug-prices-1451557981.

Even at this stage, the principal–agent problem arises in yet another odd form. Although one could describe the insurer as the principal – given that the insurer pays much of the cost – patients can work directly with pharmaceutical companies to change what *they* pay while still pushing the bulk of the cost onto the insurer. Many pharmaceutical companies provide co-pay "coupons" or "rebates" directly to patients. These incentives discount the patient's out-of-pocket costs for drugs at the point of sale, perhaps influencing the patient to purchase expensive drugs while shifting all cost (and risk) onto insurers. Thus, to paraphrase Stephen Hawking, it is principals and agents all the way down.[68]

The economic implications of such coupons are an ongoing subject of debate in pharmaceutical pricing. Massachusetts was the only state to have banned these coupons until its law was repealed (for drugs without generic equivalents) in 2012, and federal health insurance (including Medicare, Medicaid, and veterans' benefits) users are ineligible for coupon benefits under antikickback laws.[69]

If the description of the process was confusing, that is because it is. There is a complete disconnection at every step of the process. Patients require drugs, have little idea about cost, and will only pay a small percentage of it anyway, sharply affecting their ability to respond to price. Doctors also do not respond to price, given that they are tasked with a mandate of efficacy and face no financial consequence for their prescription habits. Insurers and PBMs attempt to reduce their costs by making deals with wholesalers and pharmaceutical companies, which influence the actions of doctors, pharmacists, and patients. Those insurers and PBMs, however, face the majority of the cost for the drug despite having little to no influence over its prescription by the doctor and purchase by the patient. If you were for some reason looking for a reason to feel bad for insurance companies, there it is. But perhaps you should feel only a little bad; this completely decoupled chain of pricing information and responsibility eventually leads to higher premiums, low price sensitivity, and an opportunity for pharmaceutical companies to take advantage of the complexity by raising prices for everyone.

[68] Stephen Hawking, A Brief History of Time (1988).

[69] *See* David Schultz, *Drug Coupons: A Good Deal for the Patient, but Not the Insurer*, Kaiser Health News (Oct. 1, 2012), http://khn.org/news/drug-coupons/ (noting laws preventing those on federal health insurance from using coupons and detailing the debate over co-pay rebates); Karen Weintraub, *Mass., 50th State, Now Allows Drug Coupons: What You Need to Know*, WBUR (July 16, 2012, 9:40 AM), http://commonhealth.wbur.org/2012/07/drug-coupons-massachusetts (covering repeal of Massachusetts's drug coupon law); *see also* Charles Ornstein, *Are Copay Coupons Actually Making Drugs More Expensive?* ProPublica (Jun. 30, 2016), www.propublica.org/article/are-copay-coupons-actually-making-drugs-more-expensive?utm_campaign=sprout&utm_medium=social&utm_source=twitter&utm_content=1467295822; Johnson, *Secret Rebates, Coupons, and Exclusions, supra* note 63.

Differential pricing structures around the world tend to reinforce higher prices in the United States. Along with the lower prices that must exist to serve patients in lower-income countries, many developed countries have state-run health care systems that are able to negotiate prices with drug makers unilaterally. The United Kingdom's National Health Service, for example, is the country's only drug buyer and establishes what drugs it will make available to its citizenry, encouraging companies to cut costs.[70] The diffuse configuration of buyers in the United States prevents any one buyer from gaining enough market power to make a big dent in prices. Perhaps most important, the largest American drug purchaser – the federal government – is barred by federal law from directly negotiating drug prices with pharmaceutical companies in key programs. Specifically, the U.S. government spent approximately $165 billion on prescription drugs for Medicare and Medicaid combined in 2014,[71] which amounts to roughly 55 percent of the $298 billion total spent on prescription drugs.[72] In other words, despite having $165 billion in purchasing power, the government cannot directly negotiate prices for Medicare and Medicaid![73]

In addition, the United States generally has stronger intellectual property protections than many other countries. For example, drug prices became a subject of focus during negotiations over the Trans-Pacific Partnership trade accord as the involved countries sought to harmonize intellectual property regulations. The United States argued for twelve years of exclusivities outside patents for complex biologic drugs, while countries such as Australia wanted periods as short as five years to put lower-cost generics on the market more quickly.[74] The final plan called for a flexible period that can be set between five and eight years in each country depending on

[70] Nadia Kounang, *Why Pharmaceuticals Are Cheaper Abroad*, CNN (Sept. 28, 2015), www.cnn.com/2015/09/28/health/us-pays-more-for-drugs/.

[71] Andy Slavitt & Niall Brennan, *Medicare Drug Spending Dashboard*, CENTERS FOR MEDICARE & MEDICAID SERVICES (Dec. 21, 2015), https://blog.cms.gov/2015/12/21/medicare-drug-spending-dashboard/ (noting $143 billion of spending for Medicare in 2014); MEDICAID & CHIP PAYMENT & ACCESS COMMISSION, ISSUE BRIEF: MEDICAID SPENDING FOR PRESCRIPTION DRUGS at *1 (Jan. 2016), www .macpac.gov/wp-content/uploads/2016/01/Medicaid-Spending-for-Prescription-Drugs.pdf (noting $42 billion on spending for Medicaid in fiscal year 2014, but $20 billion in rebates reduced net spending to $22 billion).

[72] CENTERS FOR MEDICARE AND MEDICAID SERVICES, NATIONAL HEALTH EXPENDITURES 2014 HIGHLIGHTS (2015), www.cms.gov/research-statistics-data-and-systems/statistics-trends-and-reports/nationalhealth expenddata/downloads/highlights.pdf.

[73] Margot Sanger-Katz, *The Real Reason Medicare Is a Lousy Negotiator: It Can't Say No*, N.Y. TIMES (Feb. 2, 2016), www.nytimes.com/2016/02/02/upshot/the-real-reason-medicare-is-a-lousy-drug-negotiator-it-cant-say-no.html?_r=0. Granted, some say the potential cost savings of allowing government negotiation would not necessarily be as large as one might think.

[74] Jonathan Weisman, *Patent Protection for Drugs Puts Pressure on U.S. in Trade Talks*, N.Y. TIMES (Jul. 30, 2015), www.nytimes.com/2015/07/31/business/international/pacific-trade-deal-drugs-patent-protection.html; Anna Maria Barry-Jester, *The Problem with Tying Health Care to Trade*, FIVETHIRTYEIGHT (Oct. 19, 2015), http://fivethirtyeight.com/features/the-problem-with-tying-health-care-to-trade/.

circumstances.[75] But even that period could have raised drug prices and decreased drug access in developing countries such as Vietnam that had signed on to the pact.[76] With the TPP, the United States, to some extent, would have been exporting its own intellectual property protections abroad. In one of his first actions in office, however, President Trump scrapped the entire Trans-Pacific Partnership, as part of an effort to move away from free trade policies.

The international debate is yet more evidence of the unique place the United States occupies in the pharmaceutical industry, both in production and in purchasing. According to the Organization for Economic Co-operation and Development, the United States is both the world's largest pharma producer, at 39 percent of global production, and the world's largest purchaser, at 45 percent of global sales.[77] In other words, domestic U.S. business sustains the pharmaceutical industry – the United States is the largest producer of pharmaceuticals, but it also provides a near-majority of the industry's sales, in part of because of high prices.

One could argue that by serving as the main profit source for pharmaceutical companies, the United States is simply subsidizing lower prices in other countries. Maybe it's Canadians who should be thanking *us* for providing the lion's share of the pharma profit margin. The answer to that question is unclear – do pharmaceutical companies actually need the amount of return we currently provide, for example? – but what is clear is that a mix of dysfunctional market dynamics, strong intellectual property protection, and regulation has led to the complicated, expensive situation we have in the United States.

In many cases, the incomplete solution we have come up with is generic competition, which we introduce next. As this book warns, however, the generic revolution has its own challenges.

D GENERICS – A BRIEF PRIMER

The magic of generic substitution usually takes place without any intervention on the part of the patient. A doctor's written prescription for Pfizer's Zoloft is substituted seamlessly for a generic bottle of sertraline by the time the patient reaches the pharmacy. Patients who have standard sinus infections will probably leave their

---

[75] Tracy Staton, *Last-Minute Deal on Drug Exclusivity Wraps Up TPP Negotiations*, FIERCEPHARMA (Oct. 5, 2015), www.fiercepharma.com/pharma/last-minute-deal-on-drug-exclusivity-wraps-up-tpp-negotiations.

[76] Julia Belluz, *How the Trans-Pacific Partnership Could Drive Up the Cost of Medicine Worldwide*, VOX (Oct. 5, 2015), www.vox.com/2015/10/5/9454511/tpp-cost-medicine.

[77] ORGANIZATION FOR ECONOMIC CO-OPERATION AND DEVELOPMENT, EXECUTIVE SUMMARY: PHARMACEUTICAL PRICING POLICIES IN A GLOBAL MARKET at 10–11 (2008), www.oecd.org/health/health-systems/41303903.pdf.

neighborhood drug store with the classic five-day boxes of azithromycin for $10,[78] rather than boxes actually branded as a Zithromax Z-Pak. Automatic substitution is led by the pharmacist, who is often allowed to substitute a generic for a branded drug when available, and the public enjoys billions of dollars of savings with no action required on the part of either patients or doctors.[79] Automatic substitution laws, known as state "drug product selection" (DPS) laws, exist in all fifty states to permit this action. In some states, automatic substitution is *required* when the generic equivalent is available. The patient's incentives are also usually aligned with those of insurers and others involved in the payment process, who wish to pay less whenever possible and thus heavily promote the use of generics in their own lists of covered drugs. When generic substitution works, it works well, and generally to the benefit of patients – given the complexity of the system, it is impressive.

Today, almost 90 percent of all prescriptions in the United States are filled using generic medication,[80] and 81 percent of all small-molecule drugs – your standard pills and potions – have a generic equivalent.[81] When a generic is introduced into a market previously monopolized by a brand-name drug, the generic drug normally enters at a 20 percent discount from the branded medication within six months of launch, and the price falls quickly from that point.[82] Eventually, most generics are priced at an 80 to 85 percent discount from their name-brand equivalents.[83] Prices can even fall to 10 percent of the original cost when many generics enter the market.[84] And, as noted previously, the brand-name drugs sold at the higher price quickly lose substantial market share. As an example, one recent study on the introduction of generic Lipitor found that the introduction of just a couple of generics decreased the number of brand-name prescriptions by 18 percent just one month

---

[78] *See Medicine Use and Shifting Costs of Healthcare: A Review of the Use of Medicines in the United States in 2013*, IMS Inst. for Healthcare Informatics at 15 (Apr. 2014), www.imshealth.com/en/thought-leadership/ims-institute/reports/use-of-medicines-in-the-us-2013#ims-form ("The average co-pay for 78.6% of all retail dispensed prescriptions was $10 or less.").

[79] *See* Michael A. Carrier, *A Real-World Analysis of Pharmaceutical Settlements: The Missing Dimension of Product Hopping*, 62 Fla. L. Rev. 1009, 1017 (2010).

[80] *See Implementation of the Generic Drug User Fee Amendments of 2012 (GDUFA): Hearing Before the H. Comm. on Oversight & Gov't Reform*, 114th Cong. 1 & chart.1 (2016) (statement of Janet Woodcock, Director, Ctr. for Drug Evaluation & Res., U.S. Food & Drug Admin.); *see also* IMS Inst. for Healthcare Informatics, *supra* note 78, at 51.

[81] *See* Ernst R. Berndt & Murray L. Aitken, *Brand Loyalty, Generic Entry and Price Competition in Pharmaceuticals in the Quarter Century after the 1984 Waxman-Hatch Legislation* 4, 6 (Nat'l Bureau of Econ. Research, Working Paper No. 16431, 2010), www.nber.org/papers/w16431.pdf.

[82] *See ibid.* at 9–10, 10 fig.2.

[83] *See Facts about Generic Drugs*, U.S. Food & Drug Admin., www.fda.gov/Drugs/ResourcesForYou/Consumers/BuyingUsingMedicineSafely/UnderstandingGenericDrugs/ucm167991.htm (last updated June 28, 2016).

[84] *See* Berndt & Aitken, *Brand Loyalty*, *supra* note 81, at 9, 10 fig. 2.

after exclusivity was lost, with brand-name prescriptions dropping another 48 percent in the month after "full" generic competition began.[85]

Perhaps most important, the FDA estimates that consumers saved more than $217 billion in 2012 alone through the use of generics,[86] with total savings of $1.68 trillion from 2005 to 2014.[87] In the Lipitor study mentioned previously, median monthly out-of-pocket spending dropped from $17.50 when only brand-name Lipitor was available to barely above $5.00 for generic versions when many generics were available.[88]

One might call the generic revolution a miracle, but it certainly did not occur naturally or serendipitously. To begin with, the modern system of generic entry has only been in place for about three decades. Generic drug entry is covered by the Drug Price Competition and Patent Term Restoration Act, commonly known as the Hatch–Waxman Act.[89] Passed in 1984, Hatch–Waxman created a pathway to generic entry meant to incentivize the speedy introduction of generic drugs to market. Before the act, generic entry into the market was slow.[90] Would-be generic manufacturers could not apply to enter the market until after the branded company's patents had expired, with the effect that brand-name companies enjoyed a de facto patent extension and ongoing monopoly profits as the generic awaited FDA approval.[91] Brand-name drugs could face no competition for years after patent expiration. Further, few generics were entering the market to begin with. The burden of the application process, which required the generic to complete its own clinical trials, and the lack of substantial profits, deterred most manufacturers.[92]

As discussed in more detail in the Introduction, Hatch–Waxman offers generics a number of incentives to enter the market as quickly as possible, creating a complex web of regulation. First, prospective generics can submit an abbreviated new drug

---

[85] Jing Luo et al., *Effect of Generic Competition on Atorvastatin Prescribing and Patients' Out-of-Pocket Spending*, J. Am. Med. Ass'n. Intern. Med. at tbl. 2 (Jun. 27, 2016), http://archinte.jamanetwork.com/article.aspx?articleid=2530416#ioi160055r28.

[86] Generic Pharm. Ass'n, Generic Drug Savings in the U.S. 1 (2013), www.gphaonline.org/media/cms/2013_Savings_Study_12.19.2013_FINAL.pdf (data supplied by IMS Health).

[87] *Implementation of the Generic Drug User Fee Amendments of 2012 (GDUFA): Hearing before the H. Comm. on Oversight & Gov't Reform*, 114th Cong. 1 (2016) (statement of Janet Woodcock, Director, Ctr. for Drug Evaluation & Res., U.S. Food & Drug Admin.).

[88] Jing Luo et al., *Effect of Generic Competition*, supra note 85, at tbl. 3.

[89] Drug Price Competition and Patent Term Restoration Act, Pub. L. No. 98–417, 98 Stat. 1585 (1984) (codified as amended in scattered sections of 21 U.S.C. and 35 U.S.C.).

[90] *See* Wendy H. Schacht & John R. Thomas, Cong. Res. Serv., Report R41114, The Hatch-Waxman Act: A Quarter Century Later, at Summary (2011), http://congressional.proquest.com/profiles/gis/result/pqpresultpage.gispdfhitspanel.pdflink/$2fapp-bin$2fgis-congresearch$2ff$2fa$2f7$2f8$2fcrs-2011-rsi-0151_from_1_to_20.pdf/entitlementkeys=1234%7Capp-gis%7Ccongresearch%7Ccrs-2011-rsi-0151.

[91] Robin Feldman, Rethinking Patent Law 159 (2012).

[92] *See* Elizabeth S. Weiswasser & Scott D. Danzis, *The Hatch–Waxman Act: History, Structure, and Legacy*, 71 Antitrust L.J. 585, 585–90 (2003) (discussing the absence of generics on the market before the adoption of Hatch–Waxman).

application ("ANDA") before the patents for the brand-name drug have expired.[93] These shorter applications only need to contain evidence that the generic is bio-equivalent and has the same characteristics as the brand-name drug; they can rely on the brand-name drug company's clinical trial data to meet the rest of the application requirements, including those related to the safety and efficacy of the drug.[94]

Second, in what is known as a Paragraph IV certification, a generic manufacturer can attempt to enter the market before the brand-name company's patent term(s) have expired. This is considered an artificial act of infringement and it generally triggers litigation over patent validity.[95] While the generic applicant has not done anything "wrong" in this case, the act of filing the application allows a brand-name company to sue and bring the dispute to a quick close. This also allows the generic applicant to face less risk in the process, since it has not actually infringed any patent and would not be liable for any damages if the patent were found valid. It is like being able to ask a court whether something would be illegal – that is, launching a generic in the face of existing patents – before actually doing so.

As a reward for facing the costs and risks of litigation, the first generic manufacturer to file a Paragraph IV certification and gain approval generally is entitled to 180 days (roughly six months) of market exclusivity alongside the brand-name drug.[96] In other words, during the six-month period, only the brand-name drug and the first generic filer are allowed to be on the market. While only six months long, this duopoly period can be extremely valuable, potentially adding hundreds of millions of dollars to the first generic's coffers before additional generics enter and drive the price down further.[97] This benefit is intended to give generic companies an incentive to challenge weak patents or patents that should not actually cover the drug at issue.

The Hatch–Waxman Act has overwhelmingly met Congress's goals of balancing adequate patent protection for original inventors with promoting the rapid introduction of generics once this patent protection has expired. Since 1984, more than 10,000 generics have entered the market,[98] and the percentage of prescriptions filled with generics rose from just 13 percent in 1980[99] to around 86 percent by 2013.[100]

---

[93] 21 U.S.C. § 355(j) (2012).

[94] 21 U.S.C. §§ 355(j)(2)(A)(i)–(v) (2012).

[95] 21 U.S.C. § 355(j)(2)(A)(vii)(IV) (2012).

[96] 21 U.S.C. § 355(j)(5)(B)(iv) (2012). Exceptions and stipulations will be discussed in the Introduction.

[97] *See* Matthew Avery, *Continuing Abuse of the Hatch-Waxman Act by Pharmaceutical Patent Holders and the Failure of the 2003 Amendments*, 60 HASTINGS L.J. 171, 178 & 178 nn.55–56 (2008).

[98] *See* Schacht & Thomas, CONG. RES. SERV., REPORT R41114, *supra* note 90, at 5; *see also Medicare Prescription Drug, Improvement, and Modernization Act: Hearing on H.R. 1 Before S. Comm. on the Judiciary*, 108th Cong. (2003) (statement of Daniel E. Troy, Chief Counsel, U.S. Food & Drug Admin.), www.fda.gov/newsevents/testimony/ucm115033.htm.

[99] CONG. BUDGET OFFICE, HOW INCREASED COMPETITION FROM GENERIC DRUGS HAS AFFECTED PRICES AND RETURNS IN THE PHARMACEUTICAL INDUSTRY 37 (1998).

[100] IMS INST. FOR HEALTHCARE INFORMATICS, *supra* note 78, at 51.

Further, generic manufacturers have the incentive and ability to enter the market immediately after (or even before) the original patent terms expire. Change did not happen overnight; nor was Hatch–Waxman the kind of legislation that engendered enormous public controversy and debate – and yet it ended up making one of the greatest changes to the health care system in modern U.S. history.

A second miracle has occurred alongside the dramatic rise of generics – for the most part, the benefits of Hatch–Waxman have held up despite its complexity and the persistent attempts at undercutting its aims. In fact, it is the complexity of Hatch–Waxman that has unfortunately created a veritable playground of opportunities that pharmaceutical companies have used to hold off generic competition. And it is these strategies that are the focus of this book.

Our goal for this book is twofold: first, to shine light on the complex strategies as they have unfolded over time, and, second, to suggest ways to cabin those behaviors and create incentives for companies to follow the path that is optimal for society. Quite simply, pharmaceutical companies should be directing their creative energies toward research and development, not toward inventing new legal challenges and regulatory obstructions.

To be clear, when pharmaceutical companies preserve their hard-earned patent exclusivity by legally knocking down generic challenges, such behavior is consistent with societal goals and important for the patent system. Rights are worth little if the rights holder cannot enforce them, and that is as true for patents as for any form of legal right. In contrast, when firms attempt to extend their monopolies unlawfully, such behavior undercuts the goals of the patent system, and the cost to society can be troubling. Patients and the general public lose, giving up billions of dollars in savings while ready-to-market generics languish on the sidelines. The energy spent on manipulation of the legal system diverts time and resources away from innovation activities.

The Introduction explains the Hatch–Waxman Act pathway to generic entry in more detail, discussing the economic incentives behind its structure and detailing amendments designed to improve the functioning of the act. The workings of Hatch–Waxman are quite complicated, even when compared to other legislation and regulatory regimes, and we will explain its principles and pathways in an easy-to-understand way that also highlights the reasoning behind each step in the process. From the beginning, Hatch–Waxman has faced issues with unintentional consequences, loopholes, and subversion. We also discuss early gaps in the act and later amendments designed to patch these holes.

Chapter 1 explains the origins of generic delay tactics, called "Generation 1.0" – the first of three "generations" the book uses to categorize the tactics that have evolved over time. The organizational system of generations that we use here is not meant to suggest that these each of these periods has taken place sequentially and separately. Some "Generation 1.0"-style settlements still survive; early "Generation 3.0" tactics have plagued generics for more than a decade – the overlap between generations can be substantial. Instead, the system serves as a helpful way of organizing sets of related tactics, and the use of "generations" implies that each era of tactics has evolved from or developed in response to strategies from previous generations.

Throughout the book, we detail examples of companies engaging in various aspects of the three generations of behaviors. The companies we describe, however, are not the only ones employing these tactics. Some companies have had the misfortune of landing in the spotlight, and some have been a tad more aggressive, but these behaviors are rampant throughout the industry.

In Generation 1.0, delay generally takes the form of "pay-for-delay," or "reverse payment," settlements, in which a potential generic manufacturer is simply paid by the pioneer drug maker, often hundreds of millions of dollars, to refrain from entering the market until a stipulated date. "Reverse payment" refers to the odd nature of the arrangement – instead of a defendant paying a plaintiff to settle a suit, brand drug companies pay off the generic to end a patent infringement lawsuit. The reasoning behind the counterintuitive direction of these settlements reflects the economics of pharmaceutical markets and unintentional incentives created by the Hatch–Waxman generic pathway. These settlements were commonplace for many years, but the Supreme Court's 2013 ruling in *FTC v. Actavis* opened the door to intense antitrust scrutiny of such agreements.

Chapter 2 describes the rise of a new generation of pay-for-delay tactics – "Generation 2.0." Beginning long before *Actavis*, these strategies generally involve the transfer of benefits from the branded firm to a generic manufacturer, but not through a simple cash settlement. Generation 2.0 agreements include patterns of multiple side deals, where two companies settle a number of Hatch–Waxman disputes at once, resulting in a net benefit for the generic firm but without any large, conspicuous payment. Other instruments include overvalued agreements wherein the generic delays entry, but it is paid handsomely to promote, manufacture, or otherwise assist the brand-name company with the sale of its drug. Finally, Generation 2.0 includes "boy scout clauses" – agreements to behave honorably that actually mask anticompetitive collusion. As described in Chapter 2, these side deals are now themselves facing antitrust scrutiny in the courts.

Chapters 3 and 4 provide a comprehensive look at emerging "Generation 3.0" strategies. Until now, these tactics have been deployed largely under the radar. Generation 3.0 tactics no longer focus on delay agreements with generic competitors, but rather on using administrative processes and drug modifications to obstruct generics from getting to market.

Many of these strategies have little justification beyond obstruction of generics, and some recent fact patterns are falling further outside the boundaries of common sense. Specifically, we will discuss delay mechanisms including drug labeling changes, using FDA safety requirements as a guise to restrict generic access, extending a drug's life through minor dosage and formula changes, as well as what we call "multiplicity tactics," in which a number of these mechanisms are exploited at once. Of course, once companies develop new obstacle strategies, they can be bargained away, and we are beginning to see new settlement agreements to that effect. Once again, the brand-name drug company can play the role of the "boy scout," agreeing to behave well but doing it in a way that prevents further competition in the market.

Despite all of the troubling anecdotes, just how prevalent are these obstructionist strategies? In Chapter 5, we will share results from our deep look into drug-related citizen petitions submitted to the FDA. We identify trends over the last decade and demonstrate empirically that a process intended to allow ordinary citizens to petition the FDA has become a key avenue for strategic behavior by pharmaceutical companies to delay entry of generic competition. We also attempt to show empirically whether generic-related petitions are timed to delay the generic approval process.

Our Conclusion finishes with ideas for reforming the generic entry pathway. These ideas borrow from systems theory – looking from the perspective of how different systems interact to create opportunities and incentives to correct suboptimal behaviors. Moreover, to move the system away from hide-and-seek games, this section proposes the addition of standards-based legal rules. Most important, to avoid "death by tinkering"[101] – that is, adjusting doctrines a little here and a little there without comprehensive logic until the entire area collapses under its own weight – this section suggests a deeper look and a more comprehensive overhaul of different intersecting regimes. We also suggest a dramatic increase in pricing and FDA transparency so regulators have the information they need to make informed decisions and the market functions better by resolving long-standing information gaps. Sunshine laws about pricing are already being considered by numerous legislatures across the United States.

Hatch–Waxman was indeed a brilliant legislative innovation, heralding nothing short of a miracle in the reduction of drug costs. Now, it is time to consider the next generation of the regime so those miracles are not swept away.[102]

---

[101] *See* Robin Feldman, *A Conversation on Judicial Decision-Making*, 5 HASTINGS SCI. & TECH. L.J. 1, 2 (2013) (introducing the phrase "death by tinkering" to describe patent jurisprudence in the Federal Circuit).

[102] *See generally* Aaron S. Kesselheim & Jonathan J. Darrow, *Hatch–Waxman Turns 30: Do We Need a Re-Designed Approach for the Modern Era?*, 15 YALE J. HEALTH POL'Y L. & ETHICS 293 (2015) (presenting a recent article reviewing the history of Hatch–Waxman and suggesting improvements).

Introduction

The Winding Road to Generic Entry

The Hatch-Waxman Act is a deeply complex piece of legislation, codified in four different sections of the United States Code.[1] While it creates a streamlined pathway for generic manufacturers to seek approval of their drug, it does so in a way that testifies to the difficulty of satisfying all stakeholders in the pharmaceutical market. The goal of protecting innovative activity, balanced with the desire to make low-cost drugs available to patients, has produced a labyrinthine series of statutes. Complexity breeds opportunity, however, and Hatch-Waxman's legacy is littered with evidence of manipulation.[2]

This chapter focuses on the core components of FDA drug approval most often implicated in generic delay, in the clearest terms possible, omitting discussions of exceptions and complex subsections where appropriate. Later chapters will introduce other sections of the act to help make sense of these intricate games of generic delay. These include descriptions of amendments meant to tighten the functioning of Hatch-Waxman (while frequently creating their own difficulties). Hatch-Waxman's establishment of a new generic drug landscape also means that an entire lexicon of jargon has developed to discuss the field, and this chapter will define the main terms and acronyms before continuing further.

Hatch-Waxman's core contribution was allowing prospective generic manufacturers to submit an Abbreviated New Drug Application, almost exclusively referred to as an "ANDA," to seek approval of a drug equivalent to one already approved by the FDA.[3] To prevent weighing the material down in endless jargon, we will refer to ANDAs as "generic drug applications" whenever possible. A generic drug application must be for a medication that is bioequivalent to the

---

[1] Drug Price Competition and Patent Term Restoration Act, Pub. L. No. 98–417, 98 Stat. 1585 (1984) (codified as amended in scattered sections of 21 U.S.C. and 35 U.S.C.).

[2] ROBIN FELDMAN, RETHINKING PATENT LAW 160 (2012) ("As so often is the case, complexity breeds opportunity, and clever lawyers have been exploiting the details of the act since its inception.").

[3] 21 U.S.C. § 355(j) (2012).

brand-name drug,[4] and it must generally have the same active ingredient(s), route of administration, dosage form, strength, use indications, and labeling information as the existing medication.[5] Disputes over these characteristics become the battleground for many of the games that are played between brand-name companies and generics, so we believe it is important to provide a few definitions before moving forward.

- Active ingredient: the ingredient in a medication that actually affects the state of the body. For example, in a capsule of omeprazole (Prilosec), an acid reducer, the shell of the capsule contains ingredients such as gelatin, butyl alcohol, and food dyes, but the only active ingredient is omeprazole. Generic drugs are commonly referred to only by their active ingredients.
- Route of administration: how the drug is introduced or absorbed into the body. An omeprazole capsule is classified by the FDA as having an "oral" route of administration, unsurprisingly referring to the fact that the medication is swallowed. Other common routes of administration, as classified by the FDA, include "injection," "intravenous," "topical," and "nasal."
- Dosage form: how the drug is packaged for use or consumption. Common dosage forms include tablets, capsules, suspensions (liquids), solutions (for injection or intravenous use), sprays, gels, films, ointments, and lotions, but less common forms are also seen, including lozenges, suppositories, and even shampoos.
- Strength: how much of the active ingredient is contained within a unit of the medication. Strength is often referenced when discussing varying capsules or tablets – 25 mg tablets, 50 mg capsules, and so on. Other strengths are more complicated (*e.g.* "3 mg/mL of active ingredient in an intravenous solution").
- Use indications: the officially stated and approved uses of the medication. A drug may be approved, for example, to treat anxiety or to relieve pain following surgery. The FDA keeps an official list of "use codes" delineating uses of medications connected to patents – literally thousands exist.
- Labeling information: any other information on a drug's label or prescribing information. Examples include warnings such as "this drug should not be taken with alcohol" and information about how the medication should be taken (*e.g.* "once a day with a high-fiber meal").

Once the generic can demonstrate these characteristics, however, the remainder of the approval process is significantly streamlined in comparison to approval of

---

[4] The Act Defines two drugs as bioequivalent when "the rate and extent of absorption of the drug do not show a significant difference from the rate and extent of absorption of the listed drug." 21 U.S.C. § 355(j)(8)(B) (2012).

[5] 21 U.S.C. § 355(j)(2)(A) (2012).

a new drug. The simplifying step is that the generic application can make use of a branded drug company's preexisting clinical trial data that prove the safety and efficacy of the drug.[6] This saves the generic applicant the years of work and great expense necessary to conduct new clinical trials.

As discussed in the Introduction, the Hatch-Waxman Act expressly allows the activity necessary to prepare a generic drug application to take place prior to the expiration of the patent on the original drug. Without such a provision, generic hopefuls had to wait until the patent expired before they could begin activity such as obtaining samples of the drug, developing their product, and engaging in the bio-equivalence testing required by the FDA. As a result, brand-name companies could enjoy a monopoly well beyond the patent term because no generic could possibly be ready to enter when the patent expired.[7] Under Hatch-Waxman, these activities are exempt from an assertion of patent infringement when used for development of a generic application.[8] The exemption allows generics to file an application well before expiration of the patent, so that they can be ready for entry when the patent expires at the latest, rather than having to wait for patent expiration and only then begin the approval process.

The entire process of drug approval has changed substantially in the last 50 years. Before 1962, FDA drug approval requirements were incredibly lax by modern standards – drugs could simply be sold 60 days after information was filed with the FDA, as long as the FDA did not object.[9] This process changed as a result of the thalidomide crisis in Europe in 1961, when thousands of babies were born with partially formed limbs and other severe birth defects after mothers were given the drug for nausea during pregnancy. In response, the U.S. Congress passed the Kefauver-Harris Amendments, which, among other changes, required manufacturers to prove the safety and efficacy of a drug before marketing approval could take place.[10] While the amendments revolutionized attitudes toward drug safety and scientific rigor, they created a bind for generic drug makers wishing to follow the brand-name drug onto the market. In the 1984 case of *Roche v. Bolar,* for example, the United States Court of Appeals for the Federal Circuit, a U.S. appeals court that often hears cases related to patents and other intellectual property, found that prospective generic manufacturers could not use patent-protected brand-name information for

---

[6] *See* Wendy H. Schacht & John R. Thomas, CONG. RES. SERV., REPORT R41114, THE HATCH-WAXMAN ACT: A QUARTER CENTURY LATER, at 1 (2011).

[7] *See Roche Prods., Inc. v. Bolar Pharm. Co.,* 733 F.2d 858, 863–64 (Fed. Cir. 1984) ("The [brand-name companies] gain for themselves, it is asserted, a *de facto* monopoly of upwards of 2 years by enjoining FDA-required testing of a generic drug until the patent on the drug's active ingredient expires.").

[8] 35 U.S.C. § 271(e)(1) (2012).

[9] *See 50 Years: The Kefauver-Harris Amendments,* U.S. Food & Drug Admin., www.fda.gov/Drugs/NewsEvents/ucm320924.htm (last updated February 26, 2016).

[10] *Ibid.*

research.[11] Hatch-Waxman, which remedied this problem, was signed into law five months later.

Now, when a brand-name drug company files for FDA approval, the law requires that the company list all patents that "could reasonably be asserted" against a generic applicant.[12] These are then recorded in an FDA document commonly referred to as the "Orange Book" because of its orange cover in print form. The document is formally known as "Approved Drug Products with Therapeutic Equivalence Evaluations."[13] ("ADP-TEE" didn't quite roll off the tongue as well as "Orange Book.") In ways both good and definitely bad, the Orange Book resembles outdated print methods of information organization, such as a phone book. The book is intended to serve as a compendium of all currently approved drugs and the information their manufacturers provide about them. In the modern world of search and data storage, the printed Orange Book is an outdated method of assembling information.

The Orange Book has played a prominent role in some of the game playing that has unfolded across time, mainly because its contents are, unbelievably, not subject to FDA verification. Drug makers can list any patent numbers they wish for a drug and any description of what those patents protect, and the FDA does not make any judgment on the validity of the contents. These listing decisions then have enormous consequences for the legal steps a generic company needs to take to reach the market. It seems strange that so much of the generic pipeline relies on an unchecked document (available only in print until recently) that is readily subject to abuse, but that is the system as it currently exists.

When a generic drug maker arrives later on the scene and files an application for approval with the FDA, the generic must make one of four "certifications" to each of the patents the brand-name drug maker has listed for the drug in the Orange Book.[14] Most of these certifications result in limited fuss and bother because they either represent that all the patents have expired, that no relevant patents are listed in the Orange Book, or that the generic company will wait until all patents expire before taking the drug to market.[15]

All the action, however, is in what is known as a "Paragraph IV" certification. A Paragraph IV certification alleges that the listed patent either (1) is invalid or

---

[11]   *Roche Prods., Inc. v. Bolar Pharm. Co.*, 733 F.2d 858, 863–64 (Fed. Cir. 1984).

[12]   21 U.S.C. § 355(b)(1) (2012).

[13]   FELDMAN, RETHINKING PATENT LAW, *supra* note 2, at 60–61; *see Orange Book: Approved Drug Products with Therapeutic Equivalence Evaluations*, U.S. FOOD & DRUG ADMIN. (May 17, 2013), www.accessdata .fda.gov/scripts/cder/ob/default.cfm.

[14]   *See* 21 U.S.C. § 355(j)(2)(A)(vii) (2012); *see also* 21 U.S.C. § 355(j)(7)(A) (2012) (describing the workings of the Orange Book).

[15]   *See* 21 U.S.C. §§ 355(j)(2)(A)(vii)(I)–(III) (2012).

(2) would not be infringed by the generic drug application.[16] The goal is to resolve questions of weak or misapplied patents so that the generic can enter as soon as possible.

A Paragraph IV certification is treated as an "artificial" act of patent infringement – as if the generic company had already started selling the drug. Thus, the brand-name drug company is permitted to initiate litigation, which it must do within 45 days of receiving notification from the generic filer. If the brand-name drug company does not litigate, the FDA is free to approve the generic's application once the Agency verifies the safety and efficacy of the generic drug.[17]

Why would a generic applicant purposely choose to invite costly and potentially damaging litigation? First, there are weak patent claims – a topic that has inspired numerous writings about the state of the modern-day patent system. Generic companies have enjoyed considerable success challenging weak drug patents. One early study reported by the Federal Trade Commission in 2002 found that generic applicants won their "Paragraph IV challenge" 73 percent of the time.[18] Another study from 2010 found that generics won fewer than 50 percent of their Paragraph IV challenges between 2000 and 2009; however, if settlements and cases eventually dropped by the brand-name company are included in the calculation, the win rate in this study rises to 76 percent for the 2000–2009 period as well.[19]

Second, baked into Hatch-Waxman is a significant incentive for the first generic to submit an application with a Paragraph IV certification to at least one of the listed patents for the drug. As long as the applicant does not lose its patent infringement case, the first generic filer generally is entitled to 180 days of marketing exclusivity alongside the brand-name drug.[20] In other words, for about six months, only the brand-name drug company and the first generic can sell the drug; no other generic company can enter the market.

This essentially creates a duopoly consisting of the brand-name drug and the first generic for 180 days. The FDA is not permitted to approve any other applications with a Paragraph IV certification until the 180-day period elapses; the period is

---

[16] 21 U.S.C. § 355(j)(2)(A)(vii)(IV) (2012).

[17] *See* 21 U.S.C. § 355(j)(5)(B)(iii) (2012).

[18] *See Generic Drug Entry Prior to Patent Expiration* FED. TRADE COMM'N 16 (2002), www.ftc.gov/ sites/default/files/documents/reports/generic-drug-entry-prior-patent-expiration-ftc-study/genericdrug study_0.pdf.

[19] *In re K-Dur Antitrust Litigation*, 686 F.3d 197, 215 n. 11 (3rd Cir. 2012), citing RBC Capital Mkts., *Pharmaceuticals: Analyzing Litigation Success Rates* 4 (2010), *available at* www.amlawdaily.typepad .com/pharmareport.pdf.

[20] *See* 21 U.S.C. § 355(j)(5)(B)(iv) (2012). After 2003 amendments to Hatch-Waxman, it is possible to forfeit the 180-day exclusivity period without losing a patent infringement case. Further, it is also possible that the brand-name drug company chooses not to bring litigation during the 45-day period. In this case, the first filer still retains its rights to 180 days of exclusivity.

generally deemed to begin when the first commercial marketing of the drug takes place.[21] Generic entry normally occurs after one of the following events: all relevant patents and exclusivities expire; the generic drug maker wins a challenge invalidating all relevant patents or finding that infringement did not occur; or the generic company reaches a settlement with the branded drug maker allowing entry. This six-month exclusivity period can easily be worth hundreds of millions of dollars to a generic, representing a substantial majority of the potential profits to be gained from generic entry.[22]

The entire Paragraph IV process is intended to give generic companies an incentive to do battle with powerful pharmaceutical companies. (This metaphor may have had stronger relevance at the start of the modern era of generics. With the tremendous consolidation in recent years, many generic companies are now subsidiaries or units of much larger pharmaceutical conglomerates. The battle is now more likely to be *Part of Goliath vs. Part of Goliath*, with fewer actual Davids on the scene.)

The Paragraph IV first-filer exclusivity is thus an enormous incentive for a generic applicant to file as soon as possible and secure the six months of exclusivity. In addition, if the generic succeeds in overturning the patent, the generic also gains market entry long before the patent would have expired. The artificial nature of the patent infringement action provides other benefits as well. It allows the generic to trigger litigation without actually entering the market and potentially accruing substantial damages. Despite its many benefits, however, this complicated and lucrative pathway has made Hatch-Waxman susceptible to abuse, due in large part to the economic incentives created by the exclusivity period.[23]

Going back to the filing process – if the patent holder chooses to initiate litigation, a 30-month stay is placed on generic approval. The goal is to allow the infringement litigation to work its way through the courts while the FDA continues reviewing the generic application.[24] The generic application cannot be approved for 30 months,

---

[21] *See* 21 U.S.C. §§ 355(j)(5)(B)(iv)(I)–(II) (2012). However, this does not entirely prevent the presence of other competition. Brand-name companies can launch their own generic version of the drug at a lower price-tier (or permit another company to do so), creating instant competition for the generic. These generics are often called "authorized generics" and are discussed later in Chapter 2.

[22] *See* Matthew Avery, *Continuing Abuse of the Hatch-Waxman Act by Pharmaceutical Patent Holders and the Failure of the 2003 Amendments*, 60 HASTINGS L.J. 171, at 178, 178 nn.55–56 (2008).

[23] When there are multiple first-filing ANDA applicants (all submitting on the same day, usually the first day that ANDAs will be accepted), all applicants are eligible for exclusivity. *See generally* U.S. Food & Drug Admin., GUIDANCE FOR INDUSTRY 180-DAY EXCLUSIVITY WHEN MULTIPLE ANDAS ARE SUBMITTED ON THE SAME DAY (2003), www.fda.gov/downloads/drugs/guidancecomplianceregulatoryinformation/guidances/ucm072851.pdf.

[24] *See* 21 U.S.C. § 355(j)(5)(B)(iii) (2012).

however, unless a court enters a final order declaring the patents at issue invalid, unenforceable, or not infringed.[25]

Although Hatch-Waxman generally is discussed in the framework of generic drugs, the act also was designed to add new protections for brand-name drug companies. Given the U.S. Patent and Trademark Office's patent approval process and the FDA's own approval process for the drug, which generally overlaps with a portion of the patent term, the effective life of a drug patent is often substantially shorter than the 20-year patent term.[26] Thus, Hatch–Waxman allows pharmaceutical companies to receive an extension of the patent term, in an effort to partially restore the time lost to the approval processes.[27] This "restoration" is the origin of the Hatch–Waxman Act's full name, the Drug Price Competition and Patent Term *Restoration* Act.

The Hatch-Waxman Act also provides some new drugs with methods of keeping others out of the market in addition to patents. These are known as nonpatent exclusivities. For example, drugs with an active ingredient never before approved by the FDA are eligible for either four or five years of what is known as a "marketing exclusivity."[28] This is not an extension of the patent term – it only means that the FDA is not allowed to accept generic applications that use the original drug maker's data for at least four years after initial FDA approval. Although a generic applicant theoretically could engage in the lengthy and expensive process of conducting its own clinical trials, the cost would be prohibitive. An original drug maker receives a 20-year patent to help recoup such costs, while the most a generic applicant could get would be six months of a duopoly.

This nonpatent exclusivity in Hatch-Waxman gives the brand-name drug maker breathing space before a generic company can start the ball rolling. The brand-name drug maker is guaranteed at least four years without direct competition, even if the patents are invalid.[29] Other exclusivities are available, for example, for new clinical

---

[25] *See ibid.* If the first Paragraph IV generic filer loses its case, it forfeits the 180-day exclusivity period, and the Paragraph IV certification is usually changed to a Paragraph III certification agreeing not to enter until the expiration of all FDA and patent exclusivity. *See Small Business Assistance: 180-Day Generic Drug Exclusivity,* U.S. FOOD & DRUG ADMIN., www.fda.gov/Drugs/DevelopmentApprovalProcess/SmallBusinessAssistance/ucm069964.htm (last updated February 11, 2016).

[26] *See* Schacht & Thomas, CONG. RES. SERV., REPORT R41114, *supra* note 6, at 3.

[27] *See* 35 U.S.C. § 156(g)(6)(A) (2012); 35 U.S.C. § 156(c) (2012). *See generally* 35 U.S.C. § 156 (describing the full patent term extension process). Although the patent can be extended by a maximum of five years, the maximum term remaining after approval cannot exceed fourteen years. *See id.* § 156(c)(3).

[28] The benefit is called a New Chemical Entity ("NCE") exclusivity. *See* 21 U.S.C. § 355(c)(3)(E)(ii) (2012); 21 U.S.C. § 355(j)(5)(F)(ii) (2012). The longer five-year right is reduced to four years, if a generic applicant files a Paragraph IV certification, declaring that the patent is invalid or would not be infringed by a generic version. *See* 21 C.F.R. § 314.108(b)(3).

[29] For an extensive discussion of the 13 forms of nonpatent exclusivities that exist for pharmaceuticals, *see* Robin Feldman, *Regulatory Property: The New IP,* 40 COLUMBIA J.L. & ARTS 53 (2016).

studies that lead to new indications or formulations of an existing drug (three years) or for drugs with indications to treat certain rare diseases (seven years, as established under the Orphan Drug Act).[30] In all, there are at least 13 forms of nonpatent exclusivities available under various statutory regimes.[31]

Important changes have been made to Hatch-Waxman and its related mechanisms since its enactment, mostly notably through the Medicare Modernization Act in 2003 and the Food and Drug Administration Amendments Act of 2007.[32] Many of the changes were aimed at curbing abuses and plugging loopholes in Hatch-Waxman, and they will be discussed in the chapters ahead.

In short, Hatch-Waxman set the stage for a new era in medicines: generic competitors were able to develop and test their products, as well as apply for FDA approval, before expiration of the brand-name drug company's patent. In addition, the Hatch-Waxman Act created incentives for generics to challenge weak patent claims. The goal, essentially, was to speed generic versions of drugs to market as quickly as possible, introducing competition and dramatically lowering prices for consumers.

---

[30]   *See* 21 U.S.C. § 355(c)(3)(E)(iii) (2012), 21 U.S.C. §§ 355(j)(5)(F)(iii)–(iv) (2012) (explaining new clinical study exclusivity); 21 U.S.C. §§ 360bb–360cc (2012) (explaining Orphan Drug Act definitions and exclusivities).

[31]   *See generally* Feldman, *supra* note 29.

[32]   *See* Medicare Prescription Drug, Improvement, and Modernization Act, Pub. L. No. 108–173, 117 Stat. 2066 (2003); Food and Drug Administration Amendments Act of 2007, Pub. L. No. 110–85, 121 Stat. 823 (2007) (codified as amended in scattered sections of 21 U.S.C.).

1

"Generation 1.0"

The Rise and Fall of Traditional Pay-for-Delay

A THE BASIC CONTOURS OF PAY-FOR-DELAY

With Hatch-Waxman enacted in 1984, the stage was set for a new era in pharmaceuticals. But the new dawn was considerably chillier for brand-name drug companies. Having spent hundreds of millions, if not billions, on research and development, the prospect of losing additional profits loomed large on the horizon. Imagine watching this impending storm of competition from the perspective of a brand-name drug maker. Suddenly, the government *wants* generics to challenge your hard-earned patents and looks *favorably* upon early entry. What can you can do to maintain exclusivity? You spent hundreds of millions, if not billions, on research and development – now, how can you ensure that the monopoly profits last as long as possible? Why not just pay the generic competition to stay out of the market?

With so much at stake, the strategy of pay-for-delay emerged. It is a darkly ingenious approach in which the brand-name drug company shares a portion of its monopoly profits with the generic company in exchange for the generic company's agreement to stay out of the market. The pay-for-delay strategy sparked conversations about antitrust, competition, and generic access that have raged in health policy and intellectual property circles for years.[1]

Specifically, in pay-for-delay, a brand-name company settles its lawsuit with the generic company, usually patent infringement litigation spurred on by a Paragraph

---

[1] *See generally* C. Scott Hemphill, *Paying for Delay: Pharmaceutical Patent Settlement as a Regulatory Design Problem*, 81 N.Y.U. L. REV. 1553 (2006); C. Scott Hemphill, *An Aggregate Approach to Antitrust: Using New Data and Rulemaking to Preserve Drug Competition*, 109 COLUM. L. REV. 629 (2009); Stacey L. Dogan & Mark A. Lemley, *Antitrust Law and Regulatory Gaming*, 87 TEX. L. REV. 685 (2009); Steve D. Shadowen, Keith B. Leffler, & Joseph T. Lukens, *Anticompetitive Product Changes in the Pharmaceutical Industry*, 41 RUTGERS L.J. 1 (2009); Matthew Avery & Mary Nguyen, *The Roadblock for Generic Drugs: Declaratory Judgment Jurisdiction for Later Generic Challengers*, 15 N.C. J.L. & TECH. 1 (2013); Jessie Cheng, *An Antitrust Analysis of Product Hopping in the Pharmaceutical Industry*, 108 COLUM. L. REV. 1471 (2008).

IV certification in a generic application. Under the terms of the settlement, the generic receives a cash payment and agrees to delay its entry into the market for a specified period. For example, "Brand" Company might have four years left on its patents on Drug X, but "Generic" Company is challenging the patents. To maintain its lock on the market for as long as possible, Brand might pay Generic $150 million to delay generic entry of Drug X for three years, by dropping the suit and agreeing on a specific date when Generic can enter.

These settlements are sometimes referred to as "reverse payment" schemes, a reference to the fact that payment is transferred from the suing brand-name drug company to the defending generic competitor. This runs counter to the standard expectation that a defendant would pay a plaintiff to settle a suit. The practice first came to light when Paragraph IV challenges significantly increased in the decades following Hatch-Waxman's enactment. Few drugs were subject to a Paragraph IV challenge immediately after the passage of Hatch-Waxman, but 55 percent of drugs approved between 2000 and 2002 were challenged.[2] By 2006, the median time from FDA approval of a brand-name drug to the first Paragraph IV challenge by a generic company had dropped to a flat four years for all categories of drugs.[3] That four-year figure is particularly significant because the FDA cannot accept a generic application with a Paragraph IV certification until four years after the brand-name drug was initially approved, for brand-name drugs with new active ingredients.[4] Thus, when drugs with new ingredients, which are likely to be popular or novel, are approved, generic challengers are filing with the FDA as soon as they are allowed under the law.

Put another way, more drug patents and drugs are challenged than ever before, and generic drug manufacturers are gathering resources to make challenges more quickly than they ever did previously. Today's new blockbuster drug generally can expect to be subject to a so-called preexpiration challenge. In response, drug manufacturers have developed responses to keep generics off the market.

The insidious element of pay-for-delay settlements is that the incentives of both the brand-name drug company and the generic company are aligned with each

---

[2]   *See* C. Scott Hemphill & Bhaven N. Sampat, *When Do Generics Challenge Drug Patents?* 8 J. EMPIRICAL LEGAL STUD. 613, 624, 624 fig. 4 (2011); *see also* Hemphill, *Aggregate Approach to Antitrust, supra* note 1, at 657–58 (noting increased intensity of antitrust enforcement and development of new strategies starting around 1997).

[3]   *See* Henry Grabowski *et al.*, *Pharmaceutical Patent Challenges and Their Implications for Innovation and Generic Competition* fig. 3 (AM. ECON. ASS'N, WORKING PAPER, 2015), www.aeaweb.org/aea/2015 conference/program/retrieve.php?pdfid=1203.

[4]   21 U.S.C. § 355(j)(5)(F)(ii) (2012). As noted in the Introduction, a generic applicant theoretically could submit an application replicating all of the brand-name company's clinical trials, but the cost of such work without the possibility of recoupment through a patent term makes that route extremely unlikely.

other – but not with society's interests. In particular, a generic may find it more lucrative to enter into a pay-for-delay settlement than actually pursuing a lawsuit to its conclusion – in fact, a generic application might even be filed with the intent (or hope) of eventually managing to secure a settlement from the brand-name drug maker. Once again, the economics of competition come into play when describing this phenomenon.

The value of a pay-for-delay settlement is best understood by realizing that both the brand-name company and the first generic can obtain substantial benefits through a settlement delaying entry.[5] When the first-filing generic enters the market, it is entitled to six months of marketing exclusivity alongside the branded drug. This period is valuable – valuable enough that it also leaves both parties open to bargaining. Unfortunately, in creating an incentive for early entry, Congress and the FDA also created a bargaining chip that can be essentially sold away to brand-name drug companies.[6]

A generic could easily prefer an agreement to delay entry over the risks of losing in court, knowing that the agreement will still *guarantee* six months of duopoly that may not otherwise be available. The generic has locked in its right to the exclusivity period by filing first, and this period generally is not forfeited absent a court judgment finding the patents valid. The six-month exclusivity benefit for first generic filers was designed so that generic filers would have an incentive to challenge the validity or the application of patents. Instead, the generic and the patent holder settle, and the generic still walks away with the benefit. In other words, the six-month exclusivity was designed for the benefit of society but operates here for the benefit of the companies alone. Instead of getting generic drugs to market as quickly as possible, society gets delays.

The incentive for the generic company to agree to delay is even stronger when the brand-name company throws in some form of payment. The generic filer still gains the benefits of the six-month duopoly period, but it receives an additional payment as well – a payment that results from inflated drug prices. Specifically, during the period in which the generic has agreed to stay off the market, the price of the drug stays at its height; the brand-name company shares some of its profit from those high prices with the generic company. Both are perfectly happy. It is consumers who lose out.

The scenario is the bizarre consequence of the 180-day exclusivity bargaining chip. Without the exclusivity incentive, a Paragraph IV challenge would have one of two endings: losing the challenge or winning the challenge and being able to

---

[5] Hemphill, *Paying for Delay, supra* note 1, at 127–28.
[6] *See ibid.* at 134–39, which offers a wonderful, clear explanation of the incentives at work for the branded and the generic.

enter the market – along with any other competitor who wishes to enter. As the first generic, your profits would be limited to what you could secure in the short amount of time before other competitors joined the market, with the price dropping quickly as more competitors enter. Today, this lead time is unlikely to be long, given that many generics are ready to submit applications as soon as such applications can be accepted for a drug.

When the six-month exclusivity period is available, suddenly the generic has the incentive to be the first entrant – but the kicker is that it does not really matter when that entry takes place! The alignment of incentives occurs because, in most cases, the actual entry date does not matter as much to the generic as does securing the entirety of the six-month marketing exclusivity period.[7] If annual sales are unlikely to fall sharply before the expiration of the patent term, selling the generic a few years later is unlikely to dramatically change the sales the first generic will garner during the six months of duopoly. In fact, as Professor Scott Hemphill notes, the case of increasing sales for a drug would present the scenario in which a generic would *prefer* later entry in order to enjoy a more profitable exclusivity period.[8]

In all, if a generic does not need to *win* its Paragraph IV challenge to hold on to the first-filer exclusivity period, and if a settlement does not lead to forfeiture of the exclusivity period, the generic might be willing to enter into a pay-for-delay agreement and guarantee its exclusivity.

Now, add in the complication that the uncertainty of litigation also applies to the branded firm under attack. Some patents are weak and some have stronger claims – so the actual picture is more complex. There are information asymmetries here in how much each party knows about the weakness or strength of the patents at hand.

In particular, the brand-name company in our example also faces uncertainty in the patent infringement suit it has brought against the prospective generic applicant. If it wins, the brand-name company will maintain its stream of monopoly profits through the end of its patent term, barring any challenges brought by other manufacturers. If it loses and patents are invalidated, duopoly competition will begin almost immediately, and both the brand-name price and sales volume will drop in the presence of the other competitor. If years of the patent term remain, this additional time could easily be worth of billions of dollars. A comparatively small payment – hundreds of millions of dollars or less – can guarantee that generic entry will be pushed back and the patents emerge unscathed.

Thus, the brand-name company's risk leads to additional payment under a pay-for-delay scheme. The brand-name company has much more to lose than the generic; that is why we see payment in the direction of brand to generic.

---

[7] Hemphill, *Paying for Delay, supra* note 1, at 139.
[8] *Ibid.*

Throughout all this strenuous negotiation, the biggest loser is destined to be the public, which continues to suffer higher prices during the period of delay. The FTC has estimated that reverse payment settlements cost consumers $3.5 billion each year.[9]

For example, suppose a branded drug is able to preserve four years of exclusivity through this type of settlement, a not at all unreasonable assumption.[10] Perhaps the brand pays the generic applicant $500 million for this delay. At $1 billion in annual sales,[11] the brand-name company retains $3.5 billion – that is, $1 billion each year minus the $500 million payment. The generic earns $500 million. Assuming a 20 percent price discount when duopoly competition takes place, and an equal sales volume before and after competition, that means consumers would lose $200 million a year in potential cost savings – 20 percent of $1 billion. Over the course of four years, consumers would forfeit $800 million in savings, an estimate likely to be conservative considering that further price drops would occur in subsequent years after generic entry, if additional generics enter as well.

B   PAY-FOR-DELAY AS A BOTTLENECK TO ENTRY

As discussed, pay-for-delay settlements are attractive because they offer substantial gains to both parties. They are also lucrative because the Hatch-Waxman incentive scheme can be used to reach a settlement *without* leaving the door open to other competition.[12] It is reasonable to ask, in a situation where a generic has agreed to delay entry, why another generic filer would not try to swoop in and enter the market. The answer is simple. Only the first generic filer making a Paragraph IV certification on a drug is eligible for the six months of exclusivity. Even if the certification is withdrawn or the generic filer loses its infringement case, the six months of exclusivity are not available to any subsequent filer.[13] Later generics with a Paragraph IV certification (arguing that a patent is invalid or improperly applied) cannot be approved until the six months of first generic exclusivity have elapsed.[14]

---

[9]   *Pay-for-Delay: How Drug Company Pay-Offs Cost Consumers Billions* FED. TRADE COMM'N 2 (2010), www.ftc.gov/reports/pay-delay-how-drug-company-pay-offs-cost-consumers-billions-federal-trade-commission-staff.

[10]   Hemphill studied 21 drugs with settlements including monetary payments (some included other stipulations, which will be discussed in Chapter 2). The average preexpiration delay for these drugs, weighted by sales, was 4.1 years. Hemphill, *Aggregate Approach to Antitrust*, *supra* note 1, at 649–50 & 649 tbl. 2.

[11]   In the 21 settlements studied by Hemphill, the average annual U.S. sales adjusted for inflation was $1.3 billion for each drug. Hemphill, *Aggregate Approach to Antitrust*, *supra* note 1, at 648.

[12]   Hemphill, *Paying for Delay*, *supra* note 1, at 129–34.

[13]   21 U.S.C. § 355(j)(5)(D)(iii)(II).

[14]   21 U.S.C. § 355(j)(5)(B)(iv)(II)(aa).

Thus, the first filer theoretically can create an absolute bottleneck by never starting the clock on its six months. In its early 2002 report on pay-for-delay, the FTC referred to this as "park[ing]" the exclusivity period.[15] Parking the exclusivity period was less of a problem before a set of Federal Circuit cases in 1998. Until that time, the FDA had ruled that a generic applicant making a Paragraph IV certification had to win its patent infringement suit in court, in order to receive the six-month exclusivity period – the "successful defense" requirement. A settlement would not be enough. Two Federal Circuit cases in 1998 ruled that this was not the case, leaving the door open to settlements in which the generic could still enjoy its exclusivity without winning a challenge.[16] This created the so-called bottleneck.[17]

As part of the 2003 Medicare Modernization Act, Congress made changes to Hatch-Waxman that can cause a generic first filer to lose its six months of exclusivity, a change that was meant to close the first-filer bottleneck.[18] This "forfeiture" provision sets out a number of scenarios that can take away the exclusivity period. Notably, exclusivity can supposedly be forfeited in certain circumstances. This should occur if commercial marketing does not take place (1) within 75 days of the drug receiving final approval, or (2) within 75 days of the generic manufacturer either winning a case or entering into a settlement finding the brand-name patents to be invalid or not infringed.[19] The generic company also may forfeit its exclusivity period if it does not secure tentative approval from the FDA within 30 months of submitting its application.[20] Provisions such as these were meant to close the pay-for-delay roadblock

---

[15] *See Generic Drug Entry Prior to Patent Expiration* Fed. Trade Comm'n 63 (2002), www.ftc.gov/sites/default/files/documents/reports/generic-drug-entry-prior-patent-expiration-ftc-study/genericdrugstudy_0.pdf.

[16] Hemphill, *Aggregate Approach to Antitrust, supra* note 1, at 658 n. 117 (citing *Granutec, Inc. v. Shalala,* 46 U.S.P.Q.2d (BNA) 1398, 1401 (4th Cir. 1998); *Mova Pharm. Corp. v. Shalala,* 955 F. Supp. 128, 130 (D.D.C. 1997), aff'd, 140 F.3d 1060 (D.C. Cir. 1998) ("The language of the statute … is plain and unambiguous. It does not include a 'successful defense' requirement, and indeed it does not even require the institution of patent litigation.")); *see also Medicare Prescription Drug, Improvement, and Modernization Act: Hearing on H.R. 1 before S. Comm. on the Judiciary,* 108th Cong. (2003) (statement of Daniel E. Troy, Chief Counsel, U.S Food and Drug Administration), *available at* www.fda.gov/NewsEvents/Testimony/ucm115033.htm.

[17] In a recent paper, Matthew Avery and Mary Nguyen discuss the possibility that later generic filers could attempt to enter the market by going on the offensive and seeking a declaratory judgment that the original drug patents are invalid – an alternative route to filing a Paragraph IV generic certification and waiting for a lawsuit from the brand-name drug maker. However, according to the authors, the Federal Circuit has blocked most of these attempts, saying that later filers do not present a legitimate Article III "case or controversy" in their attempts to seek a preliminary injunction. *See* Avery and Nguyen, *Roadblock for Generic Drugs, supra* note 1. Brand-name companies can also engage in strategies to stagger lawsuits and sue different generics on different patents so one noninfringement judgment does not open the entire market to all competitors. *See* Robin Feldman, Rethinking Patent Law 164–66 (2012).

[18] 21 U.S.C. § 355(j)(5)(D).

[19] 21 U.S.C. § 355(j)(5)(D)(i)(I).

[20] 21 U.S.C. § 355(j)(5)(D)(i)(IV).

loophole by punishing the generic for not seeing a case through and earning marketing approval by winning its patent challenges. The modified statute even allows exclusivity to be forfeited if the FTC or U.S. attorney general determines a settlement to be an antitrust violation and wins its case in court.[21]

Parties, however, have found a way to work around the new provisions in drafting pay-for-delay settlements. Academics and practitioners have discussed how the drafting of the provision leaves a glaring loophole that seems to permit many pay-for-delay settlements to continue to hold up other generic applications from approval.[22] Specifically, forfeiture from a "failure-to-market" event occurs only when the *later of* two conditions is satisfied: (1) 75 days have passed since the first generic application is approved or 30 months have passed since the generic application was submitted and (2) 75 days have passed since a final court determination that the patents in question are invalid or not infringed.[23]

In this case, "final court determination" includes court-signed settlement orders entering a final judgment that the patent is invalid or not infringed, a definition you, too, can find if you make your way to 21 U.S.C. § 355(j)(5)(D)(i)(I)(bb)(BB) in the United States Code. But if an event in (2) never occurs – if a final judgment of invalidity or infringement is not entered – the *"later of"* provision never applies and forfeiture does not occur.[24] Thus, generics and brand-name companies can craft their settlements so as not to assign a determination of blame or reach a judgment on patent validity.[25] Thus, one leg of the provision never occurs and the generic can settle without forfeiting anything.

In fact, five years after the 2003 amendment, monetary pay-for-delay settlements had instead increased, rising along with the popularity of Paragraph IV challenges.[26] The new provision did little to stem the tide.

---

[21] 21 U.S.C. § 355(j)(5)(D)(i)(V).

[22] Matthew Avery, *Continuing Abuse of Hatch-Waxman Act by Pharmaceutical Patent Holders and the Failure of the 2003 Amendments*, 60 HASTINGS L.J. 171, 191–93 (2008), www.mavery.com/academic/ Avery_Continuing_Abuse_Hatch-Waxman.pdf; *see also* Avery and Nguyen, *Roadblock for Generic Drugs, supra* note 1, at 10; *see also* Letter from Gary J. Buehler, Dir., Off. of Generic Drugs, Ctr. for Drug Evaluation and Research, FDA, to Marc A. Goshko, Exec. Dir., Teva North America, Teva Pharms. Medicines, regarding Docket No. 2007N-0389/ANDA 77–165, at 5 n. 6 (Jan. 17, 2008) (acknowledging the possibility of further exclusivity "parking"), *available at* www.fda.gov/ohrms/DOCKETS/dockets/ 07n0389/07n-0389-let0003.pdf; *see also* Hemphill, *Aggregate Approach to Antitrust, supra* note 1, at 660–61.

[23] 21 U.S.C. § 355(j)(5)(D)(i)(I). The second requirement also allows forfeiture when 75 days have passed since the patent holder delisted a patent from the Orange Book.

[24] Avery and Nguyen, *Roadblock for Generic Drugs, supra* note 1, at 11.

[25] *See ibid.* at 11. In this case, the same pathway of declaratory judgment discussed in note 17 could be used for recourse if a second filer makes a Paragraph IV certification and no lawsuit is filed in response, but it is just as unlikely to be successful as it was in the pre-2003 amendment period.

[26] Hemphill, *Aggregate Approach to Antitrust, supra* note 1, at 649 tbl.2, 660.

C IS PAY-FOR-DELAY ACTUALLY WRONG? PHARMA HEADS
TO THE SUPREME COURT

So far, we have spent this chapter describing how pay-for-delay works, the problems it can cause for generic approval, and the harm it can inflict on consumers. However, is there a sound argument that these agreements are actually unlawful? The most prevalent, and increasingly accepted, legal argument is that pay-for-delay agreements are anticompetitive given that they represent an agreement between two companies to capture the market and deny others competitive entry.

Pharmaceutical companies, however, have argued vigorously that pay-for-delay settlements are not anticompetitive, asserting that they can be understood as no more than devices by which the two parties respond to the uncertainty of patent infringement litigation – the same uncertainty we discussed in the previous section.[27] The opposing argument frames a pay-for-delay agreement as follows: Given the uncertain nature of success in the lawsuit brought on by a Paragraph IV certification, the two parties calculate what they believe their relative position is in the litigation and then settle on the basis of what they believe to be the expected value of bringing the litigation to its conclusion. Consider a very simplified example – if a generic thinks it only has a 25 percent chance of succeeding in its lawsuit, perhaps it should settle so that it does not enter until the last 25 percent of the remaining patent term. Some argue further that such settlements are even *procompetitive*, because, in many cases, the generic is allowed to enter the market before the last relevant patent expires.[28] A settlement that allows "early entry" is better than nothing, right? As a result of the settlement, the public will enjoy lower prices sooner than they would have had the Paragraph IV challenge never taken place – a result that would seemingly be consistent with the goals of Hatch-Waxman.

This argument, however, suffers from two flaws. The first is that the "procompetitive" argument about pay-for-delay lawsuits ignores the fact that Paragraph IV litigation specifically questions the validity and applicability of the patent.[29] If the patent is invalid or inapplicable to the drug, the brand-name company should have no exclusionary power.[30] In other words, there is no such thing as procompetitive "early entry" if the patent should not exist at all.

The same is true if the patent is valid but does not apply to this product. Once again, the patent should not be blocking the generic's entry at all. Thus, nothing but immediate entry would be procompetitive. Everything else is unwarranted delay.

---

[27] Feldman, RETHINKING PATENT LAW, *supra* note 17, at 163.
[28] *Fed. Trade Comm'n v. Actavis, Inc.*, 133 S. Ct. 2223, 2227 (2013).
[29] *See ibid.* at 2225; Hemphill, *Aggregate Approach to Antitrust*, *supra* note 1, at 637–38.
[30] *See Actavis, Inc.*, 133 S. Ct. at 2225.

Life would be much easier in the patent system if all patents, and all claims within a patent, were valid. The system, however, is not wired in that manner. The volume of claims submitted to the patent office and the limited amount of examiner time for each guarantee a less than perfect system.[31] One could fill an ocean with the amount of ink that has been spilled documenting and bemoaning the low quality of patents within the United States.[32] In particular, as noted in the Introduction, a Federal Trade Commission Study found that generic applicants who challenged the validity or application of a patent won their challenge 73 percent of the time.[33] Thus, one can never assume that just because a company holds a patent that the patent is either valid or validly applied to the drug at issue.

Given that a ruling in favor of the generic would allow immediate entry (as long as the FDA has also approved the generic), a settlement is practically guaranteed to delay market entry from when it would have otherwise taken place.[34] Any exclusionary power for the brand-name company – whatever its scope may be – flows from holding a valid patent. If that patent should not exist, the brand-name drug company no longer has any right to try to prevent others from entering the market. It is not unlike the thought experiment of Schrödinger's cat[35] – the patent is simultaneously valid and invalid while Paragraph IV litigation is pending. We do not know which is true until a judgment is entered. Until the point of judgment, since one of the superposed quantum states is invalidity, pay-for-delay settlements can have an anticompetitive effect if litigation is not allowed to progress to its conclusion.

Second, even if a patent is valid, it is not a license to engage in any and all activity, no matter how anticompetitive.[36] With any party that holds a legitimate monopoly

---

[31] In fact, one Federal Circuit case looking at internal patent office employee review systems reveals that a 25 percent error rate is acceptable for the quality assurance specialists who review patent examiners' decisions. *See* Brief of Petitioner Asokkumar Pal, p. 4, *Pal v. Dep't of Commerce*, 301 Fed. Appx. 984 (Fed. Cir. 2008) (No. 2008–3212), 2008 WL 3833925.

[32] *See, e.g.*, Dan L. Burk & Mark A. Lemley, THE PATENT CRISIS AND HOW THE COURTS CAN SOLVE IT (University of Chicago Press, 2009); ROBIN FELDMAN, RETHINKING PATENT LAW 76–78 (Harvard, 2012); U.S. GOV'T ACCOUNTABILITY OFFICE, GAO -13–465, *Intellectual Property: Assessing Factors That Affect Patent Infringement Litigation Could Help Improve Patent Quality* (2013) (pointing to the low quality of patents as a key cause of modern problems in patent litigation) *available at* www.gao. gov/assets/660/657103.pdf.

[33] *See Generic Drug Entry Prior to Patent Expiration* FED. TRADE COMM'N 16 (2002), www.ftc.gov/ sites/default/files/documents/reports/generic-drug-entry-prior-patent-expiration-ftc-study/genericdrug study_0.pdf.

[34] *Cf.* Robin Feldman, *Ending Patent Exceptionalism and Structuring the Rule of Reason: The Supreme Court Opens the Door for Both*, 1 MINN. J. L. SCI. & TECH. 61 (2014).

[35] Paul Halpern, *Schrödinger's Cat Lives On (or Not) at the Age of 80*, PBS NOVA, (Nov. 10, 2015), www .pbs.org/wgbh/nova/blogs/physics/2015/11/schrodingers-cat-lives-on-or-not-at-the-age-of-80/.

[36] For a detailed history of the development of antitrust limitations on behavior involving patents, see Robin Feldman, *The Insufficiency of Antitrust Analysis for Patent Misuse*, 55 HASTINGS L.J. 399, 405–17 (2003).

position in the market, the antitrust laws place limits on what one can do with that monopoly power.[37] In this context, the Supreme Court uses a variety of standard antitrust measures when judging whether a patent holder's behavior violates antitrust law.[38]

Many traditional antitrust questions are raised by pay-for-delay settlements, starting with their potential negative effects on consumers.[39] With timing set aside, in the abstract the agreements also function to allocate a market, by maintaining the brand-name drug's monopoly, and to fix prices, by essentially agreeing to let the pharma patent holder continue to charge supracompetitive prices.[40] Hemphill has referred to this as the "consumer-disregarding" effects of these settlements,[41] and similar consequences in other contexts tend to invite Sherman Act antitrust scrutiny regardless of the circumstances. These settlements are especially troubling in the context of Hatch-Waxman, which was specifically designed as a procompetitive catalyst for generic drug development and marketing. Settlements undermine Hatch-Waxman's intent to move patent bargaining into the open and therefore speed along the introductionof some generic drugs in cases of patent invalidity.[42] One should note that cases attempting to attack drug company settlements as anticompetitive are not cases pitting the generic against the brand-name company – the generic also benefits from these agreements! The generic versus brand battles are limited to the initial patent infringement cases that end up being settled. Instead, the plaintiffs are generally government agencies such as the FTC or New York attorney general, or purchasers of the drug, such as insurers, who argue that the settlement led to inappropriately higher prices and caused harm to businesses and consumers. In fact, in the following case, Actavis was the generic that entered into the pay-for-delay agreement!

After years of FTC complaints and studies, and cases that bounced around lower courts, the Supreme Court finally weighed in with its 2013 decision in *FTC v. Actavis*. The case involved a pay-for-delay settlement with the agreed-upon generic entry date occurring prior to the patent's expiration date.[43] The parties were Solvay (now

---

[37] *See generally Kimble v. Marvel Enters.* 135 S. Ct. 2401 (2015) (deciding that agreements to pay royalties on sales after the expiration of a patent are illegal). For information on limitations on monopoly power legitimately gained, see generally Robin Feldman, *Patent and Antitrust: Differing Shades of Meaning*, 13 Va. J.L. & Tech. 5 (2008).

[38] *Federal Trade Commission v. Actavis, Inc. et al.*, 133 S. Ct. 2223, 2231 (2013).

[39] Hemphill, *Aggregate Approach to Antitrust, supra* note 1, at 636.

[40] ROBIN FELDMAN, RETHINKING PATENT LAW 162 (2012); *Federal Trade Commission v. Actavis, Inc. et al.*, 133 S. Ct. 2223, 2232 (2013), citing *United States v. Line Material Co.*, 333 U.S. 287, 312 (1948) ("As the Sherman Act prohibits agreements to fix prices, any arrangement between patentees runs afoul of that prohibition and is outside the patent monopoly").

[41] Hemphill, *Aggregate Approach to Antitrust, supra* note 1, at 636.

[42] ROBIN FELDMAN, RETHINKING PATENT LAW 164 (2012).

[43] It is worth noting that the settlement in *Actavis* was not a pure cash payment. Along with a payment from Solvay to Actavis of approximately $19 million to $30 million per year for nine years, Actavis

part of AbbVie), maker of the brand-name drug AndroGel (a topical testosterone treatment), and Actavis, filer of the first application for a generic version of the drug. In 2003, when Actavis submitted its application for approval of generic AndroGel with a Paragraph IV certification, Solvay initiated patent litigation.[44] So far, so good.

In 2006, after the FDA had already approved Actavis' generic application,[45] Actavis settled with Solvay, with the parties agreeing not to bring a generic version of AndroGel to the market until 2015 – which, despite the enormous delay, was still 65 months before the 2020 patent expiration.[46] In return, Actavis was paid between $19 and $30 million for each of the nine years of delay, an agreement worth multiple hundreds of millions of dollars.[47] Actavis also agreed to help promote AndroGel as part of the settlement, but this provision was generally seen as a mostly valueless promise meant only to obfuscate the terms of the settlement.[48] (Two other generic companies, who were not first filers, also settled with Solvay for far less.) The FTC filed lawsuits against all parties alleging antitrust violations. When the case reached the Court of Appeals for the Eleventh Circuit, the appeals court affirmed a lower court decision dismissing the lawsuits.[49] It found that since the agreement was within the scope of the patent and allowed preexpiration entry, it was immune to antitrust scrutiny. By "scope of the patent," the court meant that it believed Solvay was not abusing its AndroGel patent but rather using it only for its intended purpose – to exclude competitors from the market until the expiration date. While the court acknowledged that payments not to enter a market are generally antitrust violations, it distinguished *Actavis* because it involved a patent holder with exclusionary power.[50]

agreed to promote a drug sold by the brand-name company, among other considerations. *See Actavis, Inc.*, 133 S. Ct. at 2229. See Chapter 2 for more information about settlements involving "side deals."

[44] *Actavis, Inc.*, 133 S. Ct. at 2229.

[45] *See* Letter from Gary J. Buehler, Dir., Off. of Generic Drugs, Ctr. for Drug Evaluation and Research, FDA, to Christine M. Woods, Assoc. Dir., Reg. Affairs, Watson Laboratories, Inc., regarding ANDA 76–737 (Jan. 27, 2006), www.accessdata.fda.gov/drugsatfda_docs/appletter/2006/076737ltr.pdf (approving the Actavis generic application). Although litigation had not been resolved at the time of approval, the 30-month litigation stay had expired at this point, allowing the FDA to approve the application. *See ibid.* at 2.

[46] *Actavis, Inc*, 133 S. Ct. at 2229. The agreement also included a so-called acceleration clause that would allow Actavis to enter the market immediately if someone else was able to market a generic before the agreed-upon entry date. Acceleration clauses will be discussed as a Generation 2.0 strategy in Chapter 2.

[47] *Ibid.* The other generic competitors were also paid tens of millions of dollars *total* as part of their settlements.

[48] *Ibid.* This kind of "co-promote" agreement is common to Generation 2.0 settlements described in Chapter 2, but generally without the kind of large cash reverse payments that now receive immense antitrust scrutiny after *Actavis*.

[49] *Ibid.* at 2229–30.

[50] *Federal Trade Commission v. Watson Pharmaceuticals, Inc.*, 677 F.3d 1298 (11th Cir. 2012), rev'd, *ibid.*

In a 5–3 decision with a majority opinion written by Justice Stephen Breyer, the Supreme Court reversed the Eleventh Circuit and ruled that the FTC's case against a brand-name firm should not have been dismissed, further adding that pay-for-delay settlements are open to antitrust scrutiny.[51] The Court declined to hold that reverse payment settlements are presumptively unlawful, however, preferring instead a rule of reason test to decide whether an antitrust violation has taken place.[52]

The rule of reason is a laborious standard that has been described by courts and commentators as difficult to meet and burdensome on both plaintiffs and the judicial system.[53] The classic description of the rule of reason can be found in the seminal antitrust treatise by the late Philip Areeda.[54] The plaintiff has the initial burden of establishing that the behavior restrains competition in a properly defined market, which includes delineating the relevant product and geographic markets. If the plaintiff meets this initial burden, the burden shifts to the defendant to show that its behavior serves legitimate objectives. If the defendant meets this burden, the plaintiff must then establish that the defendant could meet its objective using a less restrictive alternative. Deep breath – if the matter is *still* unresolved at this point, the court must weigh the harms and benefits of the restraint with the plaintiff shouldering the burden at this stage to show that the restraint is unreasonable on balance. Fun, right?

Together, the test involves complex economic analysis, requires extensive information about industries that may be difficult to obtain, and follows an amorphous set of standards that are difficult to pin down and establish. Thus, plaintiffs in an antitrust case try to avoid the rule of reason by framing the case to fit into one of a limited number of per se categories – categories of activities that are presumed to be illegal, such as price fixing or territorial allocation of sales territories.[55]

---

[51] *Actavis, Inc.*, 133 S. Ct. at 2237. Justice Alito recused himself from the case.

[52] *Ibid.*

[53] *See* Robin Feldman, *Defensive Leveraging in Antitrust*, for a discussion of the rule of reason and the extensive criticism of it. 87 GEO. LJ. 2079, 2107–08 (1999) (citing the following sources: *Jefferson Parish Hosp. Dist. No. 2 v. Hyde*, 466 U.S. 2, 34 (1984) (O'Connor, J., concurring) (comparing the rule of reason to the odd form of per se rule applied in tying cases and describing both as requiring extensive and time-consuming economic analysis); *Continental T.V., Inc. v. GTE Sylvania*, 433 U.S. 36, 50 (1977) (describing rule of reason as complex and burdensome on litigants and the judicial system); *Northern Pac. Ry. Co. v. United States*, 356 U.S. 1, 5 (1958) (noting that rule of reason analysis requires complicated and prolonged economic investigation into the entire history of an industry and related industries); Robert Pitofsky, *Antitrust in the Next 100 Years*, 75 CALIF. L. REV. 817, 830, 830 n.42 (1987) (explaining that the court refused to apply rule of reason given the practical difficulties of the minute inquiry required into economic organization)).

[54] *See* 7 PHILIP E. AREEDA, ANTITRUST LAW § 1502, at 371–72 (1986).

[55] *United States Attorneys' Manual, Antitrust Resource Manual* U.S. DEP'T OF JUSTICE 8 (1997), www .justice.gov/usam/antitrust-resource-manual-8-identifying-sherman-act-violations.

Although the rule of reason test traditionally has been the death knell for antitrust cases, the *Actavis* ruling actually improved the state of the field. In the decision, the Supreme Court opened the door to serious antitrust consideration by suggesting that lower courts "structure" the rule of reason in these cases.[56] Most important, the Court concluded that "a reverse payment, where large and unjustified, can bring with it the risk of significant anticompetitive effects," rebuking the Eleventh Circuit "scope of the patent" argument and giving credibility to the arguments that had long been made by academics and the FTC.[57]

In the aftermath of *Actavis*, courts and parties have taken the Supreme Court's message to heart, at least when it comes to pay-for-delay settlements that are entirely in cash.[58] In the FTC's report on agreements between brand-name and generic companies in fiscal year 2014 – the first full year after *Actavis* – the FTC found that the number of suspected pay-for-delay settlements dropped to 21, compared to 29 in fiscal year 2013 and the record-high of 40 in 2012.[59]

Pay-for-delay agreements are also under fire outside the United States. In early 2016, the United Kingdom's Competition and Markets Authority announced total fines of £45 million against pharmaceutical companies engaging in pay-for-delay settlements.[60] Between 2001 and 2004, a brand-name company had paid generics £50 million to delay entry of a popular antidepressant into the UK market.[61]

Looking again at the United States, two cases, in particular, signal the beginning of the end for traditional delay games, leaving no doubt that the guidance in *Actavis* is being used to scrutinize these settlements heavily. In the case of *In re Cipro*, the California Supreme Court applied *Actavis* to California's own antitrust law, which follows certain aspects of federal law.[62] The case concerned a pay-for-delay settlement regarding Bayer's popular antibiotic Cipro. In rendering its opinion, the court

---

[56] For analysis of the *Actavis* case, see generally Aaron Edlin et al., *Activating Actavis*, 28 ANTITRUST 16 (2013); Feldman, *Ending Patent Exceptionalism and Structuring the Rule of Reason, supra* note 34; Michael A. Carrier, *Payment After Actavis*, 100 IOWA L. REV. 7 (2014).

[57] *Actavis, Inc.*, 133 S. Ct. at 2237.

[58] For further analysis of how courts have treated the *Actavis* decision, see generally Michele M. Kang, *ANDA Reverse Payments and the Post-Actavis Landscape*, 8 HASTINGS SCI. & TECH. L.J. 73 (2016).

[59] *See Agreements Filed with the Fed. Trade Commission under the Medicare Prescription Drug, Improvement, and Modernization Act of 2003: Overview of Agreements Filed in FY 2014*, BUREAU OF COMPETITION, FED. TRADE COMM'N at 4 exhibit 1, www.ftc.gov/system/files/documents/reports/agreements-filled-federal-trade-commission-under-medicare-prescription-drug-improvement/160113mmafy14rpt.pdf. Note that under the FTC's definition of a pay-for-delay agreement, some of these agreements include side deals and "no-AG" clauses that will be discussed in Chapter 2.

[60] Press Release, U.K. Competition & Mkts. Auth., CMA Fines Pharma Companies £45 Million (Feb. 12, 2016), www.gov.uk/government/news/cma-fines-pharma-companies-45-million.

[61] The settlements included cash payments as well as supply and distribution agreements. *See* Jeff Overley, *GSK Fined $54M Over UK 'Pay-for-Delay' Deals*, LAW360 (Feb. 12, 2016, 11:03 AM), www.law360.com/ip/articles/758706.

[62] *See generally In re Cipro Cases I & II*, 348 P.3d 845 (Cal. 2015).

went to great lengths to discuss the fact that any patent might or might not be valid. "A critical insight undergirding *Actavis* is that patents are in a sense probabilistic, rather than ironclad: they grant their holders a potential but not certain right to exclude."[63] The court went on to explain that a patent is simply a legal conclusion reached by the Patent Office under time and resource pressure, which is why "Congress has elected not to make the issuance of a patent conclusive but, rather, subject to validation or invalidation in court proceedings."[64] Thus, the California Supreme Court implemented a "structured rule of reason" test for scrutiny of reverse payment settlements, one falling somewhere between the notion that such settlements are per se illegal and the amorphous rule of reason.[65] The test focuses on whether the value of that reverse payment exceeded litigation costs combined with the value of any other services the generic might agree to provide to the brand – essentially, did the brand-name company pay the generic more than what they should have received for their legal costs and any contractual services it agreed to supply to the brand.[66] Critically, the court held that in presenting any procompetitive arguments in favor of a settlement, the brand-name company may not include arguments that the patent is actually valid or that the settlement allowed preexpiration entry.[67]

Similarly, in the spring of 2015, Teva agreed to pay $512 million to settle a class action brought by purchasers of the company's drug Provigil, a widely used narcolepsy drug.[68] The lawsuit had accused Teva of paying four different generic competitors – who had all filed their generic applications for Provigil on the same day – more than $300 million to stay out of the market for six years.[69] (Confusingly, Teva was one of those generic competitors before it acquired Cephalon, the original maker of Provigil.) The settlement was the largest ever for direct purchasers in a pay-for-delay case.

---

[63] *Ibid.* at 859.

[64] *Ibid.*

[65] *Ibid.* at 865–67.

[66] *Ibid.*

[67] *Ibid.* at 870–71.

[68] Kelly Knaub, *Teva to Pay $512M to End Provigil Pay-for-Delay Dispute*, Law360 (Apr. 20, 2015, 3:38 PM), www.law360.com/lifesciences/articles/645224/teva-to-pay-512m-to-end-provigil-pay-for-delay-dispute; Katie Thomas, *Teva to Pay $512 Million to Settle Suit Over Delay of Sleep Disorder Drug*, N.Y. Times (Apr. 20, 2015), www.nytimes.com/2015/04/21/business/teva-to-pay-512-million-to-settle-suit-over-delay-of-sleep-disorder-drug.html?_r=0. The drug was originally sold by Cephalon, a company bought by Teva in 2011. Chris V. Nicholson, *Teva to Buy Cephalon for $6.8 Billion*, N.Y. Times (May 2, 2011), http://dealbook.nytimes.com/2011/05/02/teva-to-buy-cephalon-for-6-8-billion/?_r=0.

[69] *See* Rebecca R. Ruiz & Katie Thomas, *Teva Settles Cephalon Generics Case with F.T.C. for $1.2 Billion*, N.Y. Times (May 28, 2015), www.nytimes.com/2015/05/29/business/teva-cephalon-provigil-ftc-settlement.html; Matthew Bultman, *FTC Can Seek Disgorgement in Cephalon Suit, Judge Says*, Law360 (Apr. 16, 2015, 1:48 PM), www.law360.com/articles/643622/ftc-can-seek-disgorgement-in-cephalon-suit-judge-says.

A little more than a month after settling with direct purchasers, Teva agreed to settle similar antitrust claims with the FTC, raising the total settlement to $1.2 billion, by far the largest settlement ever secured by the FTC.[70] The settlement occurred five days after an unfavorable ruling from a federal judge in the case.[71]

At the end of the day, however, Teva may still have profited handsomely from its behavior – although not nearly as handsomely as it had expected. Shortly after reaching the pay-for-delay settlement in 2006, one high-level executive commented, "We were able to get six more years of patent protection. That's $4 billion in sales that no one expected."[72] Even considering the FTC's lower-end estimate of $3.5 billion in profit from the delay rather than the executive's $4 billion comment, the company was still left with at least $2 billion after settling with the class action plaintiffs and the FTC.[73] And, thus, pay-for-delay lives on in a variety of forms, as we will discover in Chapter 2.

---

[70] See Ruiz & Thomas, *Teva Settles*, *supra* note 69; Press Release, Fed. Trade Comm'n, Bureau of Competition, FTC Settlement of Cephalon Pay for Delay Case Ensures $1.2 Billion in Ill-Gotten Gains Relinquished; Refunds Will Go to Purchasers Affected by Anticompetitive Tactics (May 28, 2015), www.ftc.gov/news-events/press-releases/2015/05/ftc-settlement-cephalon-pay-delay-case-ensures-12-billion-ill; Brent Kendall, *Teva, FTC Reach $1.2 Billion Settlement on Cephalon's Provigil*, WALL ST. J. (May 28, 2015), www.wsj.com/articles/teva-close-to-ftc-settlement-on-cephalons-provigil-valued-at-roughly-1-billion-1432813288. The $1.2 billion figure includes the $512 million secured in the direct purchaser settlement.

[71] Bultman, *FTC Can Seek Disgorgement*, *supra* note 69.

[72] Complaint for Injunctive Relief at 2, *Fed. Trade Comm'n v. Cephalon, Inc.*, No. 08CV00244, 2008 WL 446785 (D.D.C. Feb. 13, 2008).

[73] Bultman, *FTC Can Seek Disgorgement*, *supra* note 69, (noting the FTC's $3.5 billion figure).

2

"Generation 2.0"

Complicating Pay-for-Delay

A ALREADY STEPS AHEAD OF *ACTAVIS*

Although *Actavis* dealt a blow to traditional pay-for-delay settlements, it was years too late. By the time the decision was handed down, drug manufacturers had long moved on to other forms of settlement. With heightened scrutiny applied to pure cash pay-for-delay agreements even before the *Actavis* ruling, drug companies quickly began to combine delay provisions with noncash provisions. These noncash deals are meant to obscure the fact that the generic firm is still receiving large considerations, valued at tens or hundreds of millions of dollars, in return for delayed entry. In these "Generation 2.0" games, the reverse payment is still very much alive – just not so clearly denoted by dollar signs.

Before moving forward, we want to reiterate that our framework of "generations" does not imply that *Actavis* completely foreclosed Generation 1.0 settlements and replaced them with Generation 2.0 controversies – *Actavis* was decided in 2013, and, as we will discuss shortly, the first Generation 2.0 settlements occurred as early as 1997. In addition, cash payment agreements continued well into the 2000s and beyond. Instead, "generations" should be thought of as marking the evolution of delay strategies and grouping them in helpful organizations. Evolution does not mean previous strategies do not exist; the branches of a multigenerational family exist simultaneously although its members are of different ages, and all generations still have their place and unique strengths within the family.

This chapter will explore the structure of standard Generation 2.0 agreements, along with examples that demonstrate the evolving complexity of such settlements. Further, we introduce some of the consequences of increasing complexity: as some generic-hampering strategies have become the norm, pharmaceutical companies will now promise to refrain from certain actions in exchange for a delay, provisions we have dubbed "boy scout clauses." The chapter also turns to a discussion of how these agreements have been interpreted by courts. Although the *Actavis* agreement itself was in part a "later generation" settlement – Actavis agreed to promote a separate drug made by the brand-name company as part of the deal – there has been a surprising amount of lower court judicial resistance to extending *Actavis* antitrust scrutiny to noncash deals. Recent decisions, however, have offered some guidance and consolidation in a confusing post-*Actavis* world.

We begin with the origins of "advanced" pay-for-delay strategies. The first Generation 2.0 settlement is generally understood to be a 1997 agreement to delay entry of K-Dur, a drug treating potassium deficiencies.[1] The drug was manufactured by Schering-Plough (now part of Merck), and, in 1995, Upsher-Smith became the first generic to file a Paragraph IV generic application for K-Dur. (If all of these pharmaceutical companies are going to consolidate, can they not at least consolidate their names as well?)

Hours before trial was set to begin in the ensuing patent infringement case, Schering and Upsher reached a settlement. Upsher agreed to delay entering the generic K-Dur market for approximately four years. What differed in this first Generation 2.0 agreement was what Schering, the brand-name drug company, added to the agreement as a noncash consideration. (In fact, Schering appeared quite fearful of signing on to a cash-only deal.)[2] Schering agreed to buy licenses to sell multiple Upsher medications – in particular, a cholesterol drug known as Niacor-SR, which Upsher had developed. Schering paid Upsher $60 million and agreed to pay royalties on Niacor-SR, depending on its sales of the product.[3] Before the settlement was even ratified, the two parties quickly abandoned their plans to make Niacor-SR, but suspiciously left the $60 million "license" payment intact.[4] (No refunds, it seems.)

In court, Schering and Upsher made an argument soon to be common in Generation 2.0 cases – that the $60 million payment was only for the licensing deal and had nothing to do with the delay of generic K-Dur.[5]

Schering and Upsher were prescient in their settlement design: the *K-Dur* case presents the archetypical form of a classic Generation 2.0 settlement.[6] As part of

---

[1] *See In re K-Dur Antitrust Litig.*, 686 F.3d 197, 205–06 (3d Cir. 2012); C. Scott Hemphill, *An Aggregate Approach to Antitrust: Using New Data and Rulemaking to Preserve Drug Competition*, 109 COLUM. L. REV. 629, 658 (2009).

[2] *Schering-Plough Corp. v. FTC*, 402 F.3d 1056, 1059 (11th Cir. 2005).

[3] *See In re K–Dur Antitrust Litig.*, 686 F.3d at 205–06.

[4] *Ibid.* at 206. Also suspicious is the following: The generic demanded cash and early entry when the settlement was first being negotiated. But, concerned about pay-for-delay antitrust scrutiny even back in 1997, the brand-name company would not agree to these more basic terms. *Ibid.* at 205.

[5] *Ibid.* at 206.

[6] Recall that *Actavis* also had elements of a Generation 2.0 settlement (*e.g.* side deals, installment payments). We associate *Actavis* with Generation 1.0 in this chapter given that the *Actavis* argument has mostly been applied only to cash deals as of now.

these generic delay agreements, the two parties agree to provide services for each other, frequently referred to as "side deals," that are frequently related to other drugs in one of the firms' portfolios. Cash is often still exchanged, but it is disguised as a payment for the other services mentioned in the agreement.

These services can include 1) promises to promote or market other drugs (the "co-promote deal" seen in *Actavis*); 2) licensing deals as in *K-Dur* that allow the brand-name drug company or the generic to manufacture the other party's drug; 3) "authorized generic" agreements permitting the generic to manufacture and/or sell the brand-name formulation as a generic without filing for generic approval, with profit-sharing or royalty deals attached; 4) agreements to share research and development duties on a future project; 5) deals to supply the brand-name company with raw materials for manufacturing; and more.[7]

In most cases, the result is that the brand-name company "overpays" the generic for the services the generic supposedly furnishes to the brand – with the difference between the market value and the actual payment constituting the cash consideration for the delay.[8] In the alternative, the generic may "underpay" for something of value it receives from the brand-name drug company, such as the right to make or sell other pharmaceuticals from the brand-name drug company's portfolio.[9] In this case, the generic has received a "deal" elsewhere in exchange for delaying entry of the drug currently under discussion.

A particularly questionable aspect of these side deals is that the services promised are often beyond the generic's capability. These generic-brand relationships are rarely, if ever, found outside the context of a settlement. For example, a generic company generally does little marketing and advertising, instead relying on the fact that pharmacists will automatically substitute a generic drug when filling a prescription listing the brand-name drug. In fact, this leaner organizational structure is what allows a generic to offer medication at substantially lower prices.

How, then, could a generic manufacturer offer marketing and promotion services that a brand-name company would find desirable? Further, it is rarely obvious that a generic firm would be the most effective manufacturing and supply partner for a large brand-name company.[10] Consider the example of Provigil, the narcolepsy drug for which Teva eventually paid $1.2 billion to settle assorted antitrust litigation that resulted from the pay-for-delay deals.[11] In one of the deals, the company agreed to purchase Provigil's active ingredient from Ranbaxy, a generic, in an agreement that

[7]   See Hemphill, *Aggregate Approach to Antitrust, supra* note 1, at 663–66.
[8]   See *ibid.* at 663–64. *See generally* Michael A. Carrier, *Payment after Actavis*, 100 IOWA L. REV. 7 (2014).
[9]   See Hemphill, *Aggregate Approach to Antitrust, supra* note 1, at 665–66.
[10]   See *ibid.* at 668.
[11]   See Chapter 1 for more on the Provigil settlements.

included delay.[12] However, Ranbaxy *did not even produce* the active ingredient and was instead sourcing it from a third-party manufacturer.[13] The brand-name company was essentially agreeing to pay higher prices by allowing the generic company to stand in as the middleman. According to the FTC, a senior manager at the brand-name company called the supply deals – which were struck with multiple generics – a "supply chain disaster."[14]

Thus, the side deals are hollow promises that may or may not ever be fulfilled. Rather, they may function purely as a façade for the pay-for-delay that lies beneath the language of the settlement. Teasing out these pay-for-delay deals, however, can be quite difficult.

Back to K-Dur – how was the story resolved? In the case of *In re K-Dur*, a case brought by drug purchasers and decided 15 years after the initial settlement, the Court of Appeals for the Third Circuit found that the Schering and Upsher licensing agreement was a "reverse payment" for generic delay, despite the fact that the cash payment was supposedly for the licenses. The circuit court ruled that a "quick look rule of reason" test, "based on the economic realities of the reverse payment settlement rather than the labels applied by the settling parties," should be applied to these settlements.[15]

It is interesting to note that the *very first instance* of a Generation 2.0 settlement facing a major court challenge led to a ruling that reverse payments could encompass more than direct cash payments. Why did the story not end there for Generation 2.0? In fact, rather than being a seminal case applying suspicion to side deal settlements, *In re K-Dur* is mostly notable for its role in advancing jurisprudence in reverse payment settlements in general. The Third Circuit's test stood in contrast to the Eleventh Circuit's decision in the *Actavis* line of cases in the same year.[16] These developments created a circuit split encouraging Supreme Court review, which concluded with the SCOTUS decision in *FTC v. Actavis*. As described in Chapter 1, the *Actavis* decision rejected the approach taken by the Eleventh Circuit, but was not as clear as the Third Circuit in delineating what kinds of reverse payments might meet its criteria for scrutiny.

---

[12] *See* Complaint for Injunctive Relief at paras. 64–68, *FTC v. Cephalon, Inc.* (settlement approved E.D. Pa. June 17, 2015) (No. 2:08-cv-2141), complaint filed D.D.C. Feb. 13, 2008, www.ftc.gov/sites/default/files/documents/cases/2008/02/080213complaint.pdf.

[13] *Ibid.* at para. 68; *see also* Hemphill, *Aggregate Approach to Antitrust, supra* note 1, at 668 n. 165.

[14] Complaint for Injunctive Relief, *supra* note 12, at para. 57.

[15] *In re K-Dur Antitrust Litigation*, 686 F.3d 197, 218 (3rd Cir. 2012).

[16] Years earlier, the Eleventh Circuit, in a case brought by the FTC rather than by private plaintiffs against K-Dur, had rejected the argument that the K-Dur deal was anticompetitive, using a line of reasoning similar to what the Eleventh Circuit would later apply in *Actavis. Schering-Plough Corp.*, 402 F.3d.

B *IN RE LIPITOR*: EVERYTHING BUT THE KITCHEN SINK

While the Court of Appeals for the Third Circuit appeared to easily see through the intent of the two parties' side deal in *K-Dur*, getting to the bottom of a settlement is not always so easy. Clarity is particularly difficult to achieve when companies settle multiple Hatch-Waxman cases at once, distributing the payoffs in a way that quickly becomes quite complex.

Consider the case of *In re Lipitor*, which involved one of the most tangled sets of agreements in all of generic delay.[17] Lipitor, a statin used to lower cholesterol, is widely known as the best-selling drug in history, with more than $125 billion in sales between 1996 and eventual generic entry in late 2011.[18] It is no surprise that Lipitor's manufacturer, Pfizer, went to unprecedented lengths to protect the monopoly on its ultrablockbuster. A protracted six-year battle between Pfizer and the first generic filer, Ranbaxy, led to a settlement including delayed entry for generic Lipitor.[19] Scrutiny of this settlement then led to multiple class action lawsuits.[20]

Together, the resulting litigation implicated issues allegedly including, but not limited to, sham litigation, sham patent obtainment through data falsification,[21] Orange Book listings (and patents not listed in the Orange Book), petitions filed with the FDA, multiple and staggered lawsuits, multiple settlements, and even purposeful generic application approval delay on the part of Ranbaxy through delays in moving generic manufacture to an FDA-approved facility.[22] For the sake of providing

---

[17] See *In re Lipitor Antitrust Litig.*, 46 F. Supp. 3d 523 (D.N.J. 2014) (dismissing direct purchasers' class actions); *see also* ROBIN FELDMAN, RETHINKING PATENT LAW 162 (2012); Hemphill, *Aggregate Approach to Antitrust, supra* note 1, at 638–39, 683.

[18] See *Lipitor Becomes World's Top-Selling Drug*, CRAIN'S N.Y. BUS. (Dec. 28, 2011), www.crainsnewyork .com/article/20111228/HEALTH_CARE/111229902.

[19] See Direct Purchasers' Amended Complaint and Demand for July Trial at para. 87, *In re Lipitor Antitrust Litig.*, 46 F. Supp. 3d 523 (D.N.J. Sept. 12, 2014) (Nos. 3:12-cv-2389 & 3:12-cv-4115), 2013 WL 5669146 (dismissing direct purchasers' class actions).

[20] See *ibid.* See generally End-Payor Plaintiffs' Amended Consolidated Class Action Complaint and Jury Demand, *In re Lipitor Antitrust Litig.*, 46 F. Supp. 3d 523 (D.N.J. Oct. 15, 2013) (No. 3:12-cv-2389), 2013 WL 7117787 (breaking down all the alleged methods of delay in the case).

[21] *AFI-AGC Building Trades Welfare Plan v. Pfizer, Inc*, No. 12–0939 (S.D.N.Y. filed Feb. 6, 2012) (arguing that Pfizer filed fraudulent and duplicate patent applications for Lipitor), cited in Laura S. Shores, *Pharmaceutical Patent Life Extension Strategies: Are REMS Next?* ANTITRUST HEALTH CARE CHRON. 20, 22 (2012).

[22] See End-Payor Amended Complaint, *supra* note 20, (breaking down all the alleged methods of delay in the case); *see also In re Lipitor Antitrust Litig.*, No. 3:12–cv–2389, 2013 WL 4780496, at *12 (D.N.J. Sept. 5, 2013) (granting in part and denying in part motion to dismiss class action claims and referencing the claims regarding Ranbaxy's purposeful negligence of data integrity and manufacturing practices); *see also* Complaint and Jury Demand, *Meijer, Inc. v. Ranbaxy, Inc.*, No. 1:15-cv-11828, 2015 WL 2219184 (D. Mass. May 12, 2015) (arguing manufacturing problems have been widespread for Ranbaxy and the result of their haste to put in ANDAs and lock in 180-day exclusivity).

some clarity, this discussion will only focus on the terms of the eventual settlement between Pfizer and the first generic filer.

In the 2008 settlement, Ranbaxy agreed to delay release of generic Lipitor until late 2011.[23] In return, Pfizer gave the generic the right to market generic Lipitor in 11 international markets. Pfizer also resolved other litigation with Ranbaxy involving the drugs Caduet and Accupril.[24]

In a class action complaint, end payors alleged that this settlement represented an unlawful reverse payment.[25] Their argument was as follows: Pfizer knew it was unlikely to win its remaining attempts to stop the launch of generic Lipitor – its hopes were hanging on an application for a patent to be reissued and a petition it had filed with the FDA.[26]

However, Pfizer had a very strong case against Ranbaxy regarding another drug, Accupril, a treatment for hypertension.[27] In fact, it was widely believed that the suit over Accupril could have easily been worth hundreds of millions of dollars in damages because Ranbaxy had *already entered the market* before a final determination was made in the Hatch-Waxman litigation, an uncommon action known as

---

[23] *In re Lipitor*, 2013 WL 4780496, at *12. The complaint alleged this aspect of the settlement created an ANDA bottleneck that blocked the approval of subsequent ANDAs. End-Payor Amended Complaint, *supra* note 20, at paras. 373–92.

[24] Press Release, Pfizer, Inc., Pfizer and Ranbaxy Settle Lipitor Patent Litig. Worldwide (June 18, 2008), http://press.pfizer.com/press-release/pfizer-and-ranbaxy-settle-lipitor-patent-litigation-worldwide; *In re Lipitor*, 46 F. Supp. 3d at 532–33. Also dismissed was a process suit over the same two patents asserted against Ranbaxy over Lipitor. *See* End-Payor Amended Complaint, *supra* note 20, at paras. 270–82.

[25] End-Payor Amended Complaint, *supra* note 20, at paras. 393–95.

[26] A district court had already enjoined approval of Ranbaxy's ANDA until March 2010 by upholding one of Pfizer's patents. *In re Lipitor*, 2013 WL 4780496, at *7; FELDMAN, RETHINKING PATENT LAW, *supra* note 17, at 162. Pfizer's infringement claim on its second patent (the subject of much controversy) was not upheld. It then turned to reissue proceedings for that second patent as well as a citizen petition to attempt to delay entry. *In re Lipitor*, 2013 WL 4780496, at *6–10. Together, complainants allege the only thing preventing generic entry in March 2010 was a patent reissue application that had a "real risk" of being "denied" and a citizen petition that was still pending. End-Payor Amended Complaint, *supra* note 20, at paras. 243, 266.

[27] In a bizarre series of events, Ranbaxy launched a generic version of Accupril at-risk in December 2004 – meaning that it launched before a judgment was made as to the validity or invalidity of Pfizer's patents and thus presenting the possibility that it could face substantial damages if the patents were later judged to be valid and infringed. *In re Lipitor*, 46 F. Supp. 3d at 532. It did so despite Pfizer's having already secured summary judgment that an earlier ANDA applicant had infringed patents related to Accupril. *Ibid.* at 531. Pfizer's sales of Accupril dropped from $534 million in 2004 to just $71 million after generic launch. End-Payor Amended Complaint, *supra* note 20, at para. 296. In light of the other Accupril decision over the first ANDA, a court granted a preliminary injunction on sales of generic Accupril, and Pfizer appeared to be very confident that Ranbaxy would be found liable for hundreds of millions of dollars in damages. In fact, they requested that treble damages be awarded under the theory that Ranbaxy willfully infringed the Accupril patents. End-Payor Amended Complaint, *supra* note 20, at paras. 310–11. Yet, as described *infra*, Pfizer was apparently willing to settle the case for only $1 million.

launching "at-risk."[28] At-risk launches sometimes occur when a generic is confident it will prevail in litigation. Ranbaxy's case looked unfavorable at this point, however, given that another generic had already lost its case regarding Accupril patents. Despite the apparent strength of Pfizer's position, Pfizer mysteriously asked for only $1 million to settle the Accupril litigation.

Thus, in exchange for letting the generic company go on the Accupril litigation for a trivial $1 million payment, the brand-name company was able to delay the launch of a far more important generic drug, Lipitor. While the Lipitor settlement involved no cash exchange, and the Accupril settlement involved only $1 million, complainants alleged that Pfizer's stunning and unexpected act of generosity regarding Accupril was actually a "massive [reverse] payment worth hundreds of millions of dollars to [the generic]."[29] In other words, Pfizer paid for the delay by giving up another case likely to be worth hundreds of millions of dollars.

Here is where the tactics get particularly crazy. To put an obfuscating bow around the entire deal, Pfizer allegedly initiated a separate sham lawsuit in order to create the illusion of a lawful settlement. At the time of the Accupril settlement, Pfizer did not have pending litigation against Ranbaxy regarding Lipitor.[30] However, if Pfizer wanted to get a settlement that included the delay of Lipitor, there had to be a pending Lipitor case to settle in the first place. Thus, Pfizer sued the generic over infringement of two small patents not even listed in the Orange Book for Lipitor – two patents for which a court had already said Pfizer had no standing to assert against the generic.[31]

One reason that the patents could not be legitimately asserted in a Hatch-Waxman suit is that they were not "Hatch-Waxman" patents listed in the Orange Book. Recall that under Hatch-Waxman, the act of filing a generic application is treated as an artificial act of patent infringement against the patents listed in the Orange Book, so that patent issues can be resolved well before a generic company directly infringes by launching its product. Ranbaxy had not entered the Lipitor market – a fact often forgotten in scrutinizing these delay settlements – so there was no direct infringement. Given that the patents were not listed in the Orange Book, no infringement – real *or artificial* – could have taken place.[32]

---

[28] End-Payor Amended Complaint, *supra* note 20, at paras. 314–18.

[29] End-Payor Amended Complaint, *supra* note 20, at para. 314.

[30] But it was waiting on the results of a pending citizen petition and an application for reissuance of one of its Lipitor patents. Plus, Ranbaxy was already enjoined from receiving ANDA approval and entering the market until 2010. *In re Lipitor*, 2013 WL 4780496, at *7.

[31] End-Payor Amended Complaint, *supra* note 20, at paras. 270–82.

[32] In more technical terms, there was no "justiciable case or controversy" since the "mere threat of [future] litigation" could not support the case for Pfizer's preliminary injunction. *In re Lipitor Antitrust Litig.*, No. 3:12-cv-2389, 2013 WL 4780496, at *10; Hemphill, *Aggregate Approach to Antitrust*, *supra* note 1, at 639 n. 39.

Three months later, Pfizer and Ranbaxy reached their "agreement" to settle the newly initiated litigation.[33] With all terms considered, some industry estimates pegged the value of the settlement at more than $1.5 billion for the generic.[34] A nice haul indeed, but how much of that figure was payment for keeping Lipitor off the market?

In 2014, this question went before a district court in New Jersey. The court dismissed one group of purchasers' class action for failure to state a claim because the plaintiffs were unable to provide "a reliable estimate" of the monetary value of the reverse payment.[35] It can indeed be difficult to tease out the value of a reverse payment, making these types of complex settlements an attractive option for pharmaceutical companies. If the test involves providing a reliable estimate of the value of the reverse payment, the plaintiff would first need to determine the market value of each piece of the settlement, including: the value to the generic of ending the (supposedly sham) litigation with Pfizer; earning the rights to market generic Lipitor in international markets; ending the Accupril case,; and ending the Caduet litigation.[36] Next, the plaintiff would have to show how much the generic actually "paid" for these pieces of the settlement and then prove that the gap between the market value and the actual value of the settlement represents the reverse payment from Pfizer to the generic to secure Lipitor delay. This presents an enormous hurdle for a plaintiff to clear, and it has led to the dismissal of other related Lipitor class actions.[37]

C THE POST-*ACTAVIS* LANDSCAPE, CONTRACT CLAUSES, AND *KING DRUG*

Lipitor was not the only set of cases dismissed for an apparent failure to define the scope of a reverse payment. In other cases, courts also have not been easily persuaded

---

[33] End-Payor Amended Complaint, *supra* note 20, at para. 279.

[34] *Ibid.* at para. 284.

[35] *In re Lipitor*, 46 F. Supp. 3d at 550.

[36] So little about the Caduet litigation was mentioned in the end-payor complaint that the district court cited it as a reason for dismissing the case, since the complaint failed to address in any way how settling the Caduet litigation factored into the global scope of the settlement. *In re Lipitor*, 46 F. Supp. 3d at 523, 533, 548.

[37] *In re Lipitor Antitrust Litig.*, No. 3:12-cv-02389 (D.N.J. Oct. 30, 2014), http://assets.law360news.com/0592000/592594//mnt/rails_cache/https-ecf-njd-uscourts-gov-doc1-11919306435.pdf (dismissing end-payors' class action suit). Appeals continued after the dismissals. *See* Kelly Knaub, *3rd Circ. Urged to Merge Lipitor, Effexor Antitrust Appeals*, Law360 (Apr. 3, 2015, 9:30 PM), www.law360.com/articles/639404/3rd-circ-urged-to-merge-lipitor-effexor-antitrust-appeals. Some argue that the standard used in *Lipitor* requiring a "ballpark" estimate of the payment sets too high a bar. Aaron Edlin et al., *The Actavis Inference: Theory and Practice*, 67 RUTGERS U. L. REV. 585, 600–01 (2015). In *Actavis*, the Supreme Court cast suspicion on settlement payments that far exceeded expected litigation costs. *Fed. Trade Comm'n v. Actavis, Inc.*, 133 S. Ct. 2223, 2237 (2013). Thus, Edlin et al. argue that a mere

that side deals constitute a reverse payment, particularly in the context of renewed debate after *Actavis* over the definition of what constitutes a "large, unjustified" payment deserving of further antitrust scrutiny.[38]

Other Generation 2.0 settlements, however, do not hinge on contracts for actual services or settling multiple cases. Instead, contract clauses themselves can serve as indirect payments and bottlenecks that prevent later generics from entering.

One popular contract item is an "acceleration clause," also known as a "coordination clause." An acceleration clause stipulates that the generic, which has agreed to delay entry, may immediately *speed ahead* to enter the market if another generic is able to jump the queue and get into the market before the first filer enters and enjoys its exclusivity period. These clauses have also been called "most favored nation" clauses, taking a page from international trade.[39] This nomenclature also makes sense, because the brand-name drug company is essentially offering more favorable terms to the first generic than it is to any other generic.

Beating an acceleration clause by cutting the line is possible through a couple of strategies that later-filing generics may be able to use in certain circumstances. We'll discuss further in Chapter 4. To simplify, with an acceleration clause, the first filer is not locked into its agreed-upon entry date if another generic is able to break through the exclusivity period fence, roadblock, bottleneck, or whatever other metaphorical barrier you prefer.

The true benefit of an acceleration clause, however, is not the reassurance it provides to the delaying generic entrant with fears that another company could somehow steal its exclusivity. Rather, it is the disincentive the clause creates for other prospective generics – what Professor Michael Carrier has called the "poison pill" effect.[40] After an acceleration clause is put in place, any generic looking for a way onto the market does so with the knowledge that, if they are successful, they will immediately face generic competition from the first filer. Each additional competitor leads to declining revenue and market share for everyone in the market, including the new competitor. Thus, entrance is less attractive, especially given the extensive legal battles necessary to secure an earlier place on the market for a

---

showing that the payment exceeded anticipated litigation costs is enough to sustain an *Actavis* claim. Edlin et al., *supra*, at 600–01.

[38] *See generally In re Effexor XR Antitrust Litig.*, No. 11–5479, 2014 WL 4988410 (D.N.J. Oct. 6, 2014) (granting in part and denying in part motion to dismiss); *In re Loestrin 24 FE Antitrust Litig.*, 45 F. Supp. 3d 180 (D.R.I. 2014) (granting motion to dismiss), vacated, No. 14–2071, 2016 WL 698077 (1st Cir. Feb. 22, 2016).

[39] *See* Complaint for Injunctive Relief at para. 58, *FTC vs. Cephalon, Inc.* (settlement approved E.D. Pa. June 17, 2015) (No. 2:08-cv-2141), complaint filed D.D.C. Feb. 13, 2008, www.ftc.gov/sites/default/files/documents/cases/2008/02/080213complaint.pdf.

[40] Carrier, *Payment after Actavis*, *supra* note 8, at 37.

later-filing generic. In turn, the chance that the first generic will be able to launch as the only generic on the market – with the six-month exclusivity period intact – is increased. (Of course, keeping other generics out also means that the brand-name drug company is more likely to enjoy the full delay period as the monopoly seller, as well as the full six-month duopoly period when the first filer finally enters.) In essence, the brand-name firm pays the generic by reducing the risk of competition in exchange for a commitment to delay.

The success of this strategy relies on other manufacturers' having knowledge that the acceleration clause exists. Unsurprisingly, this is precisely what we see happening. In some cases, the clauses are revealed as part of press releases announcing settlements. For example, acceleration clauses were mentioned in public statements regarding four Provigil settlements. Teva, as one of the generics, included in its press release "An earlier entry by Teva in any of the territories may occur based upon the entry of another generic version of Provigil."[41] Identical language was used by the brand-name company in its statements announcing settlements with Ranbaxy, Mylan, and Barr.[42]

One recent example shows how this strategy might work. In settling with three generics wishing to sell Actos, an antidiabetic drug, Takeda allegedly included acceleration clauses in each of the settlements.[43] All three generics filed on the same day, making all eligible for the six-month exclusivity. What was Takeda's impetus behind the clauses? A complaint in the case alleges that Teva, a fourth generic, wanted to enter the market by arguing that Takeda had inaccurately listed its patent information in the Orange Book. If successful, Teva might have been able to enter before the other generics.[44] Thus, the inclusion of the acceleration clauses served as a disincentive for Teva to pursue its case, as Teva would know it would face three other competitors if it managed to reach the market. And there was another clue that this was the intent: while the remainder of the three settlements were confidential,

[41] *See* Press Release, Teva Pharm. Indus. Ltd., Teva Announces Agreement with Cephalon Regarding Settlement of Provigil Patent Litig. (Dec. 9, 2005), www.tevapharm.com/news/teva_announces_agreement_with_cephalon_regarding_settlement_of_provigil_patent_litigation_12_05.aspx.

[42] *See* Press Release, Cephalon, Inc., Cephalon, Inc. Announces Agreement with Ranbaxy Labs, Ltd., Regarding Settlement of Provigil Patent Litig. (Dec. 22, 2005), www.prnewswire.com/news-releases/cephalon-inc-announces-agreement-with-ranbaxy-laboratories-limited-regarding-settlement-of-provigilr-patent-litigation-55651172.html; Press Release, Cephalon, Inc. Announces Agreement with Mylan Pharm., Inc., Ltd. Regarding Settlement of Provigil Patent Litig. (Jan. 10, 2006), www.prnewswire.com/news-releases/cephalon-inc-announces-agreement-with-mylan-pharmaceuticals-inc-regarding-settlement-of-provigilr-patent-litigation-53379057.html; Press Release, Cephalon, Inc., Cephalon, Inc. Announces Agreement with Barr Labs., Inc. Regarding Settlement of Provigil and Actiq Patent Litigs. (Feb. 1, 2006), www.secinfo.com/d11MXs.v5b4.c.htm.

[43] Consolidated Class Action Complaint and Jury Demand at paras. 214–216., *In re* Actos Direct Purchaser Antitrust Litig., No. 1:15-cv-03278, 2015 WL 4600605 (S.D.N.Y. June 4, 2015).

[44] *Ibid.* at paras. 212–213.

Takeda reportedly bestowed upon the generics the ability to tell Teva about the acceleration clauses.[45]

Of particular note among the contract clauses are we what we call "boy scout clauses." These are clauses in which the brand-name company promises good behavior but does so in a way that has anticompetitive effects. To explain boy scout clauses, we need to introduce a concept known as "authorized generics."

Brand-name companies often introduce generic, unbranded versions of their own drugs, at a lower price, to compete against the incoming first generic. Given that the brand-name company already has FDA approval, it is not subject to generic approval processes, and, therefore, its own "generic version" is not restricted from entering the market during the first filer's six-month exclusivity period. In 2005, the D.C. Circuit ruled that the six-month exclusivity does not block authorized generics because brand-name approval has already taken place. The exclusivity provision only bars *future* approvals.[46]

(As an aside, the existence of authorized generics is an example of both how cheap the marginal cost of production can be once research and development are completed, and of how extensive the markup can be on branded pharmaceuticals. It demonstrates that a brand-name company can instantly reduce the price on its drug if it so wishes toward the end of its exclusivity life span.)

Authorized generics allow a brand-name company to hold on to a portion of the profits that would otherwise go to the first generic filer, and it reduces the incentive for entering generics. This changes the Hatch-Waxman calculus for a perspective generic: if you win your patent challenge, you will now be entering a market with another generic on the shelves, not just the expensive brand-name drug. Licenses to manufacture authorized generics also tend to appear in "side deals" in Generation 2.0 agreements.[47]

Early on, commentators expressed concern about the potential anticompetitive effects of the authorized generics and whether the practice undermines the Hatch-Waxman incentive structure. After all, does it not seem to be a bit of a bait and switch? We have spent the first part of this book talking about first filers and the six-month exclusivity, only to find out that it is not so exclusive after all. If the goal of Hatch-Waxman is to incentivize generic challenges, it certainly feels as if authorized generics might hamper this goal by cutting into the monetary reward of the exclusivity period. At the same time, authorized generics pose an interesting problem. While

[45]   *Ibid.* at paras. 216.
[46]   *Teva Pharm. Indus. Ltd. v. Crawford*, 410 F.3d 51 (D.C. Cir. 2005).
[47]   For example, the authorized generic version of Lipitor (atorvastatin) was not made by Pfizer, but was instead manufactured by Watson. *See* Jing Luo *et al.*, *Effect of Generic Competition on Atorvastatin Prescribing and Patients' Out-of-Pocket Spending*, J. Am. Med. Ass'n. Intern. Med. (Jun. 27, 2016), http://archinte.jamanetwork.com/article.aspx?articleid=2530416#ioi160055128.

they might have the long-term effect of disincentivizing competition, the short-term effect of *increasing* competition will actually reduce prices for consumers.

The FTC explored these issues in a 2011 report, in which the agency concluded that authorized generics are generally procompetitive and price reducing, noting only limited cases in which the anticipated presence of authorized generic competition could have been a disincentive for generic entry. The FTC's model found that generics launched at an average 14 percent discount when no authorized generic was present, compared to a slightly larger 18 percent discount when an authorized generic was also launched.[48] The bigger hit results from decreased market share, however. In all, the FTC estimated that a generic's revenue drops between 40 percent and 52 percent when facing competition from an authorized generic during the exclusivity period.[49] Nevertheless, the FTC concluded that authorized generics are mostly procompetitive, given that the presence of authorized generics does not seem to deter patent challenges. In particular, authorized generics are often limited to best-selling drugs that are so lucrative they would incite generic challenges with or without an authorized generic present. Yes, the brand-name company makes more, but the generics are pouring in the door anyway. Perhaps this is one area where brand-name strategy generally benefits consumers: prices decrease without preventing generics from adding their own competition to the market.

Against this backdrop, however, what Big Pharma giveth, Big Pharma may taketh away. With the threat of authorized generics looming over generics, brand-name generics can entice generics to enter settlements by promising not to launch an authorized generic. This is exactly the type of "boy scout clause" found in many advanced pay-for-delay settlements today: a "no-authorized-generic agreement." In a no-authorized-generic agreement, a brand-name firm agrees not to launch a generic form of its drug until the first filer's six-month exclusivity period has expired. In return, the potential generic manufacturer delays entry. The brand-name company, of course, retains the right to continue selling the more expensive branded version of the drug throughout both the generic delay period and the six months of exclusivity. The FTC found that 39 of 157 settlements between fiscal years 2004 and 2010 included no-authorized-generic clauses, involving a total drug market exceeding $23 billion.[50] A full 60 percent of agreements in the last year of the study, 2010, contained some sort of no-authorized-generic clause.[51]

---

[48] *Authorized Generic Drugs: Short-Term Effects and Long-Term Impact* FED. TRADE COMM'N (2011), www.ftc.gov/os/2011/08/2011genericdrugreport.pdf, at ii and iii.

[49] *Ibid.* at iii.

[50] *Ibid.* at vi.

[51] *Ibid.* at vi. n. 14.

What is so clever about this form of agreement is the following: having created authorized generics, the brand-name company now stands up and faithfully swears not to engage in the practice. This, however, is when authorized generics can truly be used in an anticompetitive way. What matters is the context. The brand-name company is agreeing to shun this practice in exchange for an agreement that the generic will delay its entry. The value of forgoing authorized generic entry – the fact that the first generic's revenue will now no longer drop 40 percent to 52 percent – becomes the payment for delay. Once again, the brand-name company can provide something of value to the generic in exchange for staying off the market. The deal benefits both, but harms consumers by delaying the entry of *any* generic drug.

In short, having developed strategic behaviors, the brand-name company can now agree to forgo them, using the value of what would have been its additional sales to pay the generic. All of this is wrapped in the guise of a boy-scout-like promise to be on good behavior. It is a little like the schoolyard bully who agrees to stop hitting the younger kids in exchange for their lunch money. When hauled into the principal's office, he says in great seriousness, "But didn't you want me to stop hitting them?" In this case, however, the lunch money is mostly coming from consumers, who pay in the form of higher prices.

A later version of a boy scout clause appears in the Generation 3.0 tactics in the form of no-product-hopping agreements.[52] In that case, the comparison is even more apt because product hopping – a change in a drug product meant to obstruct generic substitution – is much more clearly an anticompetitive behavior than are authorized generics.

One silver lining of no-authorized-generic agreements, as other commentators and academics have pointed out, is that they may offer an easier argument to courts that noncash agreements violate antitrust laws. Instead of needing to demonstrate how much co-promotion or licensing deals are worth, the penalty to the brand-name company (and reward reaped by the generic) are more readily valued. Plus, an agreement *not to launch* a generic certainly seems to be a "straightforward promise not to compete."[53]

At first, two post-*Actavis* class action lawsuits on this issue, *In re Lamictal Direct Purchaser Antitrust Litigation* and *In re Loestrin 24 FE Antitrust Litigation*, were dismissed in lower courts, with both opinions focusing on what they believed to be the

---

[52] *See* Chapter 3 for more on product hopping.

[53] Laura S. Shores, *Pharmaceutical Patent Life Extension Strategies: Are REMS Next?* ANTITRUST HEALTH CARE CHRON. 20, 25 (2012); *see also* Michael A. Carrier, *Eight Reasons "No-Authorized-Generic" Promises Constitute Reverse Payment*, 67 RUTGERS U. L. REV. 697, 716 (2016), http://ssrn.com/abstract=2533720 ("It does not make economic sense to preclude antitrust scrutiny when a brand, instead of paying with cash … agrees not to compete with the generic in some other market. Or agrees not to launch an authorized generic"); *see also* Carrier, *Payment after Actavis*, *supra* note 8, at 41–44.

Actavis opinion fixation on cash.[54] In addition, the *Loestrin* court had concerns similar to the *Lipitor* case about needing the "true value" of the no-authorized-generic payment, although the court also worried that its ruling would allow pharmaceutical companies to structure settlements simply to "avoid cash payments" and antitrust scrutiny.[55]

During his tenure at the FTC, the former chairman, Jon Leibowitz, similarly articulated the absurdity of limiting the Supreme Court's *Actavis* ruling to cash payments and ignoring no-authorized-generic agreements:

> It used to be that a brand might say to a generic, "if you go away for several years, I'll give you $200 million." Now, the brand might say to the generic, "if I launch an AG, you will be penalized $200 million, so why don't you go away for a few years and I won't launch an AG."[56]

A landmark opinion in June 2015 from the Third Circuit overturned the district court ruling in *Lamictal*. With the case title having changed to *King Drug v. SmithKline Beecham*, the Third Circuit vacated the decision and rejected the trial court's logic.[57] The Third Circuit, as you may recall, was among the first to look skeptically at side deals involving cash in its opinion in the *K-Dur* case. In *King Drug*, that skepticism was extended to noncash reverse payments, including no-authorized-generic agreements. The court found that such noncash payments are not immune to *Actavis*-style scrutiny and that direct purchasers suing over the settlement in question had sufficiently pleaded their antitrust claims.[58]

To fill in the case details, *King Drug* arose out of a settlement between GlaxoSmithKline and first generic filer Teva over Glaxo's brand drug Lamictal, an anticonvulsant drug used to treat epilepsy and bipolar disorder. In the Paragraph IV litigation, the district judge invalidated the primary claim in Glaxo's patent on Lamictal.[59] One month later, the parties agreed to settle in what was, by that point, a case that the brand-name drug company was likely to lose.[60]

---

[54] *In re Lamictal Direct Purchaser Antitrust Litigation*, No. 12-cv-995 (WHW), 2014 WL 282755, (D.N.J. Jan. 24, 2014), vacated, *King Drug Co. of Florence, Inc. v. Smithkline Beecham Corp.*, 791 F.3d 388 (3d Cir. 2015); *In re Loestrin 24 FE Antitrust Litig.*, 45 F. Supp. 3d 180 (D.R.I. 2014) (granting motion to dismiss), vacated, No. 14–2071, 2016 WL 698077 (1st Cir. Feb. 22, 2016); *see also* Carrier, *Eight Reasons* "No-Authorized-Generic" Promises Constitute Reverse Payment, at 703–05; *cf. In re Effexor XR Antitrust Litig.*, No. 11–5479, 2014 WL 4988410 (D.N.J. Oct. 6, 2014) (granting a firm's motion to dismiss a generic's claims that a no-AG agreement constituted an illegal reverse payment).

[55] *In re Loestrin 24 FE Antitrust Litig.*, 45 F. Supp. 3d 180, 190 & 193 (D.R.I. 2014).

[56] Carrier, *Eight Reasons, supra* note 53, at 716, citing FTC, Statement of Chairman Jon Leibowitz on the Release of the Commission's Interim Report on Authorized Generics (June 2009), www.ftc.gov/os/2009/06/P062105authgenstatementLeibowitz.pdf.

[57] *King Drug Co. of Florence, Inc. v. Smithkline Beecham Corp.*, 791 F.3d 388 (3d Cir. 2015).

[58] *Ibid.* at 409.

[59] *Ibid.* at 397.

[60] *Ibid.* at 409–10.

No *cash* was exchanged as part of the settlement. Instead, Glaxo allowed the generic to enter the $50 million market for chewable Lamictal 37 months before the patent expired. Looks good so far. However, the settlement did not permit entry into the far more lucrative $2 *billion* Lamictal tablet market until one day before the expiration of Glaxo's patent.

Employing a no-authorized-generic agreement, Glaxo also agreed that it would not introduce its own generic version of the lucrative Lamictal tablets until after the generic's six-month exclusivity period.[61] Direct purchasers challenged this settlement in a class action, alleging that the no-authorized-generic agreement was an anticompetitive reverse payment.

The Third Circuit agreed that a no-authorized-generic agreement may represent an "unusual, unexplained reverse transfer of considerable value" under *Actavis*, allowing the antitrust claims to continue and reversing the district court's dismissal of the suit.[62] The reasoning applied was similar to that of *Actavis*, but the court also explained the ways in which a noncash payment such as this could have considerable value for both parties.

In particular, the Third Circuit explained that if the patent infringement court had reached a final judgment that Teva did not infringe the patent – which seemed likely at the time of settlement – Teva would have been able to enter the tablet market long before the settlement entry date, lowering the price at an earlier time while enjoying its six months of exclusivity.[63] In exchange for dodging this bullet, the brand-name company agreed that when the six-month exclusivity finally arose, it would not introduce an authorized generic version. It was, essentially, a promise not to compete.[64]

This "generic monopoly," as the court described it, can be worth hundreds of millions of dollars more than a market in which the generic also has to compete with an authorized generic.[65] Wealth is transferred from the brand to the generic – the brand chooses to forgo short-term profits it could earn from an authorized generic

---

[61] *Ibid.* at 397.

[62] *Ibid.* at 394. The early entry to the chewable market was largely ignored in the opinion, mainly because the size of the market is magnitudes smaller than the tablet market. Even if this agreement were slightly competitive, the court decided "plaintiffs have sufficiently alleged that [these aspects] … were outweighed by the anticompetitive harm of the no-AG agreement." *Ibid.* at 410.

[63] *Ibid.* at 405.

[64] *Ibid.* at 406–07.

[65] *Ibid.* at 405. The Court used the term "generic duopoly" to describe when the brand-name drug company and the first generic both enter the market with generic versions. It should be noted, however, that this market structure is different from what economists generally refer to as a duopoly, which occurs when the original drug maker is selling its own branded drug and the first generic is selling a generic version. In contrast, the Court's "generic duopoly" market may feature three versions of the drug on the market – the brand-name drug and two generic versions – one made by the original drug maker and one made by the first filing generic.

in order to restrict competition: that appears to be clear evidence of a problematic payment.[66]

The Third Circuit also found that a no-authorized-generic agreement cannot be written away as an "exclusive license" to a generic. This term is an evasive bit of pharma lingo popular in no-authorized-generic cases – similar to using the term "rightsizing" to describe a major round of corporate layoffs. Instead of a license, the settlement was an agreement not to compete in a certain arena – the generic market price tier.[67] Teva received a generic monopoly period it "could not capture by early entry alone" – because standard early entry these days brings with it a threat of an authorized generic. In other words, what Teva received was exclusivity it could "only hope to obtain … with the brand's self-restraint."[68] This is an agreement that only seems to favor Teva, which would certainly be a strange licensing agreement, unless you take into account the true anticompetitive nature of the clause and the benefits Glaxo gains from delayed entry. (Between this case and *Lipitor*, any pharmaceutical deal that appears to involve an act of generosity should be viewed with extreme suspicion.)

The *King Drug* ruling reverberated throughout the pharmaceutical law world, our comfy niche of choice for this book. In a ruling similar to that in *King Drug*, the First Circuit in February 2016 overturned the district court's ruling in *Loestrin*, also finding that deals with noncash considerations can violate antitrust laws, and, importantly, walking back other rulings requiring specific calculations of the value of noncash payments.[69] Instead, the First Circuit ruled that an estimate of a "large and unjustified" payment can suffice at least to plead an antitrust claim.[70] Following the *King Drug* and *Loestrin* rulings, the FTC filed a complaint in another no-authorized-generic case in March 2016, adding more intrigue to a case we will discuss further in Chapter 3.[71] This was the FTC's first formal complaint involving a no-authorized-generic noncash agreement.[72]

---

[66] *Ibid.* at 405.

[67] *Ibid.* at 406–08 & 406 n. 27.

[68] *Ibid.* at 408.

[69] *In re Loestrin 24 FE Antitrust Litigation*, No. 14–2071, 2016 WL 698077 (1st Cir. Feb. 22, 2016).

[70] *Ibid.* at *31.

[71] Complaint for Injunctive and Other Equitable Relief, *FTC vs. Endo Pharm., Inc., et al* (E.D. Pa. Mar. 30, 2016) (No. 2:16-cv-01440), www.ftc.gov/system/files/documents/cases/160331endocmpt.pdf; *see also* Ed Silverman, *Cash Is Not King: FTC Sues Drug Maker over Pay-For-Delay Deal*, STAT (Mar. 31, 2016), www.statnews.com/pharmalot/2016/03/31/patents-monopoly-antitrust/. For a description of the path of the case, see Kelly Knaub, *Endo Settles Pay-For-Delay Suit as FTC Renews Watson Case*, Law360 (Jan. 23, 2017, 11:07 pm), https://www.law360.com/ip/articles/883817?utm_source=rss&utm_medium=rss&utm_campaign=section.

[72] Press Release, FTC, *FTC Sues Endo Pharm. Inc. and Others for Illegally Blocking Lower-Cost Generic Versions of the Branded Drugs Opana ER and Lidoderm* (Mar. 31, 2016), www.ftc.gov/news-events/press-releases/2016/03/ftc-sues-endo-pharmaceuticals-inc-others-illegally-blocking-lower.

SmithKline Beecham filed a petition in February 2016 asking the Supreme Court to grant review of the *King Drug* ruling, but the Court declined to take the case.[73] This leaves the Third Circuit's ruling in place, confirming that *Actavis* scrutiny can be extended to noncash Generation 2.0 agreements.

In short, Generation 2.0 has featured lucrative side deals and strategic no-cash clauses involving brand-name drug companies and generics. These tactics allow companies to camouflage the nature of the transfer by arguing that no "pay" had been received for the "delay." According to that pharma perspective, the payment supposedly corresponds to the secondary considerations and side deals, while the primary agreement to delay generic entry is made without any value exchange. More expansive readings of *Actavis*, however, threaten to dampen the number of Generation 2.0 settlements. Instead, companies desperate to extend the monopoly life of drugs are turning toward actions in Generation 3.0, where the generic is no longer a potential friend and is instead an opponent to be attacked.

---

[73] Petition for a Writ of Certiorari, *SmithKline Beecham vs. King Drug, cert. denied*, 137 S.Ct. 446 (2016) (No. 15-1055), 2016 WL 704916.

3

"Generation 3.0"

New Tactics for Active Obstruction of Generics

A A NEW GENERATION OF PHARMACEUTICAL DELAY

As described in the prior chapters, pay-for-delay strategies appear to be on their last legs. *Actavis* and *Cipro* combined to deliver a knockout punch to rudimentary cash pay-for-delay deals. Similarly, although the trail of the large unexpected payment is harder to pin down in "Generation 2.0" deals – hidden behind multiple settlements, layers of superfluous deals, and valuable contract clauses – *King Drug* landed a major post-*Actavis* blow. When it comes to lengthy delay deals, pharmaceutical companies are on the ropes, and brand-name companies are less frequently looking to team up with their generic counterparts to extend the life of their monopoly. Instead, brand-name companies are now fighting back directly against generics with small jabs, and consumers are the unwitting recipient of the collateral damage.

The saying goes, "If you can't beat 'em, join 'em." Unsurprisingly, that is not the case for pharmaceutical companies, for which the guiding motto seems closer to, "If you can't join 'em by securing agreements to delay generic entry, *beat* 'em."

With their ability to enter into pay-for-delay deals severely diminished, brand-name drug companies are turning to new strategies no longer friendly to generics. Instead, they actively obstruct generics from entering the market. The point of obstruction can occur at different stages of generic development: before a generic application is submitted, during the generic application approval process, after a generic drug has been approved for marketing, or even once the generic has managed to enter the market.

As Chapters 4 and 5 will explain, the mechanisms of obstruction are varied and complex, but most involve strategic behavior in the generic substitution system or in the FDA regulatory process. One mechanism is known as "product hopping," whereby the brand-name drug company takes advantage of its market power to shift pharmacists, doctors, and consumers to "new" versions of drugs before a generic for the "old" version is able to reach the market.[1] A second mechanism subverts FDA guidelines meant to ensure the safe use of potentially dangerous or potent drugs. These safety protocols are used in schemes that either (1) prevent potential generic manufacturers from accessing the drug samples necessary to test for bioequivalence or (2) block collaboration on shared risk strategies. Many of these tactics take advantage of a process available to the public to raise concerns about pharmaceuticals, known as "citizen petitions." These petitions can require extensive FDA review of the assertions made – and pharmaceutical companies know full well that the FDA is likely to take months (or longer) to review even entirely groundless claims.

In this chapter, we will focus on "early" Generation 3.0 strategies that mainly take advantage of generic substitution systems and the oddities of the pharmaceutical market to obstruct generic sales. Chapter 4 will detail strategies that subvert FDA regulatory measures to achieve delay.

The new era of obstructionist strategies can result in anywhere from a few months up to a couple years of delay, in contrast to the multiple years of delay that reverse payment agreements can create. (There have been, of course, some exceptions and edge cases, particularly when it comes to product hopping and other early strategies.) The tactics are unlikely to be successful beyond the months of delay garnered by filing an FDA petition or refusing to sell drug samples to a generic hopeful, and many of the attempts are likely to be rejected by the FDA. Nevertheless, even a rejected or dismissed attempt at obstruction can be worth hundreds of millions of dollars.

Recall the figures we described for showing that pay-for-delay strategies can be extremely valuable. If a branded drug has $1 billion in annual U.S. sales, an agreement with the generic to delay entry for three to four years is worth billions to the brand-name company – even when factoring in the cost of paying the generic to delay.[2] If the brand-name manufacturer is able to broker a delay of three years for a cost of $500 million, the branded manufacturer still walks away with $2.5 billion of additional revenue out of the deal.[3] With money like this on the table, even shorter forms of delay can be valuable if the costs and risks are low.

Consider the example of a citizen petition asking the FDA to delay approval for a generic. The cost of filing a citizen petition is trivial, perhaps just tens of thousands of dollars of legal fees, compared to the expected value of the benefits, even

---

[1] *See* Herbert Hovenkamp et al., IP AND ANTITRUST: AN ANALYSIS OF ANTITRUST PRINCIPLES APPLIED TO INTELLECTUAL PROPERTY LAW § 12.5 (1st ed. 2002) (discussing and naming the phenomenon "product hopping").

[2] Of the 100 top-selling drugs in the United States in 2013, the median drug had sales exceeding $1 billion. *U.S. Pharmaceutical Sales-2013*, DRUGS.COM, www.drugs.com/stats/top100/2013/sales (last updated Feb. 2014) (reporting sales data for Lovaza and Gilenya, the 50th and 51st best-selling drugs, respectively).

[3] This does assume that branded sales drop to immediately after generic introduction.

if actually having the petition accepted is unlikely.[4] Although the most current legislation requires that citizen petitions with the potential to affect generic approval must be considered within 150 days,[5] those approximately five months of delay could be worth hundreds of millions of dollars in additional monopoly revenues as the generic sits on the sideline waiting for approval.[6] It is not billions, but it will do. In short, the new strategies might impact a shorter term with lower rewards, but their minimal cost makes them worth a try when the potential rewards are substantial.[7]

In addition, some of these strategies could conceivably approach the high-flying numbers of pay-for-delay settlements. Take the example of the events that led to *In re Flonase Antitrust Litigation*.[8] At its peak, Flonase, an extremely popular steroid nasal spray for allergy treatment, reached $1.3 billion a year in sales.[9] Through a complicated series of citizen petitions to the FDA, GlaxoSmithKline was able to stave off generic entry for 23 months.[10] Thus, the delay achieved through citizen petitions was worth approximately $2.5 billion, assuming it maintained the peak $1.3 billion in sales per year until generic entry occurred. In two class action lawsuits that were later filed against Glaxo, the company settled for a total of $185 million.[11]

---

[4]   *See* Darren S. Tucker, *FDA Citizen Petition: A New Means of Delaying Generic Entry?* 20 ANTITRUST HEALTH CARE CHRON. 10, 11 (2006) (citing Comment of the Staff of the Bureau of Competition & the Office of Policy Planning of the Fed. Trade Comm'n before the Food & Drug Admin. In the Matter of Citizen Petitions; Actions That Can Be Requested by Petition; Denials, Withdrawals, and Referrals for Other Administrative Action, FDA Docket No. 99N-2497, at *4, 6–7 (Mar. 2, 2000), www.ftc.gov/sites/default/files/documents/advocacy_documents/ftc-staff-comment-food-and-drug-administration-concerning-citizen-petitions/v000005.pdf.

[5]   21 U.S.C. §355(q)(1)(F); Food and Drug Administration Safety and Innovation Act, Pub. L. 112–44, 126 Stat. 993 (2012); *see also* U.S. Food & Drug Admin., GUIDANCE FOR INDUSTRY: CITIZEN PETITIONS AND PETITIONS FOR STAY OF ACTION SUBJECT TO SECTION 505(Q) OF THE FEDERAL FOOD, DRUG AND COSMETIC ACT 3 (Nov. 2014), www.fda.gov/downloads/drugs/guidancecomplianceregulatoryin-formation/guid ances/ucm079353.pdf (discussing Section 505(q)(1)(F)).

[6]   This calculation assumes the same $1 billion in annual sales for a top 100 drug used previously in the chapter.

[7]   Granted, the cost of these strategies could climb much higher as companies begin to face antitrust litigation for their actions and must expend millions on legal fees after the fact. Until these cases are regularly ending in settlements worth billions to the plaintiffs, however, these "games" are still valuable for brand-name drug companies.

[8]   *In re Flonase Antitrust Litig.*, 951 F. Supp. 2d 739 (E.D. Pa. 2013) (approving direct purchaser settlement); *In re Flonase Antitrust Litig.*, 291 F.R.D. 93 (E.D. Pa. 2013) (approving indirect purchaser settlement).

[9]   Tracy Staton, *GSK Reaches $150M Deal in Flonase Antitrust Case*, FIERCEPHARMA (Dec. 20, 2012), www.fiercepharma.com/story/gsk-reaches-150m-deal-flonase-antitrust-case/2012-12-20.

[10] *See* Seth C. Silber, Jonathan Lutinski, & Rachel Taylon, *Abuse of the FDA Citizen Petition Process: Ripe for Antitrust Challenge?* ANTITRUST HEALTH CARE CHRON., Jan. 2012, at 26, 33–35, www .wsgr.com/PDFSearch/silber0112.pdf (describing the delay mechanisms used by GSK).

[11] Carolina Bolado, *Judge Approves $150M Flonase Antitrust Accord*, LAW360 (June 14, 2013, 6:57 PM), www.law360.com/articles/450443/judge-approves-150m-flonase-antitrust-accord; Jonathan Randles, *Judge Gives Final OK to $35M GSK Flonase Settlement*, LAW360 (June 19, 2013, 5:00 PM), www .law360 .com/articles/451604/judge-gives-final-ok-to-35m-gsk-flonase-settlement.

Thus, even with the settlement, the delay may have been worth up to $2.3 billion for Glaxo – a tidy sum.

The value of petitioning or other obstructionist strategies is even higher when you consider the possibility that the petition might actually be accepted, forcing the generic to retool its application or withdraw from the market. For example, Michael Carrier and Daryl Wander found that the FDA granted about 20 percent of the citizen petitions filed by brands against generics between 2008 and 2010 – a small but significant number.[12]

This chapter continues with a discussion of the some of the earliest market-based Generation 3.0 delay strategies that make up the toolbox for a branded pharmaceutical manufacturer, starting with perhaps the most well-known: product hopping and evergreening.

B PRODUCT HOPPING AND THE PURPLE PILL

Commentators have written for some time on the phenomenon known as "evergreening," in which a company tries to refresh its market monopoly by making slight modifications to a drug's delivery mechanism, dosage, or other characteristics to make the drug eligible for additional exclusivity or patents.[13] One of the most dramatic forms of obstruction uses refreshed or "evergreened" patents as part of a strategy called "product hopping." With product hopping, drug companies attempt to shift the entire market for their brand-name drug to a new or improved version of the medication.

The following steps make up a product hop. First, the brand-name drug company makes a small change to its existing drug – just as its patents or regulatory exclusivities are about to expire – and introduces the new formulation as an entirely new drug. This new form generally is protected by new patents or exclusivities corresponding to the minor changes, and these new rights block generic competition from quickly moving to the new market. The strategy forces a market shift away from the old drug – just as it is approaching its patent cliff.

The brand-name drug company brings about the market shift in a number of ways. Notably, the company usually undertakes a significant promotion and advertising

---

[12] Michael A. Carrier & Daryl Wander, *Citizen Petitions: An Empirical Study*, 34 Cardozo L. Rev. 249, 276 (2012), http://cardozolawreview.com/content/34-1/Carrier.34.1.pdf.

[13] *See generally* Robin Feldman, Rethinking Patent Law 170–77 (2012); Michael A. Carrier, A Real-World Analysis of Pharmaceutical Settlements: The Missing Dimension of Product Hopping, 62 Fla. L. Rev. 1009 (2010); Jessie Cheng, Note, *An Antitrust Analysis of Product Hopping in the Pharmaceutical Industry*, 108 Colum. L. Rev. 1471 (2008); Vikram Iyengar, *Should Pharmaceutical Product Hopping Be Subject to Antitrust Scrutiny?* 97 J. Pat. & Trademark Off. Soc'y 663 (2015); Steve D. Shadowen, Keith B. Leffler, & Joseph T. Lukens, *Anticompetitive Product Changes in the Pharmaceutical Industry*, 41 Rutgers L.J. 1 (2009).

campaign to herald the benefits of the "new" medication and push doctors into writing prescriptions for the new drug. This strategy obstructs generic substitution in different ways, depending on the nature of the product hop. When the product hop involves a shift to an entirely new drug – for example, a shift from Prilosec to Nexium in the market for heartburn relief and other stomach acid–related conditions – convincing doctors to prescribe the new drug prevents generic substitution simply because there is no generic equivalent for the new drug.

Alternatively, in the case in which the product hop involves a switch to a new form of the drug – such as a shift from Suboxone tablets to Suboxone film strips, as described later – pharmaceutical representatives often ask physicians to append a note to their prescriptions asking the pharmacist to "Dispense as Written." This prevents pharmacists from dispensing the generic version of the old form of the drug since the doctor has specifically requested the new form – a form for which there is again no generic substitute.

Some companies go to extreme lengths to earn the coveted "Dispense as Written" phrase on prescriptions. Genentech manages a Web site titled "Preserve Your Branded Choice" for CellCept, a drug that prevents organ rejections after transplants. The Web site heavily encourages health care professionals to write "Dispense as Written" on prescriptions that so branded CellCept is dispensed.[14] The site includes a unique PDF for all 50 states, the District of Columbia, Puerto Rico, and *even Guam,* with specific information about the "Dispense as Written" guidelines in each jurisdiction.

While attempting to switch or preserve prescriptions, the brand-name company also provides a monetary incentive to various participants in the payment and reimbursement chain – including insurers, managed care organizations, and pharmaceutical benefit managers – to catalyze the product hop.[15] The new drug is often introduced with significant rebates and discounts to insurers, causing them to prefer the use of the new drug over the old form in the short term.[16] An insurer may even place the new drug in a preferred position in its formulary of drugs covered for patients – meaning that the patient copay for the new drug is likely to be lower compared to that of the old form. Thus, pressure for doctors to prescribe the new drug comes from all sides: from pharmaceutical reps preaching the benefits of the

---

[14] *Preserve Your Branded Choice,* CELLCEPT, www.cellcept.com/hcp/prescribing-branded-cellcept.

[15] For some additional discussion of this issue, *see* Shadowen, Leffler & Lukens, *Anticompetitive Product Changes, supra* note 13, at 17–21.

[16] Note that these rebates are really only valuable to the insurer when you compare the price of the brand's "old drug" to the rebated/discounted price of the new drug. The cheapest option for the insurer would be to pay for a generic version of the old drug at a price cheaper than even a discounted version of a patent-protected new formulation. Further, rebates and discounts are likely to disappear or diminish once the product hop is sufficiently completed.

product hop, from patients wishing to minimize their copay, from insurers who have a short-term financial incentive to prefer the new drug, and from pharmacists who ask doctors to change prescriptions to the new drug even when the old form is prescribed. As described in the Prologue, patients are also wooed with copay discounts or rebates directly offered by the drug manufacturer, which lowers patient prices while pushing the rest of the brand-tier costs onto the insurer. As of mid-2016, for example, Genentech provided a CellCept copay card to consumers on the same Web site pushing doctors to prescribe only the branded medication.[17]

To complete the product hop, brand-name companies will often discontinue the previous version of the drug, closing distribution channels and sometimes even buying back all remaining inventory of the drug.[18] In some cases, the original drug is eventually removed or excluded from the insurance formularies or national databases used to determine generic equivalence, such as First Databank MedKnowledge, formerly known as the National Drug Data File.[19]

When the original branded drug is excluded from formularies, use of an equivalent generic generally comes to a full halt. Substitution cannot take place because there is no longer a brand-name drug for the generic on the market. Even if a doctor were to write a prescription specifically for the generic instead of the new branded drug, most insurance companies will consider the generic drug to be a "branded" drug for co-pay and reimbursement purposes, given that it is the only drug on the market. This would shift more costs onto the consumer and discourage use of the drug. In sum, the result is that a generic that was supposed to create competition for the original brand-name drug can no longer gain a foothold in the market.

In perhaps the most famous product hop of all time, AstraZeneca switched the market from its original drug Prilosec to Nexium by moving Prilosec from a prescription medication to an over-the-counter drug, and then shifting the prescription market to a newly patented Nexium.

You may know Prilosec as a proton pump inhibitor used for ulcer and heartburn treatment. It contains omeprazole as its active ingredient – to dive into the biology briefly, a pill of Prilosec can be described in technical terms as a "racemic mixture"

---

17 *CellCept CoPay Card*, CELLCEPT, www.cellcept.com/hcp/patient-financial-resources/cellcept-copay-card.

18 *See* FELDMAN, RETHINKING PATENT LAW, *supra* note 13, at 175. In at least one instance, a pharmaceutical company "managed to persuade the FDA to withdraw its license" for an original branded drug right as generic competition was about to be permitted. Lars Noah, *Product Hopping 2.0: Getting the FDA to Yank Your Original License Beats Stacking Patents*, 19 MARQ. INTELL. PROP. L. REV. 161, 165 (2015).

19 *See Teva Pharm. USA, Inc. v. Abbott Lab.*, 580 F. Supp. 2d 345, 355 (D. Del. 2008) (featuring the case of TriCor, in which the brand-name manufacturer recoded earlier versions of TriCor as "obsolete" in the NDDF, allegedly blocking some substitution); *see also* Carrier, *A Real-World Analysis of Pharmaceutical Settlements*, *supra* note 13, at 1019–20 (discussing TriCor and the National Drug Data File).

because it contains both left-handed and right-handed conformations of the active molecule.[20] These right- and left-handed conformations (or "enantiomers") have the exact same molecular structure but are mirror images in their three-dimensional arrangement, similar to left and right hands.

As Prilosec approached its 2001 patent cliff, AstraZeneca made the following change to create Nexium: it simply isolated one of the enantiomers – the left-handed molecule, if you care – to create its drug.[21] In some cases, "enantiopure" drugs containing only one enantiomer of a molecule can have significantly different effects than racemic mixtures.[22]

In the case of Nexium, however, doctors and health executives alike have argued that Nexium is little different from its predecessor drug. An executive with health care provider Kaiser Permanente did not mince words with the *New York Times* back in 2004: "Nexium is no more effective than Prilosec," she said. "I'm surprised anyone has ever written a prescription for Nexium."[23] Another Kaiser physician told the *Wall Street Journal*: "Nexium is clearly no value-added drug."[24]

Thus, there was significant doubt as to whether the isolated form had *any* efficacy benefit over Prilosec. There is little to no evidence that Nexium is better for heartburn treatment, so studies focused on whether Nexium might offer better healing of the esophageal damage that acid reflux can cause. Two of four studies commissioned by AstraZeneca showed that a 40-mg dose of Nexium worked better than a 20-mg dose of Prilosec. In other words, the studies compared double the dose of the new drug to the regular dose of the old one. In the only study going nose to nose with the same dosages – comparing 20-mgs of each – Nexium demonstrated a healing rate of 90 percent versus a slightly lower rate of 87 percent for Prilosec.[25]

Regardless, the strategy was enough to earn new patents and shift the market. Nexium received FDA regulatory approval in February 2001 and began sales in March. The timing, however, was too tight. Prilosec's patents were due to expire in April of that year, and that small, two-month window of time would not be enough to switch the market to Nexium. To solve the problem, AstraZeneca secured an

[20]   *See* FELDMAN, RETHINKING PATENT LAW, *supra* note 13, at 171.

[21]   *Ibid.*

[22]   Silas W. Smith, *Chiral Toxicology: It's The Same Thing … Only Different*, 110 TOXICOLOGICAL SCI. 4, 16 (2009), http://toxsci.oxfordjournals.org/content/110/1/4.full. Using just the right-handed molecule of thalidomide, however, would not have prevented the 1950s thalidomide crisis in Europe because conversions between the left- and right-handed forms of the molecule take place while the drug is being processed in the body. *Ibid.*

[23]   Stuart Elliott & Nat Ives, *Questions on the $3.8 Billion Drug Ad Business*, N.Y. TIMES (Oct. 12, 2004), www.nytimes.com/2004/10/12/business/media/questions-on-the-38-billion-drug-ad-business .html?_r=0.

[24]   *See* Gardiner Harris, *Prilosec's Maker Switchers Users to Nexium, Thwarting Generics*, WALL ST. J. (June 6, 2002), www.wsj.com/articles/SB1023326369679910840.

[25]   *Ibid.*

additional six months of pediatric exclusivity and then added patents on a widely available coating for the drug.[26]

The generic entry window was now pushed out, and AstraZeneca could begin its switch, including massive campaigns targeted at both physicians and consumers. AstraZeneca carefully crafted a campaign that portrayed Nexium as the successor to Prilosec, giving it the "Purple Pill" moniker that Prilosec once held. "The makers of Prilosec introduce their new purple pill," a narrator announces in a commercial that aired beginning in early 2001 and featured celebrities such as Jane Lynch.[27] It directed consumers to call for a free trial alongside the classic instruction to contact your doctor about the medication.

Then, Prilosec was eventually switched to an over-the-counter drug. You might remember the omnipresent commercials featuring the comedian "Larry the Cable Guy" trumpeting the news that Prilosec was available over the counter.[28] Corresponding to that shift, Nexium commercials intensified their push to classify the drug as the prescription-level medication, for "frequent heartburn," juxtaposed with the suggested use of over-the-counter Prilosec. In a 2006 commercial, an actor describes how his doctor "prescribed Nexium," the "healing purple pill," because "he needed more than heartburn relief."[29] And, of course, there was help if the prescription was too costly: "If you can't afford your medication, AstraZeneca may be able to help."[30] As early as 2004, doctors noted that a monthly Nexium prescription could cost $200 versus $45 for a monthly supply of over-the-counter Prilosec.[31] With Nexium as the main prescription form and new patents to protect Nexium from generic competition, doctors channeled into writing prescriptions for the well-protected, new brand-name drug. (Insurance plans generally do not reimburse patients for over-the-counter medications.) It was a perfect and inspired product hop.

AstraZeneca's product hop was, and continues to be, enormously successful. Before the original patent expiration in 2001, Prilosec was the country's number one selling drug with $6 billion per year in sales.[32] In 2013, 12 years after the evergreened

---

[26] *Ibid.*

[27] AstraZeneca, Nexium advertisement (2001), www.youtube.com/watch?v=HqUmbr-lliw (scroll to 2:30 mark of the video).

[28] For example, see AstraZeneca, Prilosec OTC advertisement (2013), www.youtube.com/watch?v=-mYP7eiz5Co. *See also* Feldman, Rethinking Patent Law, *supra* note 13, at 171 (describing the over-the-counter switch). Prescription Prilosec was not completely discontinued, but the move to over-the-counter availability created a product hop because insurers excluded Prilosec from their formularies once it became available without a prescription.

[29] AstraZeneca, Nexium advertisement: The Finisher (2006), www.youtube.com/watch?v=goHWjr6eeMo.

[30] *Ibid.*

[31] Elliott & Ives, *Questions on the $3.8 Billion Drug Ad Business, supra* note 23.

[32] *AstraZeneca Holds Off Rivals as Drug Patent Dies,* USA Today (Oct. 5, 2001), http://usatoday30.usatoday.com/money/general/2001-10-05-prilosec.htm.

Nexium launched, Nexium was the number two selling drug with just below $6 billion in sales. And do not forget, a whopping $2.5 billion of that amount is paid by the government and its beneficiaries under Medicare Part D.[33]

Multiple patents still protect Nexium capsules as of early-2017. One patent will not expire until November 2019, with pediatric exclusivity pushing the cliff back to May 2020.[34] It is hard to value the savings that consumers and insurers might have enjoyed had Nexium never received additional exclusivities, but it would likely be in the tens of billions of dollars.

C NEW EXAMPLES OF PRODUCT HOPPING

Other recent cases have even more alarming fact patterns. Take Asacol, a drug used for the treatment of chronic ulcerative colitis. As the 2013 expiration of the Asacol patents approached and at least two generic companies planned to enter, the brand-name manufacturer, Warner Chilcott, undertook a number of extraordinary actions to extend its monopoly franchise.[35]

First, it developed a higher-dose, extended-release version of the Asacol tablet.[36] The new version of Asacol received two new patents, which will both expire in 2021.[37] The company then attempted a product hop before the 2013 expiration of the Asacol patents through a marketing and promotion campaign.

However, the new form of Asacol was only approved for moderately active ulcerative colitis.[38] The older form of Asacol was approved for both the moderate form and the mild form of the disease.[39] Thus, despite continued efforts to switch all patients to the new form, engendering multiple allegations that these actions represented unlawful off-label marketing (because the drug was not actually approved for all patients), the new form of Asacol did not gain substantial market share.[40]

---

[33] *U.S. Pharmaceutical Sales 2013, supra* note 2; Katie Thomas & Robert Pear, *Medicare Releases Detailed Data on Prescription Drug Spending*, N.Y. TIMES (Apr. 30, 2015), http://mobile.nytimes.com/2015/05/01/business/medicare-releases-detailed-data-on-prescription-drug-spending.html.

[34] U.S. Patent No. 6,428,810 (issued Aug. 6, 2002) (giving information about the patent that expires in 2020), www.google.com/patents/US6428810?dq=6428810&hl=en&sa=X&ved=0ahUKEwip3NDk79rNAhXJMyYKHQhpAZcQ6AEIHDAA; FDA, Orange Book: Approved Drug Products with Therapeutic Equivalence Evaluations, Patent and Exclusivity for: No21153 (last visited Sept. 1, 2016), www.accessdata.fda.gov/scripts/cder/ob/patent_info.cfm?Appl_type=N&Appl_No=021153&Product_No=001 (listing other remaining patents for Nexium).

[35] End-Payor Plaintiffs' Class Action Complaint at paras. 115–18, *Teamsters Union 25 Health Servs. & Ins. Plan v. Allergan*, PLC, No. 15-cv-12730, 2015 WL 3856331 (D. Mass. June 22, 2015).

[36] *Ibid.* at paras. 38–41.

[37] *Ibid.* at para. 40.

[38] *Ibid.* at para. 39.

[39] *Ibid.*

[40] *Ibid.* at paras. 52–57

The company was not deterred. With Asacol's patent expiration approaching, the brand-name firm developed and introduced Delzicol, a 400-mg tablet that was bioequivalent to Asacol.[41] In fact, as Internet commenters quickly discovered, Delzicol was merely an Asacol tablet surrounded by a cellulose capsule.[42] If the capsule is cut open, the original Asacol tablet falls out.[43]

Delzicol did not receive a new grant of exclusivity from the FDA because it was not considered a new molecular entity.[44] Nevertheless, the capsule allowed the company to obtain a patent – despite the fact that the capsule provides no additional therapeutic benefit.[45] Backing this point is the fact that Delzicol was approved by the FDA as bioequivalent to Asacol, so it could not have been "medically superior" in any way.

Let us dwell on this shockingly blatant product hop for a second. Delzicol consists of *Asacol tablets surrounded by a purportedly ineffective additional capsule*. The active ingredients of Asacol must be released in the gastrointestinal tract to have a therapeutic effect on ulcerative colitis, so Asacol tablets have always been covered with an enteric coating that prevents the pill from breaking down in highly acidic stomach acid. In other words, the old pill already had the necessary protective coating, so no new protective coating was needed. Complaints have alleged that the cellulose capsule in Delzicol simply and quickly dissolves in stomach acid – thus it has no effect at all on the drug's delivery.[46]

Warner Chilcott argued that the change was necessary because a slight modification was also made to an inactive coating ingredient that it believed could pose safety concerns.[47] According to a complaint, however, this ingredient remains part of Asacol tablets sold in other countries.[48] Thus, this switch may have merely been subterfuge to display concern with safety, when the real reasoning was to add the patentable but inoperable cellulose capsule and maintain the company's supracompetitive profits.

Finally, Warner Chilcott went for the hard switch – it completely removed the original Asacol from the market, sending all patients to different dosage forms of Asacol or to Delzicol. In a candid conference call, the company's CEO left no doubts about the strategy: "It's a hard conversion. We're stopping – we're going to stop the shipment of Asacol 400 shortly, and it will be all Delzicol. I think they're

---

[41] *Ibid.* at paras. 72–75.
[42] *Ibid.* at paras. 85–88.
[43] *Ibid.* at paras. 84–87.
[44] See the Introduction for a discussion of this FDA nonpatent exclusivity that provides marketing protection for new drugs with new active ingredients.
[45] End-Payor Plaintiffs' Class Action Complaint, *supra* note 35, at para. 81.
[46] *Ibid.* at paras. 80–82.
[47] *Ibid.* at paras. 89–103.
[48] *Ibid.* at para. 83.

all familiar with what's going on."[49] A legal complaint also alleges the involvement of reverse payments and citizen petitions, offering an example of how "multiplicity tactics" are often involved in generic delay.[50]

Perhaps the most notable recent case in the product hopping space is the case that may eventually begin its downfall. Litigation over a product hop involving Namenda, an important Alzheimer's disease treatment, reached the Court of Appeals for the Second Circuit in spring 2015.[51] In a May decision, a three-judge panel denied the drug manufacturer Actavis's appeal, a decision that had the effect of forcing the company to continue selling the old version of Namenda alongside its newer product, Namenda XR.[52]

The old form of Namenda is a twice-a-day treatment for moderate to severe Alzheimer's. In July 2013 – suspiciously, a full three years after it was approved by the FDA – Actavis introduced Namenda XR, a higher-dose treatment that could be taken once daily.[53] In August 2014, about one year before patents would expire on original Namenda, Actavis tried to pull the old form of the drug completely off the market. One month later, the New York Attorney General's Office filed a complaint alleging antitrust violations and seeking a preliminary injunction to force Actavis to continue selling the older formulation. The requested injunction was received in December 2014, and the decision was eventually upheld by the Second Circuit.[54]

Namenda is important, and not just because it was one of the first cases in which product hopping was found to be potentially anticompetitive. Most important, the Namenda product hop took place in a market that the company completely dominated: Namenda is the only treatment in its class available for Alzheimer's and the only treatment approved for moderate-to-severe Alzheimer's.[55] Thus, unlike other cases of product hopping where other drugs might be available as an inexact substitute, switching to Namenda XR was the only choice for Alzheimer's patients who completely depend on the treatment.[56]

---

[49]   *Ibid.* at para. 108 (citing *Warner Chilcott Management Discusses Q4 2012 Results – Earnings Call Transcript*, SEEKING ALPHA (Feb. 22, 2013, 11:50 AM)), http://seekingalpha.com/article/ 1216961-warner-chilcott-management- discusses-q4-2012-results-earnings-call-transcript.

[50]   *Ibid.* at paras. 62–64.

[51]   New York *ex rel. Schneiderman v. Actavis PLC*, 787 F.3d 638 (2d Cir. 2015).

[52]   *Ibid.* at 643.

[53]   *Ibid.* at 647–48.

[54]   *Ibid.* at 649–50.

[55]   *See Current Alzheimer's Treatments*, ALZHEIMER'S ASS'N, www.alz.org/research/science/alzheimers_ disease_treatments.asp (noting that memantine, the generic name for Namenda, is the only NMDA receptor antagonist treatment for Alzheimer's and was the only treatment approved for moderate-to-severe Alzheimer's at the time of the product hop). A newly introduced drug approved for moderate-to-severe Alzheimer's, Namzaric, combines memantine with donepezil, a cholinesterase inhibitor that had already been approved for Alzheimer's treatment in the United States in 1996. *Ibid.* The combination drug, however, is also sold by Actavis.

[56]   *Actavis PLC*, 787 F.3d at 654 n.27.

Further, while the company appeared to be offering the benevolent innovation of a once-daily medication, all other Alzheimer's treatments in different classes had already moved to a once-a-day treatment before the introduction of Namenda XR.[57] The actions raise questions of whether Actavis had waited to incorporate a known innovation in order to thwart generic entry. Specifically, Actavis failed to introduce the once-a-day form for three years after it was approved by the FDA, timed to less than a year before the patents on original Namenda would expire.[58] All of the evidence seems to point to a deliberate and long-planned product hop at the expense of consumer cost savings. Concerningly, it may have also have occurred at the expense of better patient treatment by delaying the introduction of the once-daily dosing regimen.

Our discussion of product hopping raises one major question in particular – it might be distasteful, but does it really raise antitrust concerns? In *Namenda*, Actavis raised one defense: insurers, especially managed care organizations, have an incentive to effectuate substitution to generics, even after product hopping takes place, to lower their own costs. Thus, a product hop is not coercive and not deserving of antitrust scrutiny. Said another way, a generic should be able to convince third-party payers to promote the old generic and advocate to have the drug prescribed by the organization's doctors.[59]

This argument, however, ignores the market power of the branded company in this situation. As the *Namenda* court noted, generics do not have the same power to market their medications as branded manufacturers, given the regulatory structure of the pharmaceutical industry.[60] Most important, the brand-name drug enjoys patent-protected tenure as the medicine people know and recognize. In theory, this power should end when the patent ends, but the brand recognition effects linger on.

As the district court found in *Namenda*, "competition through drug substitution laws is the only cost-effective means of competing available to generic manufacturers."[61] Branded manufacturers know this when they attempt a product hop, which essentially blocks off a generic's only cost-effective form of distribution. Quite simply, the lower cost structure of a generic drug is fueled, in part, by the fact that generics should not need to promote substitution of its drug. The generic drug substitution laws are supposed to accomplish this seamlessly. Without this distribution channel, it would rarely be worthwhile for a generic to compete at all – and thus a product hop could completely foreclose all competition.

---

[57] *Ibid.* at 647; *New York v. Actavis PLC*, No. 14 Civ. 7473, 2014 WL 7105198, at *34 (S.D.N.Y. Dec. 11, 2014) (granting preliminary injunction).

[58] *Actavis PLC*, 787 F.3d at 647–48.

[59] *New York ex rel. Schneiderman v. Actavis PLC*, 787 F.3d 638, 655 & 655 n. 29 (2d Cir. 2015).

[60] *New York ex rel. Schneiderman v. Actavis PLC*, 787 F.3d 638, 655–56 & 656 n. 30 (2d Cir. 2015).

[61] *New York ex rel. Schneiderman v. Actavis PLC*, 787 F.3d 638, 655–56 (2d Cir. 2015).

From the patient's angle, one could argue that product hopping does not limit consumer choice. The generic is not prohibited from entering the market, and consumers are not prohibited from purchasing the generic. This simplistic explanation, however, ignores the unique characteristics of the pharmaceutical market, which does not operate much like a standard market at all, as we have discussed extensively. The argument of "consumer choice" is especially spurious in the case of *Namenda*, in which Actavis controlled the entire market for memantine treatment. No substitute treatment was available for old Namenda at the time Actavis intended to pull it from the market. Actavis was *so* committed to the idea of consumer choice, apparently, that it gave up substantial short-term profits from original Namenda to remove it completely from the market before a generic became available, *forcing* patients to move to the new Namenda XR medication. This is a suspiciously odd approach if a company wants to champion consumer choice. In fact, this willingness to forgo short-term profits was offered by the circuit panel as evidence of the need for antitrust scrutiny, concluding that the drastic move "makes sense only because it eliminates competition."[62]

The panel in *Namenda* dismissed Actavis's procompetive justifications with just one paragraph in its decision, ending with a sentence that underscores just how blatantly obvious the motives behind product hopping generally are: "Based largely on [Actavis's] *own documents*, [Plaintiff] has rebutted [Actavis's] procompetitive justifications" (emphasis added).[63]

D SCOUT'S HONOR IN PRODUCT HOPPING

Unsurprisingly, the development of antagonist strategies such as product hopping has created the opportunity for brand-name firms to dip back into their pool of Generation 2.0 tactics. In particular, product hopping has spawned a new set of "boy scout" clauses, in which the brand-name drug company agrees to refrain from antagonistic behavior after developing the tactics in the first place.[64]

One such clause combining Generations 2.0 and 3.0 is an agreement not to product hop before generic entry, or to pay the generic handsomely if product hopping occurs. For example, in *In re Opana*, class action plaintiffs allege that Endo, a brand-name firm, agreed to pay a first-filing prospective generic what amounted to more than $102 million, but only if sales of the brand-name drug fell below a certain level in the quarter before the generic launch date.[65] In exchange, the generic

---

[62] *New York ex rel. Schneiderman v. Actavis PLC*, 787 F.3d 638, 659 (2d Cir. 2015) (citing *In re Adderall XR Antitrust Litigation* 754 F.3d 128, 133 (2d Cir. 2004)).

[63] *New York ex rel. Schneiderman v. Actavis PLC*, 787 F.3d 638, 658 (2d Cir. 2015).

[64] See Chapter 2 for more discussion of "boy scout" clauses.

[65] End-Payors Plaintiffs' Consolidated Amended Class Action Complaint at para. 2, *In re* Opana ER Antitrust Litig., No. 14 C 10150, 2015 WL 2182959 (N.D. Ill. May 4, 2015).

delayed its entry for more than two years.[66] However, this significant drop in sales would likely occur only if there was a product hop away from the brand-name drug; thus, the agreement essentially functioned as a promise to pay the generic in the event Endo decided to product hop.[67]

On its face, this agreement appears to promote competition by deterring a brand name from product hopping before the generic could enter. The circumstances of the *Opana* settlement, however, were actually designed to effectuate Endo's product hop. Complainants have alleged that the two companies knew before entering into the agreement that the brand-name company would product hop – and in fact, Endo began the FDA approval process for a new version of the brand-name drug just one month after the agreement.[68] Therefore, knowing that a product hop was on the horizon, the $102 million payment effectively served as a simple reverse payment to the generic in return for delaying entry until Endo had a chance to complete its product hop.[69] By the time the generic launched, 90 percent of the product's market had already switched to the new formulation.[70]

In sum, Endo's boy scout clause was only one part of a strategy in which a product hop triggered a side deal that essentially served as a reverse payment for delay. Put another way, Endo's generous invocation of scout's honor was in fact an excuse to use a new Generation 3.0 strategy to enter into a Generation 2.0 deal masking a simple Generation 1.0 reverse payment. The weapons may differ – and may be used simultaneously – but the games remain the same.

---

[66] *Ibid.*

[67] *Ibid.* at paras. 3, 143–52.

[68] *Ibid.* at para. 3.

[69] *Ibid.* at para. 149.

[70] *Ibid.* at para. 158. The generic also secured a no-AG agreement with regard to Opana ER as well as other side deal considerations, allowing the company to recover some of the profits it lost by allowing a product hop. In the absence of the settlement, the generic may have faced competition from an Endo authorized generic when it launched. Instead, it was able to launch as the sole generic product although it faced a market that had shifted to a new version of Opana. The no-AG agreement also helped to make the deal worthwhile for the generic even in the case where Endo failed to product hop and did not trigger the $102 million payment. *Ibid.* at paras. 156–57.

4

"Generation 3.0"

Continued Obstruction of Regulatory Pathways

Chapter 3 detailed complex strategies to block or delay generic entry that involve market, contract, and insurance strategies. This chapter examines new forms of obstruction that rely on distorting regulatory approval pathways.

A REMS-BASED DELAY

REMS-based delay is another strategy in the Generation 3.0 obstruction toolkit.[1] REMS (Risk Evaluation and Mitigation Strategies) are risk management and safety plans that the FDA can require a pharmaceutical company to implement beyond the standard labeling requirements that apply to most drugs.[2] The REMS program was created in 2007 after the arthritis drug Vioxx was linked to heart attacks. The FDA requests a REMS plan when it determines that a drug has severe side effects or is unusually subject to abuse.[3] Such plans are proposed by the pharmaceutical company and then approved and continuously reviewed by the FDA.[4]

---

[1]   One of the authors, Feldman, discussed these REMS abuse issues in a Senate hearing in the summer of 2016. *See CREATES Act: Ending Regulatory Abuse, Protecting Consumers and Ensuring Drug Price Competition: Hearing Before S. Comm. on the Judiciary Subcomm. on Antitrust, Competition Policy, and Consumer Rights*, 114th Cong. (2016) (statement of Professor Robin Feldman, Director of the Institute for Innovation Law, University of California Hastings College of the Law).

[2]   REMS, which stands for "Risk Evaluation and Mitigation Strategies," is a system introduced by the FDA in 2007 as part of amendments to the FDA Act in 2007. U.S. Food & Drug Admin., FDA BASICS WEBINAR: A BRIEF OVERVIEW OF RISK EVALUATION AND MITIGATION STRATEGIES (REMS) 2 [hereinafter "FDA REMS Basics"] (Aug. 12, 2015), www.fda.gov/downloads/AboutFDA/Transparency/Basics/UCM328784.pdf (presenting risk evaluation and mitigation strategies).

[3]   *See Guidance for Industry: Format and Content of Proposed Risk Evaluation and Mitigation Strategies (REMS), REMS Assessments, and Proposed REMS Modifications*, U.S. FOOD & DRUG ADMIN. (2009), *available at* www.fda.gov/downloads/Drugs/GuidanceComplianceRegulatoryInformation/Guidances/UCM184128.pdf. A company may also voluntarily submit a proposed REMS program to the FDA. *See Ibid.* at 2.

[4]   *See* FDA REMS Basics, *supra* note 2, at 4.

REMS are unique to a particular drug or class of drug; they can include the following elements: additional medication inserts to be included with the drug, a campaign or "communication plan" to inform key stakeholders about the risks of the drug, and, most notably, "Elements to Assure Safe Use" ("ETASU").[5]

ETASU are the most restrictive requirement of a REMS program because they directly influence how and when the drug can be used. ETASU can include elements such as patient monitoring or testing while taking the drug, special certification for prescribers or pharmacies, or limitations on how and where the drug can be dispensed (e.g. only in a hospital or certified infusion site).[6] REMS can be modified or completely withdrawn after further assessment.[7] While only about 75 total REMS programs exist,[8] their prevalence is increasing, with one industry group noting that 40 percent of new drug approvals are subject to some form of REMS.[9]

REMS plans affect millions of patients. Just one drug, Suboxone, had 9 million prescriptions filled in the United States in 2012, for a total of $1.5 billion in sales. As we will describe in this chapter, Suboxone is a classic drug that needs a REMS plan, given serious concerns about abuse of this particular drug. A safety plan, however, is meant to protect patients. It should not be used as a trick to block competition in the marketplace.

The fact that REMS programs can impose restrictions on the sale, distribution, or marketing a drug has made the program ripe for abuse by branded drug manufacturers seeking to prevent generics from entering the market. For example, a common safety element restricts sales of a particular medication to hospitals and specially certified pharmacies. This, however, has been used to create obstacles for companies seeking generic approval. Specifically, a generic company must prove that its drug is bioequivalent to the brand-name drug,[10] and testing for bioequivalence requires that the generic applicant use the brand-name drug as a comparison to the generic formulation.[11] Therein lies the problem. A number of cases have involved complaints that the brand-name drug company refused to sell a small amount of their drug to the generic on the grounds that the REMS plan limits the drug's distribution to

---

[5] *Ibid.* at 13.

[6] *Ibid.*

[7] *Ibid.* at 17. *See also* Press Release, Lundbeck, U.S. FDA Approves Changes to the SABRIL® (vigabatrin) REMS Program (June 23, 2016), http://finance.yahoo.com/news/u-fda-approves-changes-sabril-183500071.html (offering an example of REMS requirements being reduced).

[8] *Approved Risk Evaluation and Mitigation Strategies (REMS)*, U.S. FOOD & DRUG ADMIN., www.accessdata.fda.gov/scripts/cder/rems/ (last visited Sept. 5, 2016).

[9] Alex Brill, *Lost Prescription Drug Savings from Use of REMS Programs to Delay Generic Market Entry*, MATRIX GLOBAL ADVISORS (July 2014), at 2, www.gphaonline.org/media/cms/REMS_Studyfinal_July2014.pdf. The study was sponsored by the Generic Pharmaceutical Association.

[10] 21 U.S.C. § 355(j)(2)(A)(iv) (2012).

[11] 21 U.S.C. § 355(j)(8) (2012).

specific outlets, and the generic company, naturally, is not one of those outlets. As described later, some brand-name companies refuse, even as the FDA insists that the company is free to sell to the generic hopeful.

Actelion was one of the first cases on this subject when the suit was filed in 2012.[12] In *Actelion,* the brand-name company refused to provide samples of two drugs to potential generic companies, preventing the generic hopefuls from filing their applications.[13] The brand-name company's position is difficult to fathom. Congress anticipated this type of tactic, and the legislation establishing REMS includes a provision specifically stating that an ETASU cannot be used to block or delay approval of a generic.[14] Further, the FDA has repeatedly said that brands may sell samples to firms for bioequivalence testing without violating their REMS program, and the Agency has even issued letters to branded manufacturers specifically permitting them to give samples to prospective generics.[15]

The legal arguments in the *Actelion* case focused on whether refusal to sell samples to a generic competitor constitutes an antitrust violation.[16] Actelion asserted that it has a right to refuse to sell even in the absence of the REMS and the company has no legal duty to provide samples to a potential generic competitor.[17] The FTC filed

[12] *Actelion Pharm. LTD v. Apotex Inc.,* No. 12–5743, 2013 WL 5524078 (D.N.J. Sept. 6, 2013); *see also* Kat Greene, *Actelion Settles Row over Giving Drugs to Generic Makers,* Law360 (Feb. 28, 2014, 7:07 PM), www.law360.com/articles/514434/actelion-settles-row-over-giving-drugs-to-generics-makers. In one other previous case filed in 2008, Lannett accused Celgene of refusing to provide it samples of Thalomid. The case ended in a settlement. Verified Complaint for Mandatory Injunctive Relief, Declaratory Relief and Money Damages, *Lannett Co., Inc. v. Celgene Corp.,* No. 08-3920, 2011 WL 1193912 (E.D. Pa. Aug. 15, 2008).

[13] *Actelion Pharm.,* 2013 WL 5524078, at *1.

[14] 21 U.S.C. § 355–1(f)(8) (2012).

[15] *See* Ctr. for Drug Evaluation & Res., U.S. Food & Drug Admin., Risk Evaluation and Mitigation Strategy (REMS) Public Meeting 270–72 (July 28, 2010) (statement by Jane Axelrad, Associate Director of Policy, Ctr. for Drug Evaluation and Res.), www.fda.gov/downloads/Drugs/NewsEvents/UCM224950.pdf (asserting that REMS should not be a barrier to acquiring generic samples). In part, these letters came about after a citizen petition filed in 2009 by Dr. Reddy's asking the FDA to issue guidance regarding the use of REMS to block or delay generic entry. It also asked the FDA to establish a procedure by which the FDA would provide letters on behalf of generic applicants to explain that the generic will meet the REMS safe use requirements that might be implicated in bioequivalence testing. *See* Citizen Petition from Kumar Sekar, Senior Dir., to Div. of Dockets Mgmt., U.S. Food & Drug Admin., No. FDA-2009-P-0266-0001, at 10 (June 10, 2009), www.fdalawyersblog.com/Dr_Reddys_Laboratories,_Inc_-_Citizen_Petition.pdf. Dr. Reddy's was attempting to obtain samples of Celgene's Revlimid and Thalomid, which are also the subject of another ongoing REMS-based lawsuit described later in the chapter.

[16] *See generally* Darren S. Tucker, Gregory F. Wells & Margaret Sheer, *REMS: The Next Pharmaceutical Enforcement Priority?* 28 Antitrust 74 (2014).

[17] *See* Memorandum of Law in Support of Plaintiffs' Motion for Judgment on the Pleadings and to Dismiss Counterclaims at 8, *Actelion Pharm. Ltd. v. Apotex Inc.,* Case 1:12-cv-05743-NLH-AMD (D. N.J. Mar. 18, 2013).

a brief stating that the company's action may amount to exclusionary conduct.[18] The case ended in a settlement in early 2014.[19]

In a similar case filed against the brand-name drug manufacturer Celgene, a generic hopeful alleged that it spent five years trying unsuccessfully to get a sample of Celgene's Thalomid (thalidomide) and another five years trying unsuccessfully to obtain a sample of Celgene's Revlimid (lenalidomide), two drugs with clear safety concerns.[20] The complaint alleged that Celgene repeatedly asked for more information and FDA assurances until the generic "recognized that further engagement with Celgene would be fruitless."[21] Although the judge dismissed some claims in the generic's complaint, she allowed important antitrust claims to survive a motion to dismiss, finding that the generic pleaded with enough detail that Celgene had no "legitimate business reasons" for denying samples.[22] Celgene's actions also led to the initiation of an FTC investigation into the company's practices.[23]

Celgene went even further, however, by obtaining a patent on its method of protecting patient safety. The patent on the thalidomide REMS safety plan specifies that the company has exclusive rights in the supposedly novel invention of "delivering a drug to a patient while restricting access to the drug by patients for whom the drug may be contraindicated."[24]

This is what is known as a "business method patent," a notoriously suspect category of patents that the Supreme Court has repeatedly attacked in recent years.[25] In

[18] For a detailed analysis of the potential antitrust issues in restricted distribution cases, see Michael A. Carrier, Nicole L. Levidow, & Aaron S. Kesselheim, *Using Antitrust Law to Challenge Turing's Daraprim Price Increase*, 31 BERKELEY TECH. L.J. (forthcoming 2016), http://ssrn.com/abstract=2724604.

[19] Greene, *Actelion Settles Row*, *supra* note 12; Lance Duroni, *Actelion Denied Judgment in Tracleer Antitrust Suit*, LAW360 (Oct. 21, 2013, 8:00 PM), www.law360.com/articles/481879. Although a settlement may represent a party's rational calculation of the strength of its case and the costs of continuing to litigate, it may also represent the strategic choice to abandon a case or pay off the other side if damaging information might emerge or dangerous precedents might be set.

[20] *Mylan Pharmaceuticals v. Celgene Corp.*, No. 14-cv-2094, Transcript of Oral Opinion at *4–9 (D.N.J. Dec. 22, 2014) (denying in part and granting in part Celgene's motion to dismiss by oral opinion). The case later ended in a settlement.

[21] *Mylan Pharmaceuticals v. Celgene Corp.*, No. 14-cv-2094, Transcript of Oral Opinion at *7 (D.N.J. Dec. 22, 2014) (denying in part and granting in part Celgene's motion to dismiss by oral opinion).

[22] *Ibid.* at *17–18; *see also* Carrier, Levidow & Kesselheim, *Using Antitrust Law*, *supra* note 18, at *13–14 (discussing this case).

[23] Laura S. Shores, *Pharmaceutical Patent Life Extension Strategies: Are REMS Programs Next?* ANTITRUST HEALTH CARE CHRON. 19, 27 (March 2012) (citing Form 10-Q Quarterly Report for Celgene Corp. (filed Nov. 2, 2011)).

[24] *See* Ameet Sarpatwari, Jerry Avorn, & Aaron Kesselheim, *Using a Drug-Safety Tool to Prevent Competition*, 370(16) NEW ENGLAND J. OF MED. 1476, 1477 (April 17, 2014) (describing US Patent US 7,141,018 B2 and discussing the thalidomide REMS in the context of problems within the REMS system).

[25] *See Alice Corp. Pty. Ltd. v. CLS Bank Int'l*, 134 S. Ct. 2347 (2014); *see also Association for Molecular Pathology v. Myriad Genetics, Inc.*, 133 S. Ct. 2107 (2013); *Mayo Collaborative Servs. v. Prometheus Laboratories, Inc.*, 132. S. Ct. 1289 (2012). For a description of these cases, see Robin Feldman, *Coming*

the *Alice* line of cases, the Supreme Court rejected both ordinary business method patents and those implemented through software. In fact, the Supreme Court has emphasized repeatedly that patentability requires an inventive concept beyond combining a series of well-known conventional steps, such as testing, tracking, and informing.

Armed with that suspect patent on its REMS safety plan, Celgene then set about blocking generic entry. When a generic company applied for approval, the original drug maker, Celgene, filed a petition asking the FDA to deny the application, including on the grounds that no generic could use Celgene's patented REMS safety plan and that any other plan would compromise patient safety by compounding burdens and confusion.[26] In other words, no generic could ever exist.

The FDA denied Celgene's petition a full seven years later.[27] But the damage was done – a decade later, no generic for Thalomid exists, and after all the trouble the one beleaguered generic went through to try to reach the market, it withdrew its application in 2010.[28]

The attempt to patent a REMS program is a particularly suspect approach, but setting this aside, REMS manipulation, in theory, could be particularly dangerous for generic competition. REMS are not linked to patents on a drug's active ingredient or mechanism of action. As a result, they can continue indefinitely, even after the expiration of all patents – they are safety programs, after all. Thus, if a company, hiding behind a restrictive REMS, refuses to allow samples to generic hopefuls, the brand-name company could continue its monopoly past the end of the patent term. And even if the company is eventually forced to share samples, every month of delay is valuable.

Furthermore, a restricted distribution scheme does not even need a REMS, or even an active patent, to be effective in blocking generic competition. For example, the case of Turing Pharmaceuticals, Martin Shkreli (yes, he is back), and Daraprim involved a restricted distribution system not imposed by the FDA, as did schemes

---

of Age for the Federal Circuit, 18 GREEN BAG 2D 27 (2014); Robin Feldman, *A Conversation on Judicial Decision-Making*, 5 HASTINGS SCI & TECH. L.J. 2 (2013).

[26] See Sarpatwari, Avorn, & Kesselheim, *Using a Drug-Safety Tool*, supra note 24, at 1477 (discussing Citizen Petition from Celgene Corporation to the FDA at 17–18 (September 20, 2007), www.regulations .gov/document?D=FDA-2007-P-0113-0002).

[27] Letter from Janet Woodcock, Dir., Ctr. for Drug Evaluation & Research, FDA, to Gary L. Vernon, Sidney Austin LLP, Re: Docket No. FDA-2007-P-0113 (Sept. 30, 2014), www.regulations.gov/ document?D=FDA-2007-P-0113-0028 (denying the Celgene citizen petition).

[28] Press Release, Celgene Corp., Celgene Announces Dismissal of Suit against Barr Laboratories Following Withdrawal of Thalidomide ANDA (May 27, 2010), http://ir.celgene.com/releasedetail .cfm?releaseid=799456 (press release confirming withdrawal of the application).

run by other Skhreli companies. In other words, the company did not have an FDA-mandated REMS plan; the company simply declared that its drug had to be restricted to certain distribution channels.

Companies who restrict generic competitors from accessing samples argue that they are concerned about the safety of people who come into contact with their drug and that the generic company might not handle the medication properly. It is a tough argument to make, however, if the FDA sees no problem in giving the sample to the generic. Can a company really argue that it is better able to judge a competitor's safety than the FDA? It is a little like the fox suggesting it has deputized itself to guard a competitor's henhouse.[29] In both cases, there is somewhat of a conflict of interest.

Restricted distribution schemes, whether they involve a REMS or not, also may be deployed to prevent generic substitution by pharmacists. In another story that captured the public's attention, federal prosecutors announced an investigation of Valeant Pharmaceuticals, also pilloried for acquiring medicines (as well as companies for tax inversion purposes in foreign countries) and then substantially increasing prices of drugs.[30] In fact, that seemed to be the company's core business model, making it a darling of big-time investors.[31] That accusation, however, was only the first of a series of allegations that would unfold against Valeant. Just days later, journalists discovered that Valeant had a deep relationship with a specialty pharmacy known as Philidor that essentially filled prescriptions only for Valeant's drugs and dermatology creams.[32] This investigation in turn led to the discovery of numerous pharmacies and subsidiaries covertly linked to Valeant.[33] (All of these subsidiaries had chess-related names, a true unforced error if you are trying not to come across as a Bond villain.)

The link between Valeant and specific specialty pharmacies allowed Valeant to ensure that prescriptions would be filled using its brand-name drugs rather than

---

[29] *See* S. Comm. On the Judiciary Subcomm. on Antitrust, Competition Policy and Consumer Rights, *The CREATES ACT: Ending Regulatory Abuse, Protecting Consumers, and Ensuring Drug Price Competition* (Jun. 21, 2016), at 1:33:15, https://www.judiciary.senate.gov/meetings/the-creates-act-ending-regulatory-abuse-protecting-consumers-and-ensuring-drug-price-competition (using fox analogy in response to a Senator's question).

[30] Jonathan D. Rockoff, *Valeant Pharmaceuticals under Investigation by Federal Prosecutors*, WALL ST. J. (Oct. 15, 2015), www.wsj.com/articles/valeant-pharmaceuticals-under-investigation-by-federal-prosecutors-1444874710?mod=e2tw.

[31] Bethany McLean, *The Valeant Meltdown and Wall Street's Major Drug Problem*, VANITY FAIR (June 5, 2016), www.vanityfair.com/news/2016/06/the-valeant-meltdown-and-wall-streets-major-drug-problem.

[32] Roddy Boyd, *The King's Gambit: Valeant's Big Secret*, S. INVESTIGATIVE REPORTING FOUND. (Oct. 19, 2015), http://sirf-online.org/2015/10/19/hidden-in-plain-sight-valeants-big-crazy-sort-of-secret-story/.

[33] Bertrand Marotte, *Valeant's Sales Network: Deciphering a Complex Web of Companies*, GLOBE & MAIL (Oct. 27, 2015), www.theglobeandmail.com/report-on-business/valeants-sales-network-the-firms-and-chess-terms-tied-to-it/article27009058/.

a generic. Doctors would submit prescriptions for Valeant drugs to a mail-order specialty pharmacy, the prescription would be sent to the patient, and then the pharmacy would work with insurance companies to secure reimbursement.[34] When a prescription is sent to a specialty pharmacy that only deals a specific drug brand, it is very unlikely that any substitution will take place to dispense a generic or over-the-counter medicine instead.[35] The specialty pharmacy simply does not deal with anything but the brand-name drug. As another company using a similar business model disclosed in a regulatory filing, the mail-order prescriptions "are less likely to be subject to the efforts of traditional pharmacies to switch a physician's intended prescription of our products to a generic or over-the-counter brand."[36] That company, Horizon, reportedly charged $1,500 a month for a medication called Duexis that simply combined ibuprofen and the active ingredient in Pepcid.[37]

The brunt of the costs of these schemes falls on insurers and not patients, perhaps intentionally so that patients and doctors do not feel the sticker shock of high prices. Nevertheless, games like these certainly do not help lower insurance premiums. Moreover, when insurers balked at the high cost of Valeant prescriptions, Philidor and other pharmacies allegedly took drastic action to secure reimbursement, including modifying prescription codes to make it appear as if the doctor specifically requested that a prescription be "Dispensed as Written" with Valeant-branded medication.[38] As a result, these schemes continually blocked generic competitors from participating in the market for the medication.

When the dust settled from the scandal, Valeant's precipitous success, attained through a model of buying drugs, inverting taxes, and raising prices, had come to a crashing end. From a share price high of $262 in August 2015, Valeant's stock had hit $33 by mid-March of 2016, and was trading below $25 by the summer – a 90 percent plummet.[39] In April 2016, the U.S. Treasury Department took action to stop corporate tax inversions,[40] which most notably led to the termination of a proposed merger between pharma giants Pfizer and Allergan.[41]

[34] Andrew Pollack, *Drug Makers Sidestep Barriers on Pricing*, N.Y. Times (Oct. 19, 2015), www.nytimes.com/2015/10/20/business/drug-makers-sidestep-barriers-on-pricing.html?smid=pl-share.

[35] *Ibid.*

[36] *Ibid.*

[37] *Ibid.*

[38] Caroline Chen & Ben Elgin, *Philidor Said to Modify Prescriptions to Boost Valeant Sales*, Bloomberg (Oct. 29, 2015), www.bloomberg.com/news/articles/2015-10-29/philidor-said-to-modify-prescriptions-to-boost-valeant-sales.

[39] McLean, *Valeant Meltdown and Wall Street's Major Drug Problem, supra* note 31.

[40] Jeffrey Zients & Seth Hanlon, *The Corporate Tax Inversions Loophole: What You Need to Know*, White House Blog (Apr. 8, 2016, 6:39 PM ET), www.whitehouse.gov/blog/2016/04/08/corporate-inversions-tax-loophole-what-you-need-know.

[41] Kristen Hallam, Cynthia Koons, & Zachary Tracer, *Pfizer Confirms Termination of Proposed $160 Billion Allergan Merger*, Bloomberg (Apr. 6, 2016), www.bloomberg.com/news/articles/2016-04-06/pfizer-allergan-end-160-billion-merger-amid-new-tax-rules; Jonathan D. Rockoff, Liz Hoffman, &

Aside from restricted distribution programs run through specialty pharmacies, other REMS-based schemes have appeared. Frequently, a REMS program will ask a drug's manufacturers to develop a more detailed medication guide or a communication plan to inform doctors and patients about the elevated risks of a drug. For example, Gilenya (fingolimod), an immunosuppressant that treats relapses of multiple sclerosis, has a REMS that requires a communication plan with materials for doctors and patients, as well as an FDA-mandated pregnancy registry.[42]

When there are multiple manufacturers of a drug – for example, a brand and a generic – the FDA often requires all parties to develop and agree on the same REMS program, known simply as a Single Shared REMS program.[43] In particular, generic entry can be conditioned on FDA approval of a shared plan. The idea that a brand-name company will be willing to cooperate in the approval of a generic seems optimistic at best. Given that brand-name drug makers are able to delay entry by refusing to cooperate, it is not a surprise that some have taken advantage of it, creating another form of generic delay. The generic cannot get its drug approved until the brand-name company cooperates, and the brand-name company avoids cooperating to keep the generic off the market. It could be compared to a high school group project in which one member not only refuses to complete a fair share of the work, but also has an incentive to see the project fail in order to sabotage the grades of others in the group. And with the brand-name company already on the market, only the generics suffer from the delay.

The most notable case dealing with this strategy is *In re Suboxone*.[44] Suboxone is used for the treatment of addiction to opioids, such as heroin and oxycodone.[45] The drug has saved the lives of many addicts, but with severe consequences. Suboxone has itself become a street drug, and it carries the risk of severe side effects and withdrawal symptoms.[46] Suboxone includes both a semisynthetic opioid and a drug used to combat the effects of an opioid overdose (with unpleasant side effects), which is included for the sole purpose of deterring potential users from injecting the drug intravenously.[47]

Richard Rubin, *Pfizer Walks Away from Allergan Deal*, Wall St. J. (Apr. 6, 2016), www.wsj.com/articles/pfizer-walks-away-from-allergan-deal-1459939739.

[42] *See Approved Risk Evaluation and Mitigation Strategies (REMS): Gilenya (fingolimod)*, U.S. Food & Drug Admin. (May 14, 2015), www.accessdata.fda.gov/scripts/cder/rems/index.cfm?event=IndvRemsDetails.page&REMS=22.

[43] *In re Suboxone* (Buprenorphine Hydrochloride and Naloxone) Antitrust Litig., 64 F. Supp. 3d 665, 675 (E.D. Pa. Dec. 3, 2014) (granting dismissal of some counts and in part denying some counts).

[44] *Ibid.*

[45] Suboxone, www.suboxone.com.

[46] *See* Deborah Sontag, *Addiction Treatment with a Dark Side*, N.Y. Times (Nov. 16, 2013), www.nytimes.com/2013/11/17/health/in-demand-in-clinics-and-on-the-street-bupe-can-be-savior-or-menace.html; *Risk Evaluation and Mitigation Strategy for Suboxone*, Indivior, www.suboxonefilmrems.com.

[47] *See* Sontag, *Addiction Treatment*, *supra* note 46.

Suboxone is perhaps the poster child for a drug needing a comprehensive REMS program. Its REMS program includes a medication guide, a checklist that physicians must follow when prescribing the drug, federal authorizations for prescribers, limits on how much medication can be initially prescribed, an intensive monitoring program requiring frequent patient return visits, and monitoring on the part of manufacturers, which can even include "surveillance" and "street ethnography" to detail patterns of abuse.[48]

Suboxone is also a blockbuster with more than $1.55 billion in sales in 2012, linked to an explosion of painkiller and heroin abuse in the United States.[49] Thus, with the brand-name company, Reckitt Benckiser, nearing the end of its exclusivity for Suboxone tablets in 2009 and generic entry looming on the horizon, the company undertook an extraordinary set of actions to maintain a monopoly on the Suboxone franchise.[50] Complainants have alleged tactics including an anticompetitive product hop, sham citizen petitions, and REMS abuse.[51]

Specifically, as exclusivity was about to expire on Suboxone, complaints alleged that Reckitt began to develop a film-strip version of Suboxone (think of those breath-freshening film strips that are widely available) with the intention of product hopping from tablet to film form.[52] The timing was off for the company, however, because the final exclusivities for the tablet were scheduled to expire about 11 months before the FDA approved the film version.[53] The resulting 11-month gap could have been a prime opportunity for a generic to enter and gain market share before the FDA approved the Suboxone film.

To effectuate a product hop, complainants argued that the brand-name company undertook a massive sales and marketing campaign to "promote" the idea that the tablet version of Suboxone presented safety concerns, which would be alleviated by

---

[48] U.S. Food & Drug Admin., RISK EVALUATION AND MITIGATION STRATEGY FOR SUBOXONE, RECKITT BENCKISER PHARMACEUTICALS, INC., NDA 20–733 (Dec. 2011), www.accessdata.fda.gov/drugsatfda_docs/rems/Suboxone%20sublingual%20tablets_2011-12-22_REMS%20DOCUMENT.pdf (approving initial Risk Evaluation and Mitigation Strategy); *see* Sontag, *Addiction Treatment, supra* note 46; *see also* Phelps Hyman & PC McNamara, *Risk Evaluation and Mitigation Strategy Tracker*, FDA LAW BLOG (last visited Sept. 5, 2016), www.fdalawblog.net/fda_law_blog_hyman_phelps/files/REMS_Tracker.xls (providing extensive tracking of REMS approvals).

[49] Sontag, *Addiction Treatment, supra* note 46.

[50] Suboxone is now sold and distributed by Invidior, a specialty pharmaceutical company that Reckitt Benckiser spun off from its core business in 2014. Ashley Armstrong, *Reckitt Benckiser to Spin-Off Drug Unit into New Listing*, TELEGRAPH (Nov. 17, 2014), www.telegraph.co.uk/finance/newsbysector/epic/rbdot/11235616/Reckitt-Benckiser-to-spin-off-drug-unit-into-new-listing.html.

[51] End-Payor Plaintiffs' Consolidated Amended Class Action Complaint at paras. 3–5, *In re Suboxone* (Buprenorphine Hydrochloride and Naloxone) Antitrust Litig., No. 13-md-02445, 2013 WL 5467390 (E.D. Pa. Aug. 15, 2013).

[52] *Ibid.* at para. 15.

[53] *In re Suboxone* (Buprenorphine Hydrochloride and Naloxone) Antitrust Litig., 64 F. Supp. 3d 665, 674 (E.D. Pa. Dec. 3, 2014).

the Suboxone film version.[54] The campaign claimed that there was a high risk of pediatric overdose from a bottle of Suboxone tablets, a risk remedied by the packaging for the film version because the films are packaged individually.[55] Notably, at the time, individually packaged tablets were available in all markets where Suboxone is sold, other than in the United States.[56] In other words, the problem could have been remedied simply by modifying the packaging of the tablets, but the company had not seen fit to provide that resolution in the U.S. market.

Further, opponents argued that the film may exacerbate safety concerns regarding pediatric exposure. Since the film dissolves more quickly than the tablet, it may be difficult to prevent children from being exposed to the medication once they put it in their mouth. Moreover, the potential for abuse may increase since the film's dissolvability allows users to hide their activity more easily.[57] Speaking with the *New York Times*, a Kentucky jailer put it better than we ever could:

> "It's such a thin strip they'll put it in the Holy Bible, let it melt and eat a page right out of the good book," said Ken Mobley, a jailer in Whitley County, Ky.[58]

Despite the campaign, the possibility of generic tablet entry continued to be a problem for Reckitt. Thus, the company sent multiple letters and applications to the FDA proposing a REMS because of the risks of abuse and pediatric exposure.[59] This request was approved, and the FDA required that the generic and branded Suboxone share the same REMS.[60] Unsurprisingly, attempts at cooperation between Reckitt and the prospective generics proved unsuccessful. Eventually, the generics gave up, applying for and receiving a waiver to create a REMS without the branded drug company – the first time such a waiver had ever been granted.[61]

---

[54] *Ibid.*

[55] End-Payor Plaintiffs' Consolidated Amended Class Action Complaint, *supra* note 51, at paras. 23–26; *see also* U.S. Food and Drug Admin., NDA 20–733, Suboxone Risk Evaluation and Mitigation Strategy (Dec. 2011), www.accessdata.fda.gov/drugsatfda_docs/rems/Suboxone%20sublingual%20tablets_2011-12-22_REMS%20DOCUMENT.pdf (approving initial Risk Evaluation and Mitigation Strategy).

[56] End-Payor Plaintiffs' Consolidated Amended Class Action Complaint, *supra* note 51, at paras. 21, 28.

[57] *In re Suboxone*, 64 F. Supp. 3d at 674.

[58] *See* Sontag, *Addiction Treatment*, *supra* note 46.

[59] Letter from Judith A. Racoosin, Deputy Dir. for Safety, Ctr. for Drug Evaluation & Research, FDA, to John Song, Manager, NA Regulatory Affairs Operations, Reckitt Benckiser, at 1 (Dec. 22, 2011), www.accessdata.fda.gov/drugsatfda_docs/appletter/2011/020733s007,s008ltr.pdf (approving Risk Evaluation and Mitigation Strategy).

[60] *In re Suboxone*, 64 F. Supp. 3d at 675. This requirement is detailed in 21 U.S.C. § 355(i)(1) (2012).

[61] *In re Suboxone*, 64 F. Supp. 3d at 675–76; *see also* Kurt R. Karst, *In Case You Missed It … We Did! Prometheus Takes Action against FDA over Generic LOTRONEX Approval and REMS Waiver, and Then Promptly Drops Case*, FDA L. Blog (June 24, 2015), www.fdalawblog.net/fda_law_blog_hyman_phelps/2015/06/in-case-you-missed-it-we-did-prometheus-takes-action-against-fda-over-generic-lotronex-approval-and-.html (noting that the Suboxone REMS waiver was the first granted by the FDA); *see also Prometheus Lab. Inc. v. Burwell*, No. 15-cv-00742 (D.D.C. filed May 18,

The nine-month period during which generics and the brand-name company could not come to an agreement on a REMS may have been worth upward of $1 billion in Suboxone sales. This is an enormous sum to result from a disagreement presumably not over the medication itself, but over how its use would be monitored and how the risks would be explained to the public.[62]

In the resulting lawsuit, the judge in 2014 dismissed the generic company's stand-alone claim that Reckitt's actions regarding the REMS amounted to an antitrust violation.[63] The saga of *Suboxone* continues in Part B of this chapter, however, with further complaints of anticompetitive behavior.[64] In short, it is clear that although the FDA would like to encourage everyone "to play nicely together on the playground," mere talk is unlikely to achieve this goal.[65] When billions are on the line, the games are bound to get rough. As the FDA admitted in another REMS case, the agency simply lacks an effective mechanism to force the two parties to reach agreement.[66]

Over the last few years, legislators have begun to offer potential solutions to REMS-related delay issues. One bill, introduced in the House of Representatives in late 2015, attempted to tackle the two main forms of REMS abuse – denial of samples for generic testing and unwillingness to cooperate on single-shared REMS.[67] The bill would require brand-name drug companies to provide samples (after FDA approval) to prospective generics at a nondiscriminatory, commercially reasonable,

---

2015) (D.D.C. denied motion for temporary restraining order May 21, 2015. Prometheus dropped suit June 11, 2015 where a brand-name company filed suit against the FDA for granting a second REMS waiver in 2014.). The FDA responded by noting, in part, that the brand-name company "dragg[ed] its feet for more than three years rather than collaborate with [the generic]." *See* Federal Defendants' Opposition to Plaintiff's Motion for a Temporary Restraining Order And/Or Preliminary Injunction at 6, *Prometheus Lab. Inc. v. Burwell*, No. 15-cv-00742 (D.D.C. May 28, 2015), www.fdalawblog.net/ LOTRONEX%20-%20Roxane%20TRO-PI%20Opp.pdf. Less than a month later, Prometheus completely dropped its suit. *See* Karst, *supra*.

[62] Assuming $1.55 billion in sales of Suboxone in 2012. This assumes that the REMS delay was the only issue standing in the way of generic approval, which is not a fully unreasonable assumption. As will be discussed in the next section, immediately before the generics applied for a REMS waiver, Reckitt announced a withdrawal of Suboxone tablets from the market and filed a citizen petition asking for the generic application not to be approved. Immediately after the citizen petition was dismissed in early 2013, the generic applications were approved. Thus, it is possible that generic entry could have been approved immediately after the REMS waiver was approved had Reckitt not taken further action.

[63] *In re Suboxone*, 64 F. Supp. 3d at 688.

[64] *See* the next section for more details.

[65] *See* CTR. FOR DRUG EVALUATION & RES., *supra* note 59, at 272 (statement by Jane Axelrad, Associate Director of Policy, Center for Drug Evaluation and Research) (discussing difficulties of getting parties to work together to set up a joint REMS).

[66] Federal Defendants' Opposition to Plaintiff's Motion for a Temporary Restraining Order and/or Preliminary Injunction, *Prometheus Lab. Inc. v. Burwell*, No. 15-cv-00742, at 15 (D.D.C. May 28, 2015), www.fdalawblog.net/LOTRONEX%20-%20Roxane%20TRO-PI%20Opp.pdf.

[67] *See* Fair Access for Safe and Timely Generics Act of 2015, H.R. 2841, 114th Cong. (2015).

market-based price. It would also streamline the process by which generic applicants can receive a waiver from the single-shared REMS process if they are able to demonstrate that negotiations were not successful after 120 days.

Another bill, introduced in the Senate during the summer of 2016, also focused on the same two main forms of REMS abuse.[68] It differed from the House bill, however, in that it created a designated cause of action for litigation to be brought against offending pharmaceutical companies, as well as mandating the sale of samples and instituting a specific REMS waiver program.[69] The Senate bill adopts the approach of assigning different roles to different branches. The FDA remains responsible for evaluating safety, both the REMS plan itself and the ability of the generic to handle the drug appropriately; the courts are responsible for resolving disputes among the parties. Although the process adds complication, it echoes the assignment of roles that exists throughout the Hatch-Waxman regime.

B   DELAY VIA CITIZEN PETITION

Citizen petitions offer one of the most ubiquitous ways to create obstacles to generic entry. Such petitions connect to delay tactics ranging from product hopping to REMS abuse. Since the 1970s, the FDA has allowed the public to request that the agency "issue, amend, or revoke a regulation or order or take or refrain from taking any other form of administrative action."[70] Although the program applies to all products under the FDA's jurisdiction, the majority of citizen petitions are related to pharmaceuticals, rather than food, cosmetics, or medical devices.[71]

What was likely meant to be a mechanism for concerned citizens and scientists to raise questions about drugs, food, and FDA regulations, however, has turned into a playground for pharmaceutical companies to challenge drug applications, especially those related to generics.

Some of these petitions are relatively benign. A number ask the FDA to allow a generic to reference a drug that is no longer on the market or to allow approval of a generic that differs slightly[72] from the brand-name drug in terms of characteristics such as strength or dosage form.[73]

---

[68]   See CREATES Act, S. 3056, 114th Cong. (2016).

[69]   For commentary on the Senate bill by one of the authors, *see CREATES Act: Ending Regulatory Abuse, Protecting Consumers and Ensuring Drug Price Competition: Hearing before S. Comm. on the Judiciary Subcomm. on Antitrust, Competition Policy, and Consumer Rights*, 114th Cong. (2016).

[70]   21 C.F.R. § 10.30 (1979).

[71]   Hyman, Phelps & McNamara PC, *FDA Citizen Petition Tracker*, FDA L. BLOG (last visited Sept. 5, 2016), www.fdalawblog.net/fda_law_blog_hyman_phelps/files/CPTracker.xls.

[72]   These are known as "ANDA suitability petitions." Kurt R. Karst, *FDA Rejects Requests to Initiate Rulemaking for (505)(b)(2) NDA Therapeutic Equivalence Rating Decisions*, FDA L. BLOG (July 28, 2014), www.fdalawblog.net/fda_law_blog_hyman_phelps/2014/07/fda-rejects-requests-to-initiate-rulemaking-for-505b2-nda-therapeutic-equivalence-rating-decisions.html.

[73]   See ibid.

In many cases, however, the "concerned citizen" behind a petition is actually an enormous pharmaceutical company seeking to stop or delay approval of a generic drug through a variety of different arguments: direct attacks against the generic application and its bioequivalence or clinical data, appeals to safety, calls to preserve or add new exclusivities for the brand-name drug, and more. A number of these petitions seem frivolous or questionable in their aims, and these filings are troubling.[74] As described previously, a citizen petition is a small investment that can easily pay off. The value of the delay can be lucrative, even when the petition is quickly rejected – even a few months of additional delay can be worth hundreds of millions of dollars.

In Chapter 5, we will examine 12 years of citizen petitions; we offer here an interesting example we uncover during that research. Petition FDA-2007-P-0123, filed by the generic company Mutual Pharmaceuticals, sought to delay other generic applications for drug products containing felodipine by asking applicants to "incorporate either a prohibition/caution against co-administration of the drug with certain orange juice-containing products."[75] Felodipine, branded as Plendil, is a common treatment for high blood pressure. Apparently concerned about a study showing differential effects of Seville orange juice versus "regular" orange juice on the metabolism of the drug, the petition from Mutual requests the "innovator company of Plendil to identify for FDA *which specific orange juice* was used in the bioavailability ... studies submitted in the [application]" [emphasis added].[76]

Seville oranges are smaller, more bitter oranges often used for marmalade and liqueurs, by the way. We did not know, either.

Anyway, in this petition, Mutual is essentially arguing that different types of orange juice used in brand and generic applications could be a major impediment to the approval of a drug application. Let us be clear – Mutual wanted another generic application delayed over what kind of orange juice was used in a study, even though Mutual already held generic approval based on the same studies.

The FDA forcefully denied nearly the entire petition, clearly stating, "We do not believe that the results of the Malhotra study present a serious safety concern."[77] In fact, the FDA seems to have a clear disdain for the claims made in the petition:

---

[74] *See* Michael A. Carrier & Daryl Wander, *Citizen Petitions: An Empirical Study*, 34 CARDOZO L. REV. 249, 261 (2012).

[75] Citizen Petition from United Research Laboratories, Inc., Mutual Pharmaceutical Company, Inc., to Div. of Dockets Mgmt., U.S. Food and Drug Admin, No. FDA-2007-P-0123, at 1 (Nov. 29, 2007), www .regulations.gov/#!documentDetail;D=FDA-2007-P-0123-0002.

[76] *Ibid.* at 2.

[77] Letter from Janet Woodcock, Dir., Ctr. for Drug Evaluation & Research, U.S. Food & Drug Admin., to Robert Dettery, Vice President, Reg. Aff., Mutual Pharmaceutical Company, Inc., Re: No. FDA-2007-P-0123, at 4 (Apr. 17, 2008) [hereinafter "FDA Response to Mutual"], www.regulations .gov/ #!documentDetail;D=FDA-2007-P-0123-0009 (granting in part and denying in part Mutual's petitions). The FDA did grant Mutual's request that a portion of the brand-name Plendil labeling stating

You hypothesize that there may be clinical consequences associated with the coadminstration of felodipine and components of Seville orange juice consumed in this form. You have offered no data to support this hypothesis. In fact, we searched the Adverse Event Reporting System (AERS) database and found no reported interactions between Seville or bitter orange products and any drug product.[78]

In a passive-aggressive footnote that qualifies as an "epic burn" by FDA citizen petition standards, the FDA even questions the truthfulness of Mutual's affirmations:

You have certified that you first became aware of the information upon which you have based Petition 1 (e.g., Malhotra study) on November 5, 2007. We note, however, the Malhotra study was published in 2001 and predates approval of Mutual's [own generic application].[79]

So, the study in question was released before Mutual's generic was approved! Ah, there is nothing like a fact-based, understated jab hidden in a footnote.

Unsurprisingly, Mutual did in fact hold the first approved generic application for Plendil, with approval taking place in November 2004, making it the first generic on the market.[80] The next generic application was filed around the first quarter of 2007, just a few months before Mutual decided to file its citizen petition.[81] The citizen petition was denied on April 17, 2008 – the same day that the second applicant's generic application was eventually approved – indicating that Mutual's so-called orange juice petition was one of the last barriers to final approval.[82] As soon as the seemingly frivolous citizen petition was denied, the second generic was approved. If not for the citizen petition, it is possible, if not likely, that additional generic approval might have taken place at an earlier time. A last-minute petition about types of orange juice cost consumers untold millions in the delay it posed to the approval of a second Plendil generic.

This appears to be the modus operandi for many citizen petitions – pharmaceutical companies will make a facially interesting, scientific-sounding claim timed to the

---

that "orange juice does not appear to modify the kinetics of Plendil" be qualified to not imply that orange juice has *no* effects on the kinetics of Plendil, even though the minimal effect does not appear to impact the safety or efficacy of the drug. *Ibid.*

[78] *Ibid.*

[79] *Ibid.* at 3 n.3.

[80] *Drugs@FDA: Felodipine*, U.S. Food & Drug Admin., www.accessdata.fda.gov/scripts/cder/drug satfda/ (last visited Sept. 5, 2016) (Enter "felodipine" in search bar, submit, and click "felodipine" in list of results. The first generic [ANDA No. 75896] listed is one from Sun Pharmaceuticals, a subsidiary of Mutual. Clicking that generic application reveals that it was approved in November 2004.)

[81] Database, ANDAs and Submission Dates, ANDA No. 78855 (estimating an application filing date in the first quarter of 2007) (on file with authors).

[82] FDA Response to Mutual, *supra* note 77, at 1; *Drugs@FDA: ANDA No. 78755*, U.S. Food & Drug Admin., www.accessdata.fda.gov/scripts/cder/drugsatfda/ (Enter "78855" in search bar and click submit. The database shows that the generic application was approved on April 17, 2008).

months right before generic approval, and the claims are eventually denied by the FDA. That bitter Seville orange juice *does* increase absorption and peak drug concentration, after all. The bigger question: does it really matter? The FDA rarely thinks so. Papers by Michael Carrier, Daryl Wander, and Carl Minniti found that the FDA denied 81 percent of generic-related petitions between 2001 and 2010, and 92 percent of petitions between 2011 and 2015, with denial rates as high as 92 percent in 2005, 96 percent in 2012, and even 100 percent in 2015.[83] It is hard to argue that these pharma-authored petitions are vocalizing legitimate concerns when the denial rate is so high. In many cases, the ulterior motives are just too hard to ignore.

Citizen petitions have played a prominent role in other obstruction strategies as well. Chapter 3 described a clause in which Endo Pharmaceuticals agreed to pay a company only if sales of Endo's drug Opana ER dropped below a certain level, a threshold that would only be met if the market for the drug significantly lessened – through a product hop, for instance. It turns out that Endo's product hop involved a switch from "Opana ER" to "Opana ER CRF," a crush-resistant form of the drug. As an opioid painkiller, Opana had been abused by people snorting the drug – the crush-resistant form was meant to solve this problem. Unfortunately, this change merely led abusers to begin injecting the drug instead, leading to a severe HIV outbreak covered on NPR's *All Things Considered*.[84]

The switch, however, may have had benefits for the company and raises suspicion in a number of ways. In particular, the switch to a new formulation occurred right as Endo was nearing generic competition, and the company completely removed the old, non-crush-resistant version from the market as soon as it received approval for the new version. The company then filed a citizen petition asking the FDA to deny any non-crush-resistant generic forms of Opana ER, also asking it to certify that Opana ER was withdrawn from the market for safety reasons to block future generic certifications.[85] Then, worried about impending generic entry (while also advancing a safety-related argument), it *sued* the FDA to speed up review of

---

[83] Carrier & Wander, *supra* note 74, at 274 (2012) (examining petitions filed between 2001 and 2010); Michael A. Carrier & Carl Minniti, *Citizen Petitions: Long, Late-Filed, and At-Last Denied*, 66 Am. U. L. Rev. 305, 333 (2016) http://ssrn.com/abstract=2832319 (examining petitions filed between 2011 and 2015). "Generic-related petitions" excludes "suitability petitions" filed by generics in the 2001–2010 paper, and it also excludes any petition not designated by the FDA as a "505(q)" petition in the 2011–2015 period.

[84] Tom Dreisbach, *How a Painkiller Designed to Deter Abuse Helped Spark an HIV Outbreak*, NPR: All Things Considered (Apr. 1, 2016), www.npr.org/sections/health-shots/2016/04/01/472538272/how-a-painkiller-designed-to-deter-abuse-helped-spark-an-hiv-outbreak.

[85] Citizen Petition from Endo Pharm., Inc., to Div. of Dockets Mgmt., U.S. Food and Drug Admin., No. FDA-2012-P-0895 (Aug. 10, 2012), www.regulations.gov/document?D=FDA-2012-P-0895-0001.

the petition before generic manufacturers were able to "flood the market with non-crush-resistant generic Opana ER."[86]

The FDA failed to find Opana ER CRF significantly safer than Opana ER and even expressed concerns that it might lead to more abuse through injection. In denying the petition, the agency found that Opana ER was not removed from the market for reasons of safety or effectiveness.[87] This ruling ended a not uncommon example of companies espousing safety concerns through product hops and citizen petitions, for reasons more concerned with preserving a market than securing the public health.

Suboxone, the case that featured creative product hopping and allegations of REMS abuse, again provides yet another troubling tale related to opioids. As described in Section A of this chapter regarding REMS-based delay, the generics were forced to obtain a REMS waiver because they were unable to get the brand-name company, Reckitt, to cooperate. Immediately prior to the generic REMS waiver request, which would have allowed the generic to move forward if and when approved, Reckitt announced that it was pulling Suboxone tablets completely off the market (but did not immediately do so).[88] The company cited safety concerns related to pediatric exposure, and it followed up on the *same day* with a citizen petition asking the FDA to refrain from approving any generic application for Suboxone.[89] In its citizen petition, the brand-name company again cited pediatric exposure to demand that medications such as generic Suboxone include "targeted educational interventions on the risk of pediatric exposure" and individual-dose packaging.[90]

The FDA has a process that allows an application to move forward for a generic version of a drug no longer on the market, if the FDA determines that the drug was not removed for safety reasons.[91] The safety move coupled with the citizen petition

---

[86] Complaint for Mandatory, Declaratory, and Injunctive Relief, *Endo Pharm. Inc. v. U.S. Food & Drug Admin.*, No. 1:12-cv-01936 (D.D.C. Nov. 30, 2012), www.documentcloud.org/documents/2083598-opana-er-endo-complaint.html; *see also* Dreisbach, *How A Painkiller Designed to Deter Abuse Helped Spark an HIV Outbreak, supra* note 84.

[87] Letter from Janet Woodcock, Dir., Ctr. for Drug Evaluation & Research, U.S. Food & Drug Admin., to Robert Barto, Vice President, Reg. Aff., Endo Pharma., Inc., Re: No. FDA-2012-P-0895 (May 10, 2013) www.regulations.gov/document?D=FDA-2012-P-0895-0014 (denying Endo's citizen petition and finding that Opana ER was not withdrawn for reasons of safety or effectiveness); *see also FDA Statement: Original Opana ER Relisting Determination*, U.S. FOOD & DRUG ADMIN. (May 10, 2013), www.fda.gov/Drugs/DrugSafety/ucm351357.htm.

[88] *In re Suboxone* (Buprenorphine Hydrochloride and Naloxone) Antitrust Litig., 64 F. Supp. 3d 665, 675–76 (E.D. Pa. Dec. 3, 2014).

[89] *Ibid.*; *see* Citizen Petition from Reckitt Benckiser Pharm., Inc. to Div. of Dockets Mgmt., U.S. Food and Drug Admin., No. FDA-2012-P-1028 (Sept. 5, 2012) [hereinafter Citizen Petition from Reckitt Benckiser], www.naabt.org/documents/Reckitt_Benckiser_Pharmaceuticals_Inc_2012_FDA_Citizen_Petition.pdf.

[90] *Ibid.*

[91] 21 C.F.R. § 314.161 (2015). A generic can file a citizen petition asking for an official determination of whether the reference drug was "withdrawn for safety or effectiveness reasons." If it is determined

may have been intended to block the generic from utilizing this pathway by trying to force the FDA to make a finding that Suboxone was, in fact, removed for safety reasons.

Complainants in *In re Suboxone* alleged that this citizen petition was a sham merely meant to block generic approval.[92] Specifically, the requested labeling measures for generic Suboxone were never required for the brand-name Suboxone tablets. In addition, the FDA does not have the ability to require that a generic company add labeling not approved for the brand-name drug.[93] Most important, Reckitt continued to sell Suboxone tablets in bulk and without unit-dose packaging (versions which it had claimed were unsafe) even after it made the petition requesting these restrictions for the generic version.[94]

The FDA denied the brand-name company's citizen petition and immediately thereafter granted approval for two generic versions of Suboxone tablets – another instance of generic approval arriving directly after the denial of a citizen petition.[95] In its denial of the petition, the FDA noted that Reckitt's "own actions ... undermine, to some extent, its claims with respect to the severity of this safety issue."[96] Further, the FDA noted that the brand-name company's decision to pull Suboxone from the market so close to the arrival of generic competition "cannot be ignored," explaining in a footnote that Reckitt gained access to private information about the potential timing for generic applications because the generics volunteered this information in an attempt to persuade the company to cooperate in REMS creation.[97]

The FDA explicitly said it was not denying the petition for failing to raise a valid scientific or regulatory issue or for purposeful obstruction of a generic application, preferring to focus on the lack of merits of the petition's safety concerns. The

---

that the drug was not withdrawn for those reasons, the drug will be relisted for the purposes of ANDA submissions.

[92] *In re Suboxone*, 64 F. Supp. 3d at 676.

[93] *Ibid.*

[94] *Ibid.* at 676–77.

[95] *Ibid.* at 676.

[96] Letter from Janet Woodcock, Dir., Ctr. for Drug Evaluation & Research, U.S. Food & Drug Admin., to Tim Baxter, Glob. Medical Dir., Reckitt Benckiser Pharm., Inc. No. FDA-2012-P-1028, at 15 (Feb. 22, 2013) [hereinafter FDA Response to Reckitt Benckiser], www.regulations.gov/#!documentDetail;D=FDA-2012-P-1028-0011; Letter from Robert L. West, Deputy Dir., Office of Generic Drugs, U.S. Food & Drug Admin., to Janak Jadeja, Dir., Regulatory Affairs, Actavis Elizabeth LLC (Feb. 22, 2013), www.accessdata.fda.gov/drugsatfda_docs/appletter/2013/091422Orig1s000ltr.pdf (approving generic Suboxone tablets on the same day the citizen petition was denied); Letter from Robert L. West, Deputy Dir., Office of Generic Drugs, U.S. Food & Drug Admin., to Candice Edwards, Senior Vice President, Regulatory & Clinical Affairs, Amneal Pharm. (Feb. 22, 2013), www.accessdata.fda.gov/drugsatfda_docs/appletter/2013/203136Orig1s000ltr.pdf (approving generic Suboxone tablets on the same day the citizen petition was denied).

[97] FDA Response to Reckitt Benckiser, *supra* note 96, at 15 & n.53.

administration, nevertheless, made its opprobrium clear by referring the company's conduct to the Federal Trade Commission for review.[98]

Despite the FDA's complete rebuttal of all of the brand-name company's claims, the citizen petition resulted in five months of delay in the time it took for the petition to be denied. Given sales of approximately $1.5 billion in 2012, the five months of delay was possibly worth more than $600 million in unchallenged sales to the brand-name company.[99] That is a remarkably strong incentive for companies to engage in this type of tactic. As always, the consumer pays the cost in the form of higher health insurance premiums, taxes (to compensate for soaring Medicare costs), and prices.

The FDA and the Federal Trade Commission have long recognized that the citizen petition process could be subject to abuse, expressing concerns and proposing modifications as early as 1999.[100] Congress attempted to curb such abuse by enacting a new section of FDA regulation in 2007, frequently known as "Section 505(q)." Section 505(q) states that when a citizen petition could delay generic approval, giving it a special designation as a 505(q) petition, the FDA must take final action on the petition within 180 days, unless the delay is necessary to protect the public health.[101] The Food and Drug Administration Safety and Innovation Act ("FDASIA"), passed in 2012, further shortened the approval period to 150 days.[102] To discourage baseless or strategically timed petitions even more, petition filers must also make a certification and verification that the petition is not frivolous, acknowledging that all information favorable and unfavorable has been provided and that the petition was

---

[98] FDA Response to Reckitt Benckiser, *supra* note 96, at 16. FTC proceedings were initiated against Reckitt Benckiser. *See FTC v. Reckitt Benckiser Pharm., Inc.* No. 14-MC-005, 2014 WL 4792175 (E.D. Va. Sept. 24, 2014) (court proceedings over release of documents for the FTC's investigation).

[99] *Suboxone Sales Data*, DRUGS.COM (Feb. 2014), www.drugs.com/stats/suboxone. As with all calculations of the value of delay in this book, the assumption is made for the sake of ease that, without the delay, generic competition would immediately drop Reckitt's revenues on Suboxone to zero.

[100] *See* Darren S. Tucker, *FDA Citizen Petition: A New Means of Delaying Generic Entry?* 20 ANTITRUST HEALTH CARE CHRON. 10, 11 (2006); Citizen Petitions; Actions That Can be Requested by Petition; Denials, Withdrawals, and Referrals for Other Administrative Action, 64 Fed. Reg. 66822-01 (proposed Nov. 30, 1999) (to be codified at 21 C.F.R. pt. 10) (withdrawn); *Comment Letter on Citizen Petition; Actions That Can be Requested by Petition; Denials, Withdrawals, and Referrals for Other Administrative Action* FED. TRADE COMM'N (Mar. 2, 2000), www.ftc.gov/sites/default/files/documents /advocacy_documents/ftc-staff-comment-food-and-drug-administration-concerning-citizen-petitions/ v000005 .pdf.

[101] Codified at 21 U.S.C. § 355(q) (2012), *amended by* Improving Regulatory Transparency for New Medical Therapies Act, Pub. L. No. 114–89, 129 Stat. 698 (2015); 21 U.S.C. § 355(q)(1)(A)(ii) (2012) (establishing the public health exception); *see also* Kurt R. Karst, *The Coming 505(q) Citizen Petition Cliff and Some Interesting Petition Strategies*, FDA L. BLOG (Sept. 4, 2012), www.fdalawblog.net/ fda_law_blog_hyman_phelps/2012/09/the-coming-505q-citizen-petition-cliff-and-some-interesting-petition-strategies.html (presenting more details about the 2007 and FDASIA changes).

[102] 21 U.S.C. § 355(q)(2)(A) (2012) (establishing the 150-day deadline for agency action).

not intentionally delayed, while also providing the date when the filer first became aware of the concern and the names of those funding the petition.[103]

Finally, the FDA also was granted the power to deny a petition at any time if it believes a petition was "submitted with the primary purpose of delaying the approval of an application and the petition does not on its face raise valid scientific or regulatory issues."[104]

In the case of *Suboxone*, however, the regulatory process worked entirely as intended, and the brand-name company's petition was denied exactly 150 days after the date it was filed. Nevertheless, the petition resulted in five months of delay and an estimated $600 million of higher priced sales for the company.[105] Thus, even when the bell rings on time as Congress intended, brand-name companies still can use the process to engage in costly delays.

Moreover, the various amendments do not seem to have discouraged the filing of nonmeritorious citizen petitions that request the delay of a generic. Between fiscal years 2008 and 2014 – the period during which the amendments have been in place and for which data are available – 149 delay petitions were filed and *only* 8 were fully granted.[106] Thirty-nine of these petitions were granted in part. However, as Carrier and Wander note, these "mixed decisions" are often a formality and not truly a partial finding in favor of the petitioner, with the stunning "orange juice" petition we found serving as an illuminating example.[107] The requests "granted in part" are often trivial requests for bioequivalence studies that either have already been completed, are in progress, or would certainly be required by the FDA even in the absence of the citizen petition. It is like asking a teacher to assign homework – when the homework is listed on the board – yet the teacher is forced to spend months reaching a conclusion, and, in the meantime, everyone but the teacher's pet is indefinitely banished to detention.

The number of citizen petitions requesting delay also has not declined since passage of the 505(q) amendments.[108] As we will discuss further in Chapter 5, we have undertaken our own extensive empirical study of the timing of citizen petitions. In simply collecting petitions for our database, a clear trend emerged – the number

---

[103] 21 U.S.C. §355(q)(1)(H)-(I) (2012).

[104] 21 U.S.C. § 355(q)(1)(E) (2012).

[105] *See Suboxone Sales Data, supra* note 99 (listing Suboxone sales as $1.5 billion in 2012, or $600 million over five months).

[106] U.S. Food & Drug Admin., Sixth Annual Report to Congress on Delays in Approvals of Applications Related to Citizen Petitions and Petitions for Stay of Agency Action for Fiscal Year 2013, at 6–7 (2014) [hereinafter FDA Sixth Annual Report for FY 2013], www.fda.gov/down loads/AboutFDA/CentersOffices/OfficeofMedicalProductsandTobacco/CDER/ReportsBudgets/UCM423291.pdf. Carrier & Wander, *supra* note 74, at 266–68.

[107] Carrier & Wander, *supra* note 74, at 266–68.

[108] FDA Sixth Annual Report for FY 2013, *supra* note 106, at 5; *see generally* Carrier & Wander, *supra* note 74.

of generic-related citizen petitions each year has not decreased. In 2003, 12 generic delay-related petitions were filed; in 2010, that number had more than doubled to 31. In that same time frame, delay-related petitions had also doubled as a proportion of *all* citizen petitions, with delay-related petitions filed by pharmaceutical companies constituting 20 percent of *all* citizen petitions by 2010, including those related to food, cosmetics, and medical devices. We will return to the rest of our empirical research on citizen petitions in Chapter 5.

The 505(q) amendment's most biting provision also has proven difficult to apply. Recall that the statute allows the FDA to deny petitions summarily, but only when they are both 1) submitted for the main purpose of delay and 2) raise no valid scientific or regulatory issues on their face. Proving both of these requirements concurrently has turned out to be quite difficult, with the FDA calling it a standard that is "extremely difficult to meet."[109] In fact, since the amendments took effect in fiscal year 2008, the FDA has *never* applied the summary denial provision.[110]

In theory, the wounded would-be generic could file a lawsuit asserting that the brand-name company engaged in anticompetitive behavior by submitting a sham citizen's petition. Such a lawsuit is unlikely to succeed, however.[111] The difficulty flows back to *Noerr-Pennington*, a line of Supreme Court cases from the 1960s that establishes a general right to petition the government without fear of antitrust liability.[112] *Noerr-Pennington* does carve out an exception that allows antitrust liability when petitioning the government constitutes a sham filing that is meant merely to interfere with a competitor.[113] The Supreme Court, however, has set an extremely high standard for demonstrating that a legal petition is a sham. Specifically, the petition must be objectively baseless – which means that no reasonable petitioner can realistically expect success on the merits – as well as subjectively baseless – which means that the petition tries to conceal an attempt to interfere directly with

---

[109] U.S. Food & Drug Admin., Seventh Annual Report to Congress on Delays in Approvals of Applications Related to Citizen Petitions and Petitions for Stay of Agency Action for Fiscal Year 2014, at 9 (2015) [hereinafter FDA Seventh Annual Report for FY 2014].

[110] FDA Sixth Annual Report for FY 2013, *supra* note 106, at 7. *See generally* Seth C. Silber, Jonathan Lutinski & Rachel Taylon, *Abuse of the FDA Citizen Petition Process: Ripe for Antitrust Challenge?* 25 Antitrust Health Care Chron. 26 (2012).

[111] *See* Silber, Lutinski & Taylor, *Abuse of the FDA Citizen Petition Process, supra* note 110, at 30.

[112] For a detailed description of the development of *Noerr-Pennington*, see generally Robin Feldman, *Federalism, First Amendment, and Patents: The Fraud Fallacy*, 17 Colum. Sci. & Tech. L. Rev. 30 (2015).

[113] *United Mine Workers v. Pennington*, 381 U.S. 657, 669–72 (1965); *E. R.R. Presidents Conf. v. Noerr Motor Freight, Inc.*, 365 U.S. 127, 144 (1961); *see also* Silber, Lutinski & Taylon, *supra* note 110, at 30; Robin Feldman, Rethinking Patent Law 166 (2012); Robin Feldman, *Intellectual Property Wrongs*, 18 Stan. J.L. Bus. & Fin. 250, 301–05 (2013) (suggesting that there may be a pathway for proving sham litigation, at least with actions that demonstrate multiplicity).

competition through the administrative process.[114] This burden on plaintiffs is crushing.

Still other pathways exist for abusing the citizen petition process, despite the limitations imposed by the amendments. As the FDA itself has noted, the 150-day clock applies only when a citizen petition has the power to delay generic approval.[115] If a citizen petition is filed before any generic application is submitted or before any generic application is "ready" for approval under the Hatch-Waxman rules, the 150-day deadline does not apply, a scenario that the FDA says is the case in "many instances."[116] Thus, citizen petitions filed before a generic application is ready can serve as yet another obstacle, perhaps combined with strategies already in play.

Finally, the 150-day limit applies to consideration of each petition, rather than providing a 150-day maximum for how long generic approval can be put on hold. That leaves the door open for what the FDA has called "serial" petitions, in which multiple petitions are filed about the same drug, frequently from the same petitioner.[117] In the FDA's 2011 report on citizen petitions, for example, it noted the following:

> For example, the agency received its fourth [delay-related] petition relating to the approval of ANDAs for topical ophthalmic products and a third [delay-related] petition related to Doryx (doxycycline). The various submissions raised different scientific issues, requiring serial review of different arguments, rather than one comprehensive review of all pertinent arguments.[118]

By filing separate petitions at staggered times on disparate issues, a brand-name company can force the FDA to spend time responding to each petition, thereby potentially lengthening the total delay by citizen petition far beyond 150 days.[119]

In our own review of citizen petitions, we came across a number of these petitions related to Doryx, an antibiotic and antimalarial drug, revealing how staggered petitions can tax FDA resources and lead to substantial delay. One petition, filed in 2004, suggests that a generic would need to file a suitability petition if its capsules

---

[114] *Professional Real Estate Inv'rs. v. Columbia Pictures Indus.*, 508 U.S. 49, 60–61 (1993); *see also* Silber, Lutinski & Taylon, *Abuse of the FDA Citizen Petition Process*, *supra* note 110, at 30–31; FELDMAN, RETHINKING PATENT LAW, *supra* note 113, at 166–67.

[115] FDA SIXTH ANNUAL REPORT FOR FY 2013, *supra* note 106, at 6.

[116] Wilson Sonsini Goodrich & Rosati, CITIZEN PETITIONS AIMED AT DELAYING GENERIC COMPETITION REMAIN A CONCERN 1 (2015), www.wsgr.com/publications/PDFSearch/wsgralert-citizen-petitions.pdf; *see also* FDA SIXTH ANNUAL REPORT FOR FY 2013, *supra* note 106, at 6–7.

[117] FDA SIXTH ANNUAL REPORT FOR FY 2013, *supra* note 106, at 7.

[118] U.S. Food & Drug Admin., FOURTH ANNUAL REPORT TO CONGRESS ON DELAYS IN APPROVALS OF APPLICATIONS RELATED TO CITIZEN PETITIONS AND PETITIONS FOR STAY OF AGENCY ACTION FOR FISCAL YEAR 2011, at 6 (2012), www.fda.gov/downloads/AboutFDA/CentersOffices/OfficeofMedicalProductsandTobacco/CDER/ReportsBudgets/UCM369782.pdf.

[119] *Ibid.*; WILSON SONSINI GOODRICH & ROSATI, CITIZEN PETITIONS AIMED AT DELAYING GENERIC COMPETITION REMAIN A CONCERN, *supra* note 116, at 2.

contained "powder" instead of "pellets."[120] A decision was never reached on this petition, in part because many of the same issues were raised in later 2008 petitions, using the same issue to occupy the FDA's time and slow the process again and again.

Another citizen petition, filed multiple times in 2008, demands additional bioequivalence testing and suggests that a generic version of Doryx must be "scored" the same way as Warner Chilcott and Mayne's ("Warner's") brand-name pill. No, that is not a request for an accompanying film soundtrack masterfully composed by John Williams, but rather a petition suggesting that the generic pill should have a line down the middle for easier splitting.[121] The FDA reached a mixed decision on this petition, denying a majority of Warner's arguments. The brand-name company won something on this round, however, given that the new scoring requirements were eventually imposed on generics. At least one generic was delayed because of the change.[122]

A third petition, submitted in 2009, requests that the FDA delay approval of at least five different generic applications.[123] At one point, Doryx had been classified as an "old antibiotic" not subject to Hatch-Waxman because the active ingredient was approved before 1997. In the petition, Warner argues that new legislation eliminated this distinction and thus a 30-month litigation stay should apply to the generic applications. The FDA denied this petition.

The *fourth* petition from 2011 returns once again to the scoring issue, demanding that a generic version of 150-mg delayed-released Doryx tablets have *two* score

---

[120] Letter from Lyle D. Jaffe, Div. of Dockets Mgmt., U.S. Food & Drug Admin., to Anthony Bruno, Warner Chilcott, Re: No. FDA-2004-P-0150 (Sept. 14, 2004), www.regulations.gov/docket?D=FDA-2004-P-0150 (describing Warner's 2004 petition).

[121] Citizen Petition from Mayne Pharma International Pty Ltd & Warner Chilcott to Div. of Dockets Mgmt., U.S. Food & Drug Admin., No. FDA-2008-P-0374 (Jun. 25, 2008) [hereinafter "2008 Mayne & Warner Citizen Petition"], www.regulations.gov/document?D=FDA-2008-P-0374-0001 (representing one version of the petition; Letter from Janet Woodcock, Dir., Ctr. for Drug Evaluation & Research, U.S. Food & Drug Admin., to Michael Halstead, Assoc. Gen. Counsel, Warner Chilcott, Re: No. FDA-2008-P-0586 (May 1, 2009), www.regulations.gov/document?D=FDA-2008-P-0586-0005 (denying in part and granting in part one of Warner's petitions).

[122] Letter from Keith Webber, Dep. Dir., Off. of Pharm. Sci., U.S. Food & Drug Admin., to Michelle P. Wong, Sen. Dir., Reg. Aff., Impax Lab, Inc., Re: ANDA 90505, at 3 n. 3 (Dec. 28, 2010), www.accessdata .fda.gov/drugsatfda_docs/appletter/2010/090505s000ltr.pdf (announcing that Impax was able to maintain its exclusivity although it missed the 30-month deadline). The generic missed its 30-month deadline for its generic application to be approved, which would usually mean that the generic would forfeit its 180-day exclusivity. An exception was made in this case because a change was made to the FDA review requirements while the application was pending – that is, approval was delayed because of the newly scored brand-name tablet.

[123] Citizen Petition from Covington & Burling LLP on behalf of Mayne Pharma Int'l Pty Ltd & Warner Chilcott to Div. of Dockets Mgmt., U.S. Food & Drug Admin., No. FDA-2009-P-0038 (Jan. 29, 2009), www.regulations.gov/document?D=FDA-2009-P-0038-0001.

lines allowing the tablet to be broken into three 50-mg pieces.[124] This petition is particularly suspicious: Warner received approval to change the 150-mg tablets from a single-scored version to a dual-scored version just 10 days before it submitted the petition and promised to withdraw the single-scored version from the market after receiving approval. About five months later, the FDA responded with what can only be called a governmental agency smackdown, denying every aspect of the brand-name petition. The language tiptoes close to directly alleging that the brand made the dual-scored change to delay a generic:

> Looking at the facts and circumstances of this case (including the fact that the RLD made scoring changes on the eve of expected generic approval and marketed the scored and unscored tablets concurrently without any added warnings, and the fact that the risk of medication error due to substitution of a single-scored tablet for a dual-scored tablet is low), we deny your request[.][125]

This denial also provides at least one confirmation of what is often thought to be true – that a last-minute citizen petition is often the final roadblock to generic approval. On the date of denial, the FDA approved a 150-mg *single-scored* tablet version of generic Doryx. In the end, Warner filed four unique petitions related to Doryx over seven years, and not a single one received a truly favorable decision from the FDA.

Thus, as with REMS delay, codified congressional condemnations of a practice[126] are just a new rule for which manufacturers must find a work-around – impose a deadline for responding to a petition, for example, and manufacturers will just file more petitions. Often, new rules are about as effective as admonishing schoolchildren to play nicely with each other on the playground.

C PREVENTING THE "SKINNY LABEL": BLOCKING CARVE-OUTS

As Generation 3.0 games advance, an additional tactic relates to "the skinny label." Before getting into the nitty-gritty of the different patents that may cover a drug, here is a general example of a "skinny label": say a hypothetical, panaceaic drug can be used for both the treatment of allergy symptoms and back pain. The brand-name drug company, however, has a patent only on the use of the drug for back pain and

---

[124] Citizen Petition from Warner Chilcott & Mayne Pharma Int'l Pty Ltd to Div. of Dockets Mgmt., U.S. Food & Drug Admin., No. FDA-2011-P-0702 (Sept. 23, 2011), www.regulations.gov/document?D=FDA-2011-P-0702-0001.

[125] Letter from Janet Woodcock, Dir., Ctr. for Drug Evaluation & Research, U.S. Food & Drug Admin., to Izumi Hara, Sen. Vice President & Gen. Counsel, Warner Chilcott, Re: No. FDA-2011-P-0702, at 8 (Feb. 8, 2012), www.regulations.gov/document?D=FDA-2011-P-0702-0003 (denying Warner & Mylan's petition).

[126] Referring to the REMS statute passed by Congress clarifying that a REMS cannot be used to block an ANDA and Section 505(q) for citizen petitions.

nothing else. In this case, a generic may be able to get on the market by declaring the generic form of the drug will only be sold to treat allergies, since that use of the drug is not patent protected. The protected use is "carved out," as it is called in pharmaceutical parlance, and what remains is a "skinny label" specifying only use for allergy symptoms.

In fact, many patents on pharmaceuticals do not cover substances and chemical formulas, but particular uses of a drug. Hatch-Waxman, however, expressly allows a generic applicant to seek approval for a "skinny label" version that only covers uses of the drug not protected by patents or FDA exclusivities.[127] Applicants also can ask permission to omit some of the brand-name drug's other labeling language from the generic label if that language relates to uses that are protected.[128] Along with the "skinny label" term, these requests are often known as "Section viii carve-outs," referring to a section in Hatch-Waxman.

For example, the brand-name company's only patent on a drug could be a "method-of-use" patent, which protects only certain indications of the drug, with "indication" referring to a reason why the drug is administered (e.g. "for treatment of *Helicobacter* infections"). This scenario might occur when the drug's chemical formula had been patented or used in the past, and the company could receive only a more limited patent for a new indication of the medicine. Under these circumstances, the generic could request approval for uses of the medication that had already gone off patent.[129]

Request for a "skinny label" could also apply when the brand-name drug company has received special FDA exclusivities available for circumstances such as use of a drug for orphan categories or new pediatric indications. A generic could file a request indicating that it does not seek approval for the protected uses.[130]

Generally, these carve-out requests are approved unless they cause the generic to be less safe or effective than the brand-name drug for all remaining, nonprotected uses.[131] Such carve-outs can be an effective way for generics to bypass weak or limited

---

[127] 21 U.S.C. § 355(j)(2)(A)(viii) (2012).

[128] 21 C.F.R. § 314.127(a)(7) (2015).

[129] Remember how there are still active Nexium patents, some of which grant exclusivity that does not expire until 2020? One of those patents protects a specific use of the drug. While Nexium made its name on acid reflux treatment, the patent is associated with the example use of the drug named in the previous paragraph – "for treatment of *Helicobacter* infections" – referring to bacterial infections often associated with stomach ulcers and cancer. The patent was filed more than 10 years after Nexium first received FDA approval. *See* Patent and Exclusivity Search Results from *Orange Book: Approved Drug Products with Therapeutic Equivalence Evaluations*, U.S. FOOD & DRUG ADMIN., https://perma.cc/TJ9B-HUWL (last updated Mar. 2016) (patent no. 8,466,175 at the bottom of the list); U.S. Patent No. 8,466,175 (filed Nov. 17, 2011).

[130] 21 C.F.R. § 314.127(a)(7) (2015).

[131] *Ibid.*

patents (or exclusivities) that brand-name companies may add near the end of a drug's patent term in the hopes of holding on to its exclusive market position for a drug.

For every action, however, there is an equal and opposite reaction, and that is certainly the case for carve-outs. Under Hatch-Waxman, when a generic application requests only Section viii carve-outs and contains no Paragraph IV certifications, that application does not trigger the artificial act of patent infringement that allows for litigation and a 30-month stay of approval. Thus, the generic application should theoretically be eligible for immediate approval.[132] Undaunted, brand-name companies file citizen petitions, arguing that the carve-out should be disallowed. These petitions generally argue that the requested carve-out contains information related to the safety or efficacy of the drug, and that such information cannot be removed from the label.[133]

A generic could, indeed, be attempting disingenuously to get around the Hatch-Waxman litigation process by removing certain uses from the label knowing that physicians may prescribe the drug for all uses, nonetheless. The off-label use of medication is a widespread phenomenon that affects many aspects of pharmaceutical law, and one of the authors has expressed serious concerns about the practice.[134] In the case of carve-outs, brand-name drug companies have expressed concern that carve-outs only remove uses and indications in name only – once on the market, the generics could be prescribed and used "off-label" for all uses approved for the brand-name version.[135] The FDA, however, has refused to accept this as a rationale for not approving a carve-out, even when the reference listed drug holder says off-label use could implicate safe and effective

---

[132] Lisa Barons Pensabene & Dennis Gregory (on behalf of Fitzpatrick, Cella, Harper, and Scinto), *Hatch-Waxman Act: Overview*, PRACTICAL L. CO. 4 (2013), www.fitzpatrickcella.com/DB6EDC/ assets/files/News/Hatch-Waxman%20Act%20Overview%20lpensabene_dgregory.pdf. There are also scenarios where an ANDA filer uses a Paragraph III or IV certification for some patents and carves out other patents via a section viii statement.

[133] *See, e.g.*, Citizen Petition from Ernest Lengle, Exec. Dir. Regulatory Affairs, Watson Labs., Inc., to Div. of Dockets Mgmt., U.S. Food & Drug Admin., No. FDA-2008-P-0069-0001, at 2 (Jan. 29, 2008), www.regulations.gov/#!documentDetail;D=FDA-2008-P-0069-0001 (requesting that the FDA refrain from allowing a carve-out for irinotecan hydrochloride on grounds that it would render the generic less safe or effective than the listed drug).

[134] *See* Robin Feldman, *Regulatory Property: The New IP*, 40 COLUMBIA J.L. & ARTS 53 (2016). For example, pharmaceutical companies have enjoyed considerable success in recent years in convincing courts that FDA restrictions on truthful statements about off-label uses of drugs may violate free speech. *See generally United States v. Caronia*, 703 F.3d. 149 (2d Cir. 2012); *Amarin Pharm., Inc. v. U.S. Food & Drug Admin*, 119 F. Supp. 3d 196 (S.D.N.Y. 2015). For a discussion of the widespread off-label uses of drugs, see *Amarin*, 119 F. Supp. 3d at 200–01.

[135] *See* Citizen Petition from Robert Church & David Fox, Hogan Lovells US LLP on behalf of Spectrum Pharmaceuticals, Inc., to Div. of Dockets Mgmt., U.S. Food & Drug Admin., No. FDA-2014-P-1649, at 12 (Sept. 30, 2014), www.regulations.gov/#!documentDetail;D=FDA-2014-P-1649-0001.

use of the drug.[136] In a response to a recent citizen petition, the FDA said requiring this type of "foreseeable use" analysis is "inconsistent with our long-standing policy of not interfering with the practice of medicine" and noted that a circuit court already rejected this argument as a bar to generic approval.[137]

Nevertheless, there are clear instances of brand-name companies making small labeling changes or securing weak method-of-use patents and then filing citizen petitions to block the carve-out requests that follow.[138] Admittedly, these tend to be some of the more complex examples in this book. Everything we have discussed so far builds up to this point, so let us dive in.

The history of Skelaxin, while complicated, is one of the most illustrative in this area, showing how adding one or two method-of-use patents along with clever labeling can lead to years of delay. Skelaxin, the brand name for the well-known muscle relaxant metaxalone, was first approved back in 1962.[139] The drug did not face the threat of generic competition for more than 30 years, even though the initial patent on the active ingredient expired in 1979.[140] The competitive landscape changed, however, in 2001, when a company filed for approval to market generic Skelaxin.[141]

With generic competition on the horizon, King, the brand, went to work on extending the monopoly market for the drug. In 2001, King conducted a study measuring bioavailability – how much of the drug actually reaches the desired destination over

[136] *See* Letter from Janet Woodcock, Dir., Ctr. for Drug Evaluation & Research, U.S. Food & Drug Admin., to Robert Church & David Fox, Hogan Lovells US LLP, No. FDA-2014-P-1649, at 13–14 (Feb. 24, 2015), www.regulations.gov/#!documentDetail;D=FDA-2014-P-1649-0005.

[137] *See ibid.* at 14 n.27 (citing *Sigma-Tau Pharm., Inc. v. Schwetz*, 288 F.3d 141 (4th Cir. 2002)).

[138] Brand-name companies also have sought to block carve-outs by modifying the "use codes" associated with a given patent in the Orange Book. Use codes provide a brief description of what use of the drug is covered by the listed patent, and brand-name companies have been accused of trying to broaden the scope of use codes to prevent a Section viii carve-out. Like the patents listed in the Orange Book, use code information is not verified by the FDA. In *Caraco v. Novo Nordisk*, 132 S. Ct. 1670 (2012), however, the Supreme Court found that generic manufacturers can file a statutory counterclaim seeking correction of an inaccurate use code.

[139] *FDA Approved Drug Products*, U.S. FOOD & DRUG ADMIN., www.accessdata.fda.gov/scripts/cder/drugsatfda/index.cfm?fuseaction=Search.Label_ApprovalHistory#apphist (Enter drug name [Skelaxin] in search bar and click "submit.").

[140] Consolidated Class Action Complaint and Jury Demand at 10, *United Food & Commercial Workers Union & Midwest Health Benefits Fund v. King Pharm., Inc.*, No. 12-cv-00085 (E.D. Tenn. Mar. 8, 2012), ECF No. 1, *consolidated into* Skelaxin (Metaxalone) Antitrust Litig., No. 12-md-02343 (E.D. Tenn. June 14, 2012), *class certification denied* 299 F.R.D. 555 (2014).

[141] CTR. FOR DRUG EVALUATION & RESEARCH, U.S. FOOD & DRUG ADMIN., APPLICATION NO. ANDA 40–445, APPROVAL PACKAGE FOR ABBREVIATED NEW DRUG APPLICATION APPROVAL 211 (Mar. 31, 2010) [hereinafter ANDA 40–455 APPROVAL PACKAGE], www.accessdata.fda.gov/drugsatfda_docs/anda/2010/040445Orig1s000.pdf (indicating, in the "Factual Background" of a 2010 Memorandum from Martin Shimer to the Dep't of Health & Human Servs., that ANDA 040445 was submitted on September 5, 2001. Although all relevant patents had expired at the time of filing, the generic did not receive immediate approval because of chemistry and bioequivalence problems that caused at least two years of delay before the relevant saga begins. *Ibid.*

time – when Skelaxin is taken on a full stomach compared to its bioavailability in a fasting state.[142] The study showed that the bioavailability of Skelaxin increases when taken with food; in particular, bioavailability increased when taken with a "high-fat meal."[143] Next, King filed for and received two patents in 2002 on the method of "increasing the bioavailability of metaxalone" by taking it with food – yes, the company received two patents for this finding.[144] In June 2002, the FDA approved a labeling amendment for Skelaxin, adding a "pharmacokinetics" section to the drug's labeling with information about the food effect study.[145] With two new patents acquired having expiration dates in 2021, the brand-name company was primed to keep the generic out and hold on to the Skelaxin market for years.[146]

In the face of these two new method-of-use patents that were now blocking generic approval, the generic company filed a citizen petition with the FDA in January 2003 asking the agency to restore the previous labeling without the bioavailability data. It also suggested an alternative: make a declaration that the old label was not withdrawn for safety or effectiveness concerns; in essence, a finding in favor of the generic would allow the generic to ask for a labeling carve-out.[147] While not approving the generic company's citizen petition to restore the original labeling, the FDA filed a "Dear Applicant" letter in 2004, confirming that the bioavailability information could be carved out of generic labeling.[148]

This was a novel case for the FDA. Skelaxin has only one approved use – "relief of discomforts associated with … musculoskeletal conditions."[149] Thus, the generic company was not asking simply to carve out one patent-protected use; it was instead seeking to remove labeling information.[150] The FDA ruled, nevertheless, that

---

[142] Letter from Gary J. Buehler, Dir., Office of Generic Drugs, to Applicant, King Pharm. Inc., at 3 (Mar. 9, 2004) [hereinafter Dear Applicant Letter from Gary J. Buehler], www.fda.gov/ohrms/dockets/dailys/04/mar04/031904/04p-0140-cp00001-07-Tab-06-vol1.pdf.

[143] *Ibid.*

[144] U.S. Patent No. 6,407,128 (filed Dec. 3, 2001); U.S. Patent No. 6,683,102 (filed Mar. 25, 2002).

[145] Letter from Lawrence Goldkind, Deputy Dir., Div. of Anti-Inflammatory, Analgesic, & Ophthalmic Drug Prods., U.S. Food & Drug Admin., to Linda B. Fischer, Dir. Regulatory Affairs, Elan Pharm., Inc. (June 20, 2002), www.accessdata.fda.gov/drugsatfda_docs/appletter/2002/13217s044ltr_2.pdf (approving new labeling); *see also* U.S. Food & Drug Admin., Approved Label For Skelaxin (2002), www.accessdata.fda.gov/drugsatfda_docs/label/2002/13217s036lbl.pdf.

[146] In 2004, the brand-name drug company complicated matters by withdrawing the 400-mg form of Skelaxin and replacing it with a newly approved 800-mg version. While another way in which generic competition was frustrated, it is outside the scope of this current discussion (and, as discussed later, eventually became moot in the generic approval discussion).

[147] ANDA 40–455 Approval Package, *supra* note 141, at 213 (indicating in row 3 of the table in "Factual Background" of a 2010 Memorandum from Martin Shimer to the Dep't of Health & Human Servs. that there was a citizen petition in January 2003 requesting that the original label of Skelaxin be restored).

[148] Dear Applicant Letter from Gary J. Buehler, *supra* note 142, at 1.

[149] *Ibid.* at 1.

[150] *Ibid.* at 3.

removing the data would not render generic Skelaxin less safe or effective than the brand-name drug, once again allowing the carve-out to move forward.[151] The FDA's response hints at how little credence the agency gave to the brand-name company's "scout's honor" insistence that it was protecting patient safety.

In rendering its decision, the FDA relied on the fact that the study did not result in any changes to the dosing instructions or the warnings and precautions in the label.[152] The agency also noted that the brand-name company's own label specifically states that "the clinical relevance of these effects is unknown," referring to the increased bioavailability after eating a high-fat meal, and no issues of safe use were implicated.[153] (A footnote appended to this argument in the "Dear Applicant" letter said that the brand-name drug company's argument might have had more merit had the company conducted clinical trials demonstrating a clinical effect from the differences in bioavailability.)[154] With the "Dear Applicant" letter in hand, the generic appeared to have a clear path to a successful carve-out.

Immediately thereafter, however, King submitted multiple citizen petitions challenging the contents of the FDA's "Dear Applicant" letter.[155] At this point, instead of wading into a new battle over Section viii carve-outs, the generic applicant filed Paragraph IV certifications for the two new patents in late 2004, triggering litigation with the brand-name company under the more standard Hatch-Waxman pathway.[156] While the lawsuit was under way, King worked to strengthen its labeling position. The company received approval for a new label in 2006 that removed the sentence about unknown clinical relevance and added the following sentence to the Precautions section of the label: "Taking SKELAXIN with food may enhance general [central nervous system] depression; elderly patients may be especially susceptible to this CNS effect."[157]

Now, King had a label with its patent-protected information about bioavailability in the Precautions section, implicating safe use of the drug. Further, the drug only had one indication, meaning that the generic could not simply carve out the language as related to a particular use of the drug. This posed a difficult problem

---

[151] *Ibid.* at 1–5.

[152] *Ibid.* at 3.

[153] *Ibid.* at 3.

[154] *Ibid.* at 3 n.3.

[155] ANDA 40–455 APPROVAL PACKAGE, *supra* note 141, at 213; *see, e.g.*, Citizen Petition from Peter Mathers, Stacy Ehrlich & Jennifer Davidson, Kleinfeld, Kaplan and Becker, LLP on behalf of King Pharm., Inc. to Div. of Dockets Mgmt., U.S. Food & Drug Admin. (Mar. 18, 2004), www.fda.gov/ohrms/dockets/dailys/04/mar04/031904/04p-0140-cp00001-01-vol1.pdf.

[156] ANDA 40–455 APPROVAL PACKAGE, *supra* note 141, at 212.

[157] U.S. FOOD & DRUG ADMIN., APPROVED LABEL FOR SKELAXIN (2006), www.accessdata.fda.gov/drugsatfda_docs/label/2006/013217s046lbl.pdf (including the new sentence in the precautions section); *see also* Letter from Bob Rappaport, Div. of Anesthesia, Analgesia & Rheumatology, U.S. Food &

for the generic and the FDA. As the FDA admitted, "Carving out patent-protected language from the Precautions section of a label that pertains to a labeled use would generally not be permitted."[158]

The FDA, at an impasse, essentially chose to punt on the issue, making no decision on the brand-name company's citizen petitions. Instead, a resolution eventually arrived through the courts five years later, when a Brooklyn-based district court judge invalidated the two bioavailability patents.[159] The judge held that, given what was already known about the drug, it was obvious that Skelaxin would be better absorbed if taken with food.[160] The supposed innovation named in the patents was nothing new at all. Thus, the generic won its Paragraph IV challenge, and the FDA approved the generic application in 2010, making the carve-out discussion entirely moot.[161]

The delay earned by King, however, was not a moot point. From the date that the FDA accepted the first generic application to the date of approval, King's tactics delayed the entry of generic Skelaxin for almost a decade, despite the fact that the company eventually found its new patents invalidated. The delay may have been worth as much as $3 billion in sales[162] – all over one sentence on a label and two patents claiming the supposedly novel finding that Skelaxin is better absorbed when taken with food.

A more recent carve-out conundrum shows how exclusivities can create confusion in the carve-out process. In 2014, AstraZeneca received an Orphan Drug Designation for Crestor, a popular cholesterol-lowering statin.[163] The designation was granted because studies found that Crestor could be used for the treatment

Drug Admin., to Douglas Dewar, Senior Dir., Regulatory Affairs, King Pharm., Inc. (Nov. 4, 2006), www.accessdata.fda.gov/drugsatfda_docs/appletter/2006/013217s046ltr.pdf (noting that the only label change was to the pharmacokinetics information).

[158] ANDA 40–455 APPROVAL PACKAGE, *supra* note 141, at 217.

[159] *King Pharm., Inc. et al. v. Eon Labs, Inc.*, 593 F. Supp. 2d 501 (E.D.N.Y. 2009).

[160] *See ibid.*

[161] ANDA 40–455 APPROVAL PACKAGE, *supra* note 141, at 227.

[162] The figure of $3 billion was calculated as follows: First, 2002 sales figures of $238 million and 2009 sales of $476 million for Skelaxin were averaged to produce an estimate of average yearly Skelaxin sales of $357 million. The first full year in which Skelaxin faced a pending generic application was 2002, while 2009 was the last full year before generic approval. Then, $357 million was multiplied by 9, representing approximately nine years of delay, to reach a total value of $3.2 billion. Press Release, King Pharm., King Pharmaceuticals Acquires Primary Care Business Unit from Elan (Jan. 30, 2003), www.sec.gov/Archives/edgar/data/1047699/000095014403000944/g80411exv99w1.txt (noting 2002 sales of $238 million); Press Release, Sandoz, Sandoz Announces Launch of First Generic Version of Leading Muscle Relaxant Skelaxin (May 20, 2010), www.fiercepharma.com/press-releases/sandoz-announces-launch-first-generic-version-leading-muscle-relaxant-skelaxin-anda-e (noting 2009 sales of $476 million).

[163] Citizen Petition from AstraZeneca Pharm. LP to Div. of Dockets Mgmt., U.S. Food and Drug Admin., No. FDA-2016-P-1485, at 1 (May 31, 2016) [hereinafter "AstraZeneca Petition"], www.regulations.gov/document?D=FDA-2016-P-1485-0001.

of pediatric homozygous familial hypercholesterolemia ("pediatric HoFN"), a rare, severe generic disorder that heightens cholesterol levels and can cause premature death.[164] The Orphan Drug Designation provided Crestor with an additional seven years of marketing exclusivity, but only for that orphan use. Notably, it is not as if it was found that Crestor has a unique effect on treating HoFN – AstraZeneca simply found that it could reduce cholesterol as the drug was generally intended to do, which could then mitigate the effects of HoFN.[165] AstraZeneca, in essence, was collecting additional exclusivities for confirming that a drug used for reducing cholesterol could help treat a pediatric disease marked by high cholesterol. We do not intend to denigrate the real therapeutic benefit that Crestor may have on patients with pediatric HoFN, but the finding was not particularly novel – it is not as if AstraZeneca suddenly discovered that Crestor had therapeutic effects not related to lowering cholesterol levels. Plus, the study suspiciously (as always) did not begin until years after Crestor was first approved in 2003.[166] Numerous commentators have expressed concerns about pharmaceutical companies' attempting to game the Orphan Drug Act by getting approval for their otherwise very popular drugs to treat rare diseases long after the drugs are first approved.[167]

AstraZeneca filed a supplementary new drug approval application to gain full marketing approval for the pediatric use, which was granted in May 2016, just a little more than a month before generics would have otherwise entered the market.[168] This allowed information about the orphan pediatric use of the drug to be included on a revised label.

Here is where matters get tricky. As we explored in the Skelaxin snafu, labeling information generally can be carved out unless it pertains to the safety and efficacy of the drug. By adding information about a pediatric, orphan drug use to the label, AstraZeneca argued in a citizen petition that this information was safety related and may not be carved out for any reason, in part because physicians might overtreat children by prescribing too high of a dose if the pediatric labeling information is removed while the adult labeling information remains.[169]

---

[164] Ed Silverman, *AstraZeneca Sues FDA to Prevent Generic Versions of Crestor*, STAT (Jun. 28, 2016), www.statnews.com/pharmalot/2016/06/28/astrazeneca-fda-crestor/.

[165] AstraZeneca Petition, *supra* note 163, at 1.

[166] *Ibid.* at 3.

[167] *See, e.g.*, Feldman, *Regulatory Property: The New IP, supra* note 134.

[168] Silverman, *AstraZeneca Sues FDA to Prevent Generic Versions of Crestor, supra* note 164.

[169] AstraZeneca Petition, *supra* note 163, at 13–14. In a twist that makes this even more confusing, AstraZeneca also argued that pediatric HoFN patients could be *undertreated* using a generic because Crestor is also approved for the treatment of another pediatric disorder, *HeFN*. That labeling information, however, is not exclusivity-protected, but it suggests a lower dose than would be needed for pediatric *HoFN*. Thus, AstraZeneca presented the concern that physicians could become confused, which, given those head-spinning sentences, may be true. *Ibid.*

AstraZeneca believes the authority for its argument stems from the unique interplay between laws governing all pharmaceutical labeling and those that specifically apply to pediatric treatment, which the company says prevents any of the pediatric labeling from being omitted from a generic label.

This was not the first time such pediatric labeling problems had arisen during the generic application process. In December 2014, with exclusivity expiring in just a few months, the brand-name company Otsuka received a pediatric Orphan Drug Designation for Abilify, a blockbuster antipsychotic drug used for treatment of depression, bipolar disorder, and schizophrenia, among other illnesses.[170] The approved supplementary new drug application allowed Otsuka to market Abilify for the pediatric treatment of Tourette's disorder.[171]

Just as AstraZeneca did more than a year later, Otsuka argued that the pediatric Tourette's indication could not be carved out of the label. The legal argument is from 21 U.S.C. § 355A(o), added in 2002's "Best Pharmaceuticals for Children Act," which states that generics are not barred from approval if "the labeling of the drug omits a *pediatric indication* or any other aspect of labeling pertaining to *pediatric use* when the omitted indication or other aspect is protected by patent or by exclusivity under clause (iii) or (iv) of Section 355(j)(5)(F) of this title" (emphasis added).[172] Clauses (iii) and (iv) of Section 355(j)(5)(F) refer to new drug and new study exclusivities that are provided for under Hatch-Waxman – notably, it does not expressly mention orphan drug exclusivity, which is contained in a different section of the Food, Drug, and Cosmetic Act.[173] (That would be Sections 360aa to 360ff, by the way.)[174] Thus, Otsuka argued that the absence of the Orphan Drug Act from the statutes precludes the FDA from allowing a carve-out of a pediatric indication – a novel argument, to say the least.[175]

Otsuka also argued that the FDA went to unprecedented lengths to stop it from blocking generics with the pediatric indication, adding a complicated twist to an already labyrinthine story. In a complaint, it argues that, a few months after

[170] Ed Silverman, *FDA is Sued by Otsuka for 'Unlawfully' Widening the Market for Abilify*, WALL. ST. J. (Mar. 26, 2015), http://blogs.wsj.com/pharmalot/2015/03/26/fda-is-sued-by-otsuka-for-unlawfully-widening-the-market-for-ability/.

[171] Federal Defendants' Opposition to Plaintiffs' Motion for a Temporary Restraining Order and/or Preliminary Injunction, *Otsuka Pharmaceutical Co., Ltd., et al. v. Burwell et al.*, No. 8:15-cv-00852, at 7–8 (D. Md. Apr. 20, 2015), www.pharmamedtechbi.com/~/media/Supporting%20Documents/The%20Pink%20Sheet%20DAILY/2015/April/Otsuka%20v%20Burwell%20FDA%20opposition%20to%20TRO%20PI%20042015.pdf.

[172] 21 U.S.C. § 355A(o).

[173] 21 U.S.C. § 355(j)(5)(F)(iii)–(iv).

[174] 21 U.S.C. § 360aa-ff.

[175] Amended Complaint, *Otsuka Pharm Co., Ltd., et al. v. Burwell et al.*, No. 8:15-cv-00852, at 11 (D. Md. Apr. 15, 2015), http://assets.fiercemarkets.net/public/lifesciences/complaint76-1.pdf.

approval, the FDA said it made an error and changed its orphan drug approval to cover Tourette's disorder in *all patients* instead of just pediatric patients.[176] This likely would have hurt Otsuka's generic-blocking argument under § 355A(o), since the orphan use would have no longer been a specific pediatric use, but rather a general-population indication.[177] It is also amusing, because Otsuka was essentially suing the FDA for approving the use of Abilify for *too wide* a population, a move that also points to the pediatric indication as a targeted addition by Otsuka to block generics. The FDA denies this change ever took place, and says any communication to the contrary was an error and not an official change.[178] Nevertheless, Otsuka filed a motion to stop generic approval, and by April 2015, it was clear that the indication was only for pediatric Tourette's despite any action the FDA may or may have not taken.[179]

Matters did not work out so well for Otsuka. The FDA approved generic versions of Abilify, and a federal judge denied Otsuka's motion for a preliminary injunction.[180] He found that § 355A(o) does not preclude the FDA from allowing Orphan Drug Act pediatric carve-outs, but instead seems to clarify that the FDA *can* in fact allow carve-outs related to Hatch-Waxman exclusivities. And the judge had a point. The language of the statute does say that applications "shall not be considered ineligible for approval," an extremely confusing double negative that supports the judge's finding, by broadening what is eligible for a carve-out rather than restricting it. The FDA made a similar determination in its denial of Otsuka's argument, finding that Otsuka's arguments regarding § 355A(o) turn the section "on its head."[181] Statutory interpretation has not been this interesting since the Supreme Court tackled the definition of an Affordable Care Act "Exchange" in *King v. Burwell!*[182]

Moving back to Crestor, AstraZeneca tried to argue that this time was different, making a very similar assertion regarding pediatric labeling and the Orphan Drug Act. Along with arguing that the decisions made by the FDA and the federal court were incorrect, the company tried to differentiate itself from Otsuka's Abilify debacle. Another deep breath – okay, ready? Abilify was only approved for

---

[176] *Ibid.* at 13–14.
[177] Silverman, *FDA Is Sued by Otsuka for 'Unlawfully' Widening the Market for Abilify, supra* note 170.
[178] Federal Defendants' Opposition to Plaintiffs' Motion, *supra* note 171, at 8–10.
[179] *Ibid.* at 9; Amended Complaint, *supra* note 175, at 14 (both referring to April 2015 letter).
[180] *Otsuka Pharm Co., Ltd., et al. v. Burwell et al.,* No. 8:15-cv-00852, at 13–14 (D. Md. Apr. 29, 2015) (memorandum opinion) (denying Otsuka's motion for temporary restaining order or preliminary injunction).
[181] Letter from John R. Peters, Acting Dir., Off. of Generic Drugs, U.S. Food & Drug Admin., to Ralph S. Tyler, Venable LLP, at 9–12, 15 (Apr. 28, 2015), www.fda.gov/downloads/Drugs/DevelopmentApprovalProcess/HowDrugsareDevelopedandApproved/ApprovalApplications/AbbreviatedNewDrugApplicationANDAGenerics/UCM444858.pdf (discussing Otsuka's arguments regarding Abilify generics).
[182] *King v. Burwell,* 135 S. Ct. 2480 (2015).

pediatric Tourette's, so carving out that part of the label leaves no indication related to Tourette's. For Crestor, eliminating the pediatric HoFN designation still leaves the adult HoFN dosage on the label, and AstraZeneca argued that this presents a potential safety problem in accidentally overtreating children.[183]

In July 2016, after several senators, representatives, and the Department of Justice weighed in to support generic approval,[184] AstraZeneca lost all of its labeling-related challenges. The FDA denied the citizen petition in a ruling very similar in structure to its letter denying Otsuka's challenges, finding that the adult HoFN dosing information is not "significantly different" from the carved-out pediatric HoFN information, and reiterating its interpretation of § 355A(o).[185] A federal judge also denied an injunction that would have prevented generic sales.[186]

That finally brings a conclusion to the sagas of Crestor and Abilify. If anything, these two complex scenarios show the lengths that brand-name companies are willing to go to block generics in Generation 3.0 of pharmaceutical delay, combining exclusivities with citizen petitions, lawsuits, and issues of statutory interpretation. They are perhaps the best example of legal resources being deployed in place of research and development, as brand-name pharmaceutical companies turn to obstruction and delay tactics that attempt to distort regulatory processes.

---

[183] AstraZeneca Petition, *supra* note 163, at 11–12.

[184] Ed Silverman, *Sanders, Other Lawmakers Urge FDA Approval of Generic Crestor*, STAT (Jul. 7, 2016), www.statnews.com/pharmalot/2016/07/07/bernie-sanders-fda-generics-cholesterol/.

[185] Letter from Janet Woodcock, Dir., Ctr. for Drug Evaluation & Research, U.S. Food & Drug Admin., to Joseph A. Cash, Jr., AstraZeneca Pharm., Re: No. FDA-2016-P-1485, at 15 (Jul. 19, 2016), www .regulations.gov/document?D=FDA-2016-P-1485-0007 (denying AstraZeneca's citizen petition).

[186] Ed Silverman, *AstraZeneca Loses Court Battle to Prevent Generic Versions of Crestor*, STAT (Jul. 20, 2016), www.statnews.com/pharmalot/2016/07/20/astrazeneca-generics-crestor-fda/.

5

Empirical Evidence of a Citizen's Pathway Gone Astray

Chapter 4 described anecdotes and concerns that have swirled around the citizen petition process at the FDA. The FDA's citizen petition process and similar programs at other agencies were created in the 1970s. The movement was part of an effort to fashion more participatory regimes, in which ordinary citizens could have a say in the decisions made by regulatory agencies.[1] The hope was that such a participatory structure would prevent regulatory agencies from being captured by the very industries they were intended to police. Evidence suggests, however, that the FDA's citizen petition process may have taken a different turn.

In contrast to its lofty goals, this mechanism designed for citizens and scientists to raise concerns about food, drugs, and FDA regulations has turned into a playground for pharmaceutical companies to challenge drug applications, especially those related to pending generic applications. In many cases, the "concerned citizen" behind a petition is actually a large pharmaceutical company, seeking to stop or delay approval of a generic drug through a variety of different means. These include direct attacks against the generic's application and its bioequivalence or clinical data, appeals to safety, and calls to preserve or add new exclusivities for the brand-name drug. Some petitions raise important or necessary issues; many others, however, seem frivolous or questionable in their aims.

In this chapter, we examine what is happening on a systemwide basis, looking beyond cases and anecdotes to undertake an empirical analysis. (Numbers are all

---

[1] The following germinal texts describe the movement and debate its consequences. Christopher Edley Jr., ADMINISTRATIVE LAW: RETHINKING JUDICIAL CONTROL OF BUREAUCRACY (Yale 1990); Antonin Scalia, *Vermont Yankee: The APA, the D.C. Circuit, and the Supreme Court,* 1978 SUP. CT. REV. 345 (1978); Clark Byse, *Vermont Yankee and the Evolution of Administrative Procedure,* 91 HARV. L. REV. 1823 (1978); *see also* Sidney Shapiro & Richard Murphy, *Eight Things Americans Can't Figure Out about Controlling Power,* 61 ADMIN. L. REV. 5 (2008); Paul Verkuil, *The Wait Is Over: Chevron as the Stealth Vermont Yankee II,* 75 GEO WASH. L. REV. 921 (2007); Reuel Schiller, *Rulemaking's Promise: Administrative Law and Legal Culture in the 1960s and 1970s,* 53 ADMIN. L. REV. 1139 (2001).

the rage these days!) In particular, we present the results of a study in which we explored whether drug companies are systematically using citizen petitions to try to delay the approval of generic competitors. Our hypothesis was that such petitions are being used as a last-ditch effort to delay generic entry as long as absolutely possible.

Assembling this information was difficult, to say the least. As with all information about strategic behavior in pharmaceutical pricing, the information must be painstakingly pieced together from scattered and incomplete public records. This chapter describes key aspects and results of our extensive research that assembled this picture of a citizen's pathway being used by drug companies as a delay tactic. It is a remarkable picture, indeed.

Following are the key findings from the study:

- The FDA's citizen petition process is one of the key pathways involved in the modern generation of generic drug delay, playing a role in various game-playing strategies.
- Citizen petitions from competitor companies – brand names and generics seeking to delay competitors – have essentially doubled since 2003.
- Citizen petitions with the potential to delay generic entry occupy a striking amount of the process in recent years. Of all citizen petitions at the FDA (including those concerning tobacco, food, dietary supplements, medical devices, etc.), nearly 15 percent have the potential to delay generics, climbing to 20 percent in some years.
- Many citizen petitions from competitor companies appear to be an eleventh-hour effort to hold off generic competition. In fact, the most common category of delay-related petitions were those filed within six months of generic approval. This is particularly noteworthy given that *the overwhelming majority of citizen petitions are denied.*[2]
- In short, the results suggest that many competitor petitions are filed late in the game, as a last-ditch attempt to delay competition just a little longer, even though they are unlikely to be successful.
- Congressional reforms enacted in 2007 have not stemmed the tide.

The study provides empirical evidence that citizen petitions at the FDA have become a new focus of strategic behavior by pharmaceutical companies to delay

---

[2] *See* Michael A. Carrier & Carl Minniti, *Citizen Petitions: Long, Late-Filed, and At-Last Denied*, 66 Am. U. L. Rev. 305, 333 tbl. 4 (2016) http://ssrn.com/abstract=2832319 (finding that between 2011 and 2015, the FDA denied 92 percent of section 505(q) citizen petitions, the type most often employed to oppose generic entry); Michael A. Carrier & Daryl Wander, *Citizen Petitions: An Empirical Study*, 34 Cardozo L. Rev. 249, 274 (2012) (finding that the FDA denied 81 percent of all citizen petitions filed by competitors against drug companies between 2001 and 2010).

entry of generic competition, now that the pay-for-delay route appears less and less promising. And, as described in Chapter 4, the delay achieved through a citizen petition, even if the petition is ultimately unsuccessful, can be worth hundreds of millions of dollars in revenue for a drug company.

A METHODOLOGY

1 Overview

As described previously, anecdotal evidence has emerged over the years suggesting that drug companies are abusing the citizen petition process as a delay tactic to keep generics off the market.[3] We set out to take a quantitative look.

To approach the question, we analyzed the timing of when citizen petitions are filed during the generic drug approval process and the frequency with which certain petitions – those that have the potential to delay – are filed. We hypothesized that such petitions would be filed toward the end of the approval process to put up one more roadblock in the path of successful approval of a generic drug.

Assembling the information from the FDA's publicly available materials is tremendously difficult. Although the FDA publishes a large amount of information on its public website, and more in hard copy, much important information is missing. The necessary information often must be pieced together or estimated; in some cases, it simply cannot be located.

Some of these gaps are downright puzzling. For example, the FDA does not always publicly reveal the date on which a generic application was filed. We tracked down many of those dates by reading through PDFs of thousands of letters in the files, looking for places in which the dates were mentioned in passing. For many others, however, we had to develop a method of identifying the likely quarter in which an application was filed by working backwards from the FDA's complicated file numbering systems. It just should not be that hard for the public to get basic information.

The FDA files also do not always link to or indicate which specific generic application a citizen petition relates to, information that is important for tracking the timing of citizen petitions in relation to the application process for a particular drug.

---

[3] *See, e.g.*, Ameet Sarpatwari, Jerry Avorn, & Aaron S. Kesselheim, *Using a Drug-Safety Tool to Prevent Competition*, 370 NEW ENG. J. OF MED. 1476, 1476-77 (2014) (discussing, as an aside, a citizen petition from Celgene Corporation to the FDA 17-18 (September 20, 2007)), www.regulations.gov/document?D=FDA-2007-P-0113-0002). Most important, Carrier and Wander, who documented a rise in citizen petitions in general, suggested that the rise might be a sign of delay behavior. *See* Carrier & Wander, *Citizen Petitions, supra* note 2, at 269-270, 283-286 (documenting empirically a rise in citizen petitions and detailing two anecdotal examples of petitions that resulted in delay, one related to the depression drug Wellbutrin and one related to the insomnia drug Ambien).

Moreover, prior to 2007, the FDA files did not explicitly denote when a citizen petition targeted a generic application.

Despite these challenges, we set out to assemble a data set of citizen petitions that had the potential to delay generic applications, along with links to the relevant generic application and timing data. All of this information had to be assembled by hand, piecing together information from citizen petition letters and various generic application files.

Through this approach, we assembled several data sets that allowed us to analyze the timing of when citizen petitions are filed during the generic drug approval process. It also allowed us to see the frequency with which petitions that have the potential to delay are filed.[4] As we describe the method we used to painstakingly piece the information together, we will do our best to include interesting tidbits and insights along the way. (We have to entertain you somehow.)

2 Compiling All Citizen Petitions from 2000 to 2012

To begin our analysis, we compiled all documents related to citizen petitions that were filed with the FDA between the beginning of 2000 and the end of 2012, using publicly available FDA databases. We limited our data set to citizen petitions filed prior to 2013 because test analyses indicated that citizen petitions filed after that time frequently related to drugs that had not yet been approved. Without final approval files, one cannot find much of the information necessary for the analysis. One also cannot reach timing conclusions about events within the approval process, given that the process is still underway.

For the period from 2000 to 2012, we obtained 19,520 documents. Multiple documents, however, can correspond to a single citizen petition. For example, supplemental data, support letters, and the FDA's actual response are different types of

---

4   For an in-depth discussion of the methodology, see Robin Feldman, Evan Frondorf, Andrew K. Cordova, & Connie Wang, *Empirical Evidence of Drug Pricing Games – A Citizen's Pathway Gone Astray* STAN. TECH. L. REV. (forthcoming 2017), http://ssrn.com/abstract=2833151. In simplified form, the process can be described as follows: (1) We compiled all citizen petitions and related documents filed between 2000 and 2012; (2) We identified citizen petitions related to pharmaceuticals, with a particular focus on generic drugs; (3) We read each remaining citizen petition and determined which of these petitions were related to generic drugs or had the power to delay generic approval, regardless of the merits or circumstances of the petition; (4) We constructed a data set of all generic applications approved between 2006 and 2015, recording the approval date for each application; (5) We compiled filing dates for the generic applications, pulling them when available from PDFs of letters within the FDA's databases. When filing information was not publicly available, we were able to estimate a filing date down to the quarter-year for most drugs; (6) We matched each citizen petition with the generic application most relevant to the requests made in the petition; (7) Using these citizen petition–generic application pairs, we constructed metrics with the goal of isolating the timing of petitions during the generic drug approval process.

documents that may be listed separately but correspond to a single citizen petition. The 19,520 documents are linked to a total of 1,790 citizen petitions filed between 2000 and 2012 and archived online.

3 Identifying Citizen Petitions That Could Delay Generic Competition

With the full data set of citizen petitions in hand, we turned to identifying citizen petitions with the power to delay pending or forthcoming generic applications. This process involved two steps for removing nonrelevant petitions: 1) removing petitions whose titles or categories indicated that they were unrelated to delay of generic competition, and 2) removing petitions by viewing the content of the petition and related documents in full.

After removing citizen petitions not relevant to our study, the remaining citizen petitions were those with the potential to delay a pending or forthcoming generic competitor. The decision to include a citizen petition in the data set was based solely on the topic of the petition, and no attempt was made to judge the merits of the issues raised in the petitions.

Many of the citizen petitions in the final pool specifically ask the FDA to stay or delay approval of a generic application. These frequently raise concerns about safety or incomplete bioequivalence or clinical testing, with bioequivalence testing a particularly prevalent topic. Many of these petitions ask the FDA to stay the approval of a generic drug until the generic applicant presents evidence that the FDA already requires. This type of petition essentially forces the FDA to make a redundant ruling that a certain type of testing is required, when in fact, that testing is already required.

These redundant petitions lead to a number of FDA rulings that grant petitions while not actually imposing any new requirements on the generic applicant. The result may be a petition that is granted in part and denied in part, with the granted portion no more than a formality that lacks practical significance.[5]

Consider the FDA's response to a citizen petition that requested a stay of generic versions of Argatroban, a drug to prevent blood clotting. In its response, the FDA acknowledges that the actions granted in the petition are merely those already required under FDA policy, stating that "[t]o the extent it is consistent with our current policies, we grant your request."[6] In plain terms: we already require this, so we grudgingly agree.

---

[5] *See* Carrier & Wander, *Citizen Petitions, supra* note 2, at 261, 266; *see also ibid.* at 261 (noting that the FDA's director of the Office of Generic Drugs has made a similar observation, saying, "when petitions are granted, in whole or in part, it is often because the FDA already has the proposed scientific or legal standard in place or is already planning to take the action that the petition requests").

[6] Letter from Janet Woodcock, Dir., Ctr. for Drug Evaluation & Research, U.S. Food & Drug Admin., to Richard D. Kelly, Oblon Spivak, on behalf of Mitsubishi Tanabe Pharma Corp., Re: No. FDA-2009-P-0115, at 8–9 (Aug. 19, 2009), www.regulations.gov/#!documentDetail;D=FDA-2009-P-0115-0006.

Other citizen petitions remaining in the pool ask that the FDA direct a generic applicant to refile its application in a different form, changing it from an ANDA (the category for generic applications that reference an existing drug) to a 505(b)(2) (the category for generic applications that reference an existing drug but differ slightly in formulation, dosage, treatment indication, etc.). Still others demand that a generic applicant revise its application to encompass additional patents. All of the requests would add burdens on a generic applicant to comply. Thus, they are best classified as petitions with the potential to delay generics.

Another category of petitions has a less direct link to delaying generic approval. On occasion, pharmaceutical companies do not address specific generic applications or even the topic of generic approval in their citizen petition. Rather, the brand-name company requests that its drug receive additional exclusivities from the FDA or retain exclusivities that the company perceives to be under threat.[7] We have chosen to categorize these petitions as potentially related to generic delay because gaining exclusivity pushes back the window for generic entry. Interestingly, one petition filed by a pharmaceutical company even identifies the relationship between its exclusivity request and delay of generic competitors trying to enter the market.[8]

The final pool of citizen petitions with the potential to delay introduction of generic drugs consisted of 249 citizen petitions filed between 2000 and 2012. This number represents a striking portion of the citizen petitions filed at the FDA during that period. In fact, in our dataset, 22 percent of citizen petitions related in some way to drugs[9] and 14 percent of all citizen petitions filed on any topic at the FDA – including those related to food, medical devices, tobacco, and (everyone's favorite) dietary supplements – had the potential to delay the entry of generics.[10] Thus, the FDA is spending an inordinate amount of its time responding to citizen petitions aimed at delaying generic entry.

---

[7] For example, Petition No. FDA-2010-P-0188 asks the FDA to "confirm," among other related requests, that the "FDA will grant 180-day marketing exclusivity to Actavis' ANDA No. 77–302." *See* Citizen Petition from Axinn, Veltrop & Harkrider LLP, on behalf of Actavis Elizabeth LLC, to Div. of Dockets Mgmt., U.S. Food & Drug Admin., No. FDA-2010-P-0188, at 2 (Apr. 6, 2010), www.regulations.gov/#!documentDetail;D=FDA-2010-P-0188-0001.

[8] *See* Petition for Stay of Action from Arnold & Porter LLP, on behalf of Medicis, to Div. of Dockets Mgmt., U.S. Food & Drug Admin., No. FDA-2007-P-0295, at 1 (Apr. 20, 2007) (stating that "the requested stay would ... prevent the approval of any ANDA or Section 505(b)(2) application referencing the Ziana™ NDA during the 3-year [*sic*] of market exclusivity that would be earned by the Ziana™ application if [the petitioner's other] citizen petition is granted") www.regulations.gov/#!documentDetail;D=FDA-2007-P-0295-0003.

[9] That is, 249 of 1,158 citizen petitions filed were related in any way to pharmaceuticals; 65 percent of all petitions (1,158 of 1,790) were related to pharmaceuticals.

[10] That is, 249 of 1,790 citizen petitions filed on any topic at the FDA.

4 Timing of the Citizen Petitions Relative to Generic Applications

For each of the 249 citizen petitions, we attempted to glean information about the timing relationship between the petition and the generic application most implicated by the petition. Namely, we wanted to know how much time had passed between when the relevant generic application was filed and when the citizen petition was filed. We also wanted to track how much time had passed between when the citizen petition was filed and when the generic application was approved.

Calculating these statistics required information on when generic applications were filed and approved. Although one would expect such information to be readily available in the FDA's public information, that is not the case.

i Filing Dates for Generic Applications

The FDA's searchable database contains readily available information regarding approval dates for most generic drugs, to the specificity of month and day. Filing dates, however, are not so transparent.[11] Assembling information on when a generic application was filed required a combination of sleuthing through the various letters in the generic drug's public file and estimating based on information known from other drug applications. The process allowed us to determine with reasonable

---

[11] Approval dates are, for the most part, readily available through the FDA's searchable database of approved drugs, known as Drugs@FDA. For example, anyone can search Drugs@FDA for information on ANDA No. 90153 (a generic version of Ambien CR), and the page clearly denotes an approval date of March 25, 2013. But *filing* dates are not so transparent. The FDA does not have a standard data field in Drugs@FDA for ANDA filing date – clicking the "Approval Date(s) and History, Letters, Labels, Reviews" link on the page for ANDA No. 90153 results in no history, letters, or documents whatsoever other than a table displaying the approval date for the drug. This was the case for the majority of generic applications we explored in the Drugs@FDA database. The only way we were able to obtain filing dates was through rarely posted approval documents on a drug's "Approval Date(s) and History, Letters, Labels, Reviews" page. For example, the Approval History table for ANDA No. 202958 (a generic version of Keppra XR, an antiepileptic) stores PDFs of the final approval letter and approved label for the generic. In the first line of the approval letter from the FDA to generic manufacturer Apotex, it references ANDA letter dated March 31, 2011, indicating the generic filing date. *See* Letter from William P. Rickman, Office of Generic Drugs, U.S. Food & Drug Admin., to Kiran Krishnan, Vice Pres., Reg. Aff., Apotex Corp., Re: ANDA 202958 (Feb. 25, 2015), www.accessdata.fda.gov/drugsatfda_docs/appletter/2015/202958Orig1000ltr.pdf. This – a brief mention in a PDF-only approval letter – appears to be the only way that filing dates have been made available to the public. We note that even that date may be slightly off. *See, e.g.,* Citizen Petition from Foley Hoag LLP, on behalf of Fresenius Medical Care North Am., to Div. of Dockets Mgmt., U.S. Food & Drug Admin., No. FDA-2012-P-0184, at 2 (Feb. 21, 2012), http://www.regulations.gov/#!documentDetail:D=FDA 2012-P-0184-0001 (date stamp one day later than the date of the letter). Other sources agree that this is the only location for filing dates. In late March of 2016, however, FDA commentators began to notice that the FDA had started to remove *all* filing dates from approval letters, eliminating the only public source of approval dates. (This also means that our study range cannot be extended past 2015.) *See* Bob Pollock, *Do You Notice Something Missing? What the Heck!* LACHMAN CONSULTANTS.COM (Mar. 31, 2016), www.lachmanconsultants.com/2016/03/do-you-notice-something-missing-what-the-heck/.

certainty the quarter in which an application was filed for nearly three-quarters of the generic applications in our pool.

In particular, the way docket numbers are assigned to generic applications makes it possible to estimate filing dates for those generic applications that do not have publicly available approval letters containing the filing date. To do this, however, we needed to look at the full set of generic applications approved by the FDA between the beginning of 2006 and the end of 2015, which consists of 4,222 applications.[12] 2006 was the starting point because we determined that very few drugs approved before this year were implicated in our set of citizen petitions filed between 2000 and 2012. 2015 was the ending point because it was the latest year for which generic approval data was available at the time we began collecting relevant information.[13]

Of the 4,222 generic applications approved between 2006 and 2015, 980 had exact filing dates available in approval letters, representing 23 percent. A further 2,108 filing dates were estimated using the process described above. In all, the quarter-year in which the generic application was filed was found or estimated for 3,088 generic applications, a success rate of 73 percent.

ii Matching Citizen Petitions to Relevant Applications

Having constructed the data set of filing and approval dates for generic applications, we then matched the data set of approximately 249 citizen petitions with the generic applications implicated by those petitions. In other words, what generic application would be most directly impacted, and potentially delayed, by the filing of that particular citizen petition?

Occasionally, the "offending" generic application would be explicitly named in the citizen petition.[14] In most cases, however, the target of the citizen petition's complaint was not so clear, perhaps because drug companies want to spread a wide net over all potential generic applications related to their existing drug. Similar to many citizen petitions, for example, Petition FDA-2009-P-0364 states, "Graceway respectfully requests that FDA refuse to approve any ANDA for a generic imiquimod cream

---

[12] We also matched the generic applications to the brand-name drug that was listed as the reference drug using the FDA's Orange Book data.

[13] In rare exceptions, we discovered a citizen petition in our data set related to a generic application that was approved prior to 2006. We were able to use the same techniques described in this section to fill in filing dates for the relevant generic application. Similarly, the FDA database of generic applications does not include approved 505(b)(2) applications. Thus, those applications were added as well, when necessary, for the 249 citizen petitions.

[14] For example, Petition FDA-2012-P-0184 specifically asks that the FDA "refuse to accept Cypress ANDA No. 20–2820 for filing (or find ANDA No. 20–2820 not approvable if already accepted for filing)." *See* Citizen Petition from Foley Hoag LLP, on behalf of Fresenius Medical Care North Am., to Div. of Dockets Mgmt., U.S. Food & Drug Admin., No. FDA-2012-P-0184, at 2 (Feb. 21, 2012), www .regulations.gov/#!documentDetail;D=FDA-2012-P-0184-0001.

product that seeks to rely on FDA's prior approval of Aldara, unless the application contains data from [bioequivalence studies, among others]."[15]

When a specific generic application was not identified, we turned to our generic application data set to find the first generic application filed that referenced the petitioner's drug.[16] The first filer is significant for a number of reasons – it opens the floodgates to generic competition, generating an initial drop in price and market share, as well as more substantial reductions as other generics enter later on. Thus, the first generic application is the most lucrative milestone for a brand-name company to delay or block.

Although we generally looked for the first-filed generic application as the appropriate reference point for a citizen petition, in a few instances the first filer could not have been the subject of the citizen petition, such as when the first filer was approved before the citizen petition was even filed. In those cases, appropriate steps were taken to identify the most relevant generic application.

At the conclusion of this process, 164 citizen petitions of the 249 originally identified were linked to a generic application that had data available – either a filing date, an approval date, or both.[17] This is a success rate of nearly two-thirds, or 65.9 percent, among the citizen petitions identified as having the potential to delay generic entry. Of those 164 petitions, 152 (or 61 percent of the total 249) were linked to generic applications with both the filing date and approval date.[18] In sum, out of the 249 citizen petitions with the potential to delay generic entry, we were able to establish at least partial timelines for the generic applications with which they were most likely associated for nearly two-thirds, and full timelines for 61 percent.

iii Establishing Key Metrics
Using our final data set of 164 citizen petitions paired with relevant generic applications with timing information, we were able to create a set of helpful metrics. The metrics we established included the following:

---

[15] *See* Citizen Petition from Graceway Pharm. LLC to Div. of Dockets Mgmt., U.S. Food & Drug Admin., No. FDA-2009-P-0364, at 2 (Jul. 30, 2009), www.regulations.gov/#!document Detail;D=FDA-2009-P-0364-0001.

[16] If multiple ANDAs were explicitly named in a petition, we identified the first-filed petition of those mentioned.

[17] In rare circumstances, a filing date was available but not an approval date. This occurred when a drug had only been tentatively approved but was still posted on the FDA's website with an attached letter noting the filing date.

[18] There were a total of 157 delay-related citizen petitions with filing information (including those with only a filing date and those with both a filing and approval date) and 159 delay-related citizen petitions with approval information (including those with only an approval date and those with both a filing and approval date).

- The number of quarters between when the generic application was filed and when the citizen petition was filed ("Quarters Since Generic Filing");
- The number of months between when the citizen petition was filed and the eventual approval of the relevant generic drug ("Months Before Approval");
- The total time it took for the generic drug to gain approval, from start to finish (its "Total Approval Time").[19]

We used quarter-years as the standard measurement basis for "Quarters Since Generic Filing" and "Total Approval Time," because those metrics required generic filing dates, many of which had to be estimated. For estimating generic filing dates, a year was not specific enough to tease out useful insights, and we did not have enough information to measure time in monthly increments. Meanwhile, we were able to use months rather than quarters for the "Months Before Approval" metric because, unlike with generic filing information, exact dates to the specificity of month and day were available for both citizen petition filing and generic approval.

Examining these core metrics will reveal trends of how citizen petitions interact with the generic approval process.

B RESULTS

As described in the opening section, the results of the study provide empirical evidence that the citizen petition process at the FDA has become a key avenue for strategic behavior by pharmaceutical companies to delay entry of generic competition. The following sections describe the core results.[20]

1 *Rise in Citizen Petitions with the Potential to Delay*

First, as Table 5.1 demonstrates below, it is notable just how many citizen petitions seem to have the potential to delay generic entry. Looking at the overall number of citizen petitions filed at the FDA on any topic, fourteen percent have the potential to delay a generic drug application, climbing to roughly twenty percent in some years. That means one in five of *all* citizen petitions to the FDA – not just those

---

[19] As an example, Petition FDA-2007-P-0418 was filed on November 9, 2007, the fourth quarter of 2007. We estimated that its relevant generic application, ANDA No. 78441, was filed in the third quarter of 2006. It was approved on May 14, 2009, the second quarter of 2009. Between the third quarter of 2006 (generic application filing) and the fourth quarter of 2007 (citizen petition filing), five quarter-years had passed, so the value of "Quarters Since Generic Filing" for this citizen petition is "5." Eighteen months and five days passed between November 9, 2007 (citizen petition filing) and May 14, 2009 (generic approval), so "Months Before Approval" for this petition is "18." Its "Total Approval Time," from the third quarter of 2006 to the second quarter of 2009, is eleven quarter-years.

[20] For a full reporting of the results, *see* Feldman, Frondorf, Cordova, & Wang, *supra* note 4.

TABLE 5.1 *All Delay-Related Petitions, by Year*

Year	Number of Delay-Related Petitions	Percentage of Yearly Total Petitions
2000	2	$2/47 = 4.3\%$
2001	4	$4/63 = 6.3\%$
2002	5	$5/106 = 4.7\%$
2003	12	$12/120 = 10.0\%$
2004	26	$26/178 = 14.6\%$
2005	15	$15/148 = 10.1\%$
2006	24	$24/184 = 13.0\%$
2007	25	$25/160 = 15.6\%$
2008	23	$23/166 = 13.9\%$
2009	32	$32/171 = 18.7\%$
2010	31	$31/149 = 20.8\%$
2011	22	$22/157 = 14.0\%$
2012	28	$28/141 = 19.9\%$
Total	**249**	$249/1{,}790 = 13.9\%$

concerning pharmaceuticals – have the potential to delay generic competition in those years.

This table also shows that petitions rose in popularity as a way to delay generics or raise issues about generics starting in 2003 and 2004. Not only did the number of citizen petitions rise noticeably after 2002, but the number of delay-related petitions also has sharply increased as a proportion of all petitions.

2 When Are Citizen Petitions Filed in Relation to Final Approval?

We now turn to the timing of when competitors file citizen petitions and the implications of that timing. The results we describe below show that many drug companies are filing citizen petitions as a last-ditch effort just months before generic approval. Moreover, many of these citizen petitions may be the *very last barrier* standing in the way of final generic approval.

These implications emerged when we graphed the amount of time between when a citizen petition was filed and when the generic application was approved. Our original hypothesis was that if citizen petitions are being used systematically to delay the approval of generics, citizen petitions might be deployed most effectively for that purpose near the end of a generic approval cycle. If filed earlier, a citizen

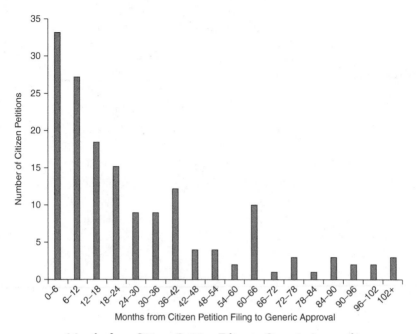

FIGURE 5.1 Months from Citizen Petition Filing to Generic Approval, 2000–2012

petition would merely introduce a review process running parallel to the rest of the generic approval process.

Figure 5.1 shows the results of this timing inquiry. First, we graphed the distribution of how many months passed between when the citizen petition was filed and when the generic received approval.

There is a clear trend in favor of citizen petitions filed shortly before the FDA approves a generic. Almost half were filed within a year and a half of generic approval.[21] In fact, the most common category was "0–6 months," with 33 petitions, or 21 percent of the total,[22] filed with *up to six months or less* remaining before the FDA approved the generic. Considering that the average length of time from generic filling to approval is roughly four years, this category occurs most often during the final leg of the approval process.

[21]   To clarify, we noted above that we had 164 citizen petitions with at least partial time line information. Of these, we had approval dates for 158 and thus could measure the time between filing of the citizen petition and approval of the generic. Of the 158 petitions, 78 petitions (or 49 percent) were filed within eighteen months of generic drug approval.

[22]   The number of citizen petitions filed six months before generic drug approval was 33 out of a total of 158 petitions (21 percent).

In other words, the trend is toward an increasing number of petitions as one moves closer to the final approval date. Thus, this histogram suggests that delay-related citizen petitions are often filed in the final stages of generic approval to raise concerns at the last minute, rather than early or midway through the process. This pattern potentially extends the length of the generic application approval process, thus delaying the market entry of generic competition.

3 How Did the 2007 Amendments Affect Citizen Petition Timing?

After years of hearings and debate on numerous FDA issues, Congress passed a large package of amendments in 2007. The 2007 Amendments included the largest reform of the citizen petition process in the petition program's thirty-year history.[23] These changes attempted to address concerns with citizen petitioning at the FDA, ranging from growing petition backlogs to signs that the process was being used inappropriately.[24]

Specifically, the 2007 Amendments added subsection "(q)" to the section of the code where most of the legislation relating to generic applications already resided. This new provision generally is called "505(q)" in academic and regulatory discussions, and the petitions that fall under it are called "505(q) petitions."

The added section applies a new set of regulations to all citizen petitions that ask the FDA to take action related to a pending generic application.[25] The section requires that the FDA respond to all such petitions within 180 days, a period that was shortened to 150 days in 2012.[26] Most important, Section 505(q) contains provisions intended to deter those who would file citizen petitions to delay generic competition. If a citizen petition relating to a generic application falls under 505(q), the person filing the petition must certify that the petition is not frivolous, all information favorable and unfavorable has been provided, and the petitioner did not intentionally delay filing the petition. The citizen petition also must provide the date when the

---

[23] FDA Amendments Act of 2007, Pub. L. No. 110-85, 121 Stat. 823 (2007) (codified as amended in scattered sections of 21 U.S.C.).

[24] *See* Carrier & Wander, *Citizen Petitions, supra* note 2, at 263 (quoting 153 Cong. Rec. 25,047 (2007)) (discussing testimony of Senator Edward Kennedy that "[t]he citizen petition provision is designed to address attempts to derail generic drug approvals. Those attempts, when successful, hurt consumers and the public health").

[25] Section 505(q) covers citizen petitions related to two categories of FDA approval applications. These are abbreviated new drug applications (ANDAs) and other forms of applications that rely on investigations not performed by or for the applicant. The latter form is referred to as 505(b)(2) applications. *See* Ctr. for Drug Evaluation & Research, FDA, Guidance for Industry: Applications Covered by Section 505(b)(2) (Oct. 1999), http://www.fda.gov/downloads/Drugs/.../Guidances/ucm079345.pdf.

[26] 21 U.S.C. § 355(q)(1)(f) (2015); Food and Drug Administration Safety and Innovation Act, Pub. L. No. 112-144, 126 Stat. 993 (2012) (codified as amended in scattered sections of 21 U.S.C.).

filer first became aware of the concern and the names of those who are funding the petition.[27]

Finally, 505(q) grants the FDA the power to summarily deny any petition it believes was filed with the "primary purpose" of delaying generic approval *if* the petition also does not "on its face raise valid scientific or regulatory issues."[28] Together, the provisions of section 505(q) were meant to end the abuse of citizen petitions by pharmaceutical companies.

The major changes to the citizen petition process beginning in 2007 serve as a natural break point in our data, allowing us to observe any effects of the legislation along with trends across time. In addition, some of the data reports mandated by the 2007 Amendments provided interesting information for our exploration.

Figure 5.2 looks specifically at the period before the 2007 Amendments. In this period, 41 percent of petitions were filed within a year and a half of approval.[29]

For the period after the 2007 Amendments, the trend is even more dramatic (see Figure 5.3). Fifty-six percent of the petitions were filed within a year and a half of generic approval.[30] In fact, a remarkable 46 percent of petitions (41 petitions) were filed within a year of generic approval. The "0–6 months" and "6-12 months" categories were by far the most popular, garnering 24 percent and 22 percent of the total, respectively.[31]

The biggest exogenous shift between the 2000 to mid-2007 histogram (Figure 5.2) and the mid-2007 to 2012 histogram (Figure 5.3) is, of course, the enactment of the 2007 Amendments. Its most notable change – requiring that the FDA respond to citizen petitions within 180 days – may explain why the post-2007 graph (Figure 5.3) paints such a dramatic picture of citizen petition timing.

Here is the observation: The FDA's 180-day time limit for responding to citizen petitions equates to six months, which aligns exactly with our smallest category of

---

[27] *Ibid.*

[28] *Ibid.*

[29] A total of 69 citizen petitions were filed in the period before the 2007 Amendments. Twenty-eight of them (41 percent) were filed within eighteen months of generic drug approval.

[30] In the post-2007 Amendments period, we measured a total of 89 citizen petitions relating to generic drug applications with approval dates available. Of those 89 petitions, 50 were filed (56 percent) within eighteen months of generic drug approval.

[31] In the post-2007 Amendments period, the number of citizen petitions filed within six months of generic approval was 21 out of a total of 89 petitions (24 percent). The number of citizen petitions filed between six and twelve months of generic approval was 20 out of a total of 89 petitions (22 percent). Our findings are consistent with another study using a different methodology. In their examination of generic-related citizen petitions filed between 2011 and 2015, Carrier and Minniti found that 39 percent of drugs named in petitions were subject to a citizen petition within six months of a brand-name drug's "exclusionary date" – the date when a brand-name patent or FDA exclusivity would expire. Carrier & Minniti, *Citizen Petitions, supra* note 2, at 338, 339 tbl.8; 98 percent of these "late-filed" petitions were denied. *Ibid.* at 341 & tbl.8. The choice of sample in this study was slightly different – Carrier and Minniti focused only on petitions given a "505(q)" designation by the FDA.

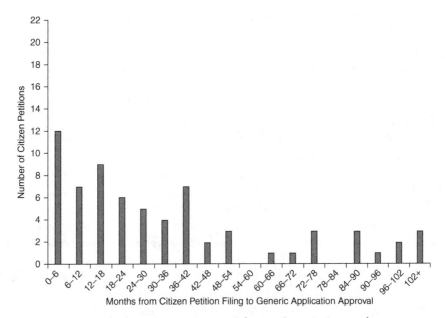

FIGURE 5.2 Months from Citizen Petition Filing to Generic Approval, 2000–2007

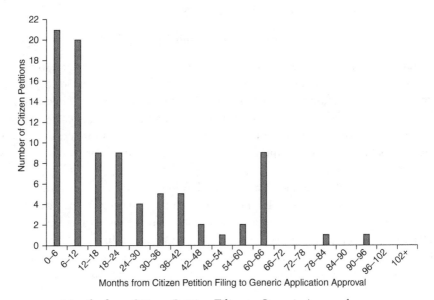

FIGURE 5.3 Months from Citizen Petition Filing to Generic Approval, 2007–2012

0-6 months. From this perspective, one can see that for a remarkable percentage of citizen petitions filed after 2007, approval for the relevant generic is occurring right around the time when the FDA must respond to the citizen petition. Specifically, from the middle of 2007 to 2012, we see a plurality of citizen petitions filed within six months of final generic approval.

This has two implications: first, many drug companies are filing citizen petitions as a last-ditch effort just months before generic approval; and, second, many of these citizen petitions may be the *last barrier* in the way of final generic approval. Anecdotally, this has certainly been the case for some petitions, as we saw in Chapter 3.

Put another way, when so many generic applications are approved within six months – the equivalent of 180 days – of when a citizen petition is filed, and the FDA had 180 days to respond to a citizen petition, the relationship does not seem to be mere coincidence. This may also explain why the trend toward late citizen petitions is not as pronounced in the period before the 2007 Amendments: citizen petitions may have still been filed during the late stages of the FDA's consideration of generic applications, but since the FDA was not held to a specific deadline for responding to citizen petitions, lengthy petition reviews could have pushed back the horizon for final generic approval by more than six months. Delving deeper into this striking correlation between the FDA's deadline of 180 days and the plurality of citizen petitions filed within 180 days of generic approval would be an interesting avenue for future research.

4 Did the 2007 Amendments Do the Job?

As described earlier, the 2007 Amendments require the FDA to respond to citizen petitions concerning generic applications within 180 days (shortened to 150 days in 2012); require those filing petitions to certify that the petition was not intentionally delayed and provide the date when the filer became aware of the concern; and give the FDA the power to deny petitions summarily in certain circumstances. Our study suggests that the 2007 Amendments have failed to stem the tide of citizen petitions intended to delay generic entry.

Imposing a deadline of 180 days for the FDA to respond may have reduced the length of the delay, but has by no means deterred the behavior. As detailed above, many competitor petitions continue to be filed late in the game, as a final attempt to delay competition just a little longer, even though they are unlikely to be successful. The same is likely true of the 2012 Amendments shortening the FDA's deadline to 150 days. The time is slightly shorter, but the incentives remain the same.[32]

---

[32] We cannot draw conclusions about the effects of the 2012 Amendments because our citizen petition data set only goes up to 2012. As discussed in Section A.2. above, we limited our data set to citizen

In particular, the FDA's power to dismiss frivolous petitions summarily appears toothless. In its own annual reports, the FDA has mentioned several times that the requirement that the petition both intend to delay a generic *and* raise no valid scientific or regulatory issue is a standard that is "extremely difficult to meet."[33] In fact, as of fiscal year 2014, the FDA had *never* denied a petition under this provision.[34]

The FDA has further complained about "serial petitioning," in which the Agency must respond to multiple petitions submitted sequentially about the same drug, a strategy that can delay approval for a considerable amount of time even though the FDA must respond to each petition within 150 days.[35] We examined one extreme instance in Chapter 4, with Doryx, when the brand-name company filed at least four citizen petitions over seven years. In a similar vein, the Federal Trade Commission (FTC) in early 2017 filed an antitrust action against Shire ViroPharma, alleging that the company abused regulatory processes by filing 43 submissions at the FDA (including 24 meritless citizen petition filings) in an effort to hold off generic competition for its gastrointestinal drug, Vancocin.[36] According to the complaint, the behavior resulted in hundreds of millions of dollars of cost to patients and other purchasers.[37]

In its annual reports, the FDA must show how many generic applications were delayed by citizen petitions.[38] On its face, the picture looks quite rosy. Of the relevant citizen petitions that the FDA has resolved in seven years of reporting (2008–14), only six petitions technically resulted in delay under the FDA's definition.[39] The problem, however, lies in the FDA's definition of a generic application delayed by a citizen petition. First, a citizen petition filed before the relevant generic application is submitted or pending is not subject to 505(q).[40] Second, if a generic application is not

---

petitions filed prior to 2013 when test analyses indicated that citizen petitions filed after that time frequently related to drugs that had not yet been approved.

33 U.S. Food & Drug Admin., *Seventh Annual Report to Congress on Delays in Approvals of Applications Related to Citizen Petitions and Petitions for Stay of Agency Action for Fiscal Year 2014*, at 10 (2015) [hereinafter "FDA Seventh Annual Report for FY 2014"].

34 *Ibid.*

35 *Ibid.* at 10.

36 Complaint for Injunctive and Other Equitable Relief, Fed. Trade Comm'n v. Shire ViroPharma, Inc., Case 1:17CV00131 (D. Del Feb. 7, 2017), https://www.ftc.gov/system/files/documents/cases/viropharma_file-stamped_redacted_complaint.pdf [hereinafter FTC Complaint]; *see also* Citizen Petition from ViroPharma, Inc., to Div. of Dockets Mgmt., U.S. Food & Drug Admin., No. FDA-2006-P-0007 (Mar. 17, 2006), https://www.regulations.gov/docket?D=FDA-2006-P-0007 (key citizen petition cited in the FTC's complaint).

37 FTC Complaint, *supra* note 36, at 2.

38 21 U.S.C. §355(q)(3)(B).

39 FDA Seventh Annual Report for FY 2014, *supra* note 33, at 9.

40 Wilson Sonsini Goodrich & Rosati, *Citizen Petitions Aimed at Delaying Generic Competition Remain a Concern*, at 1 (Feb. 11, 2015), www.wsgr.com/publications/PDFSearch/wsgralert-citizen-petitions.pdf.

ready for *immediate* approval at the 150-day response deadline, the Agency reports no delay.[41] Thus, the Agency finds no delay even if responding to the petition diverted focus from approving the application, slowing the process. Additional important categories of petitions also are not included under 505(q), including petitions that relate to the six-month exclusivity for the first generic filer or petitions about one's own application.[42] Painted this way, the citizen petition picture does not look so rosy.

In short, all of the trends we observed were stronger when examining the period after the 2007 Amendments in isolation. Part of this difference is likely due to the fact that the 180-day response deadlines enacted in the 2007 Amendments mean that some petitions are resolved more quickly. Thus, the period from citizen petition submission to generic approval is not stretched out as much by petitions as it often was before the 2007 reforms. However, considering we also found that the time between generic application filing and approval has not decreased since the 2007 Amendments – and may have actually increased – it appears that the reforms have not led to a systematic decrease in the length of time to get a generic application to market. Preventing delay, of course, was the goal of the 2007 Amendments. Finally, the number of delay-related petitions has not decreased over time, according to both our own analysis and the FDA's slightly different classification.[43]

These findings do not mean that the changes enacted in 2007 have been totally ineffective. The 180-day (and later 150-day) response deadlines for petitions certainly prevent any one citizen petition from extending the generic approval process for a significant time, a huge improvement over the days when petitions could be pending for years.[44] Nevertheless, while the potential magnitude of abuse may have been limited, the amount of abuse taking place does not seem to have declined. Many petitions are still filed very late in the approval process, the number of petitions has not declined, and there is evidence that petitions are filed even later after the passage of

---

[41] FDA Seventh Annual Report for FY 2014, *supra* note 33, at 9.

[42] *See Guidance for Industry: Citizen Petitions and Protests for Stay of Action Subject to 505(q) of the Federal Food, Drug, and Cosmetic Act*, U.S. Food & Drug Admin., at 4 (2014); *see also* 21 U.S.C. § 355(q)(4).

[43] In November 2016, the FDA promulgated a new rule on citizen petitions, strengthening some of the language and requirements, as well as ever so slightly widening the number of petitions that must make certifications by requiring certifications on petitions that "may" be subject to section 505(q). *See* U.S. Food & Drug Admin., Amendments to Regulations on Citizen Petitions, Petitions for Stay of Action, and Submission of Documents to Dockets (Nov. 8, 2016), http://www.federalregister.gov/documents/2016/11/08/2016-26912/amendments-to-regulations-on-citizen-petitions-petitions-for-stay-of-action-and-submission-of. The language follows the same general approach, however, without changing the incentive structure or enhancing the deterrent. Thus, it is unclear that the changes will lead to the desired effect.

[44] *See* Carrier & Wander, *Citizen Petitions, supra* note 2, at 285–86 (detailing a citizen petition that delayed the introduction of a generic version of the insomnia drug Ambien for more than three years at a cost of $3.1 billion).

the 2007 Amendments. As long as the benefits of 180 days of delay (or even 150 days of delay) can be worth hundreds of millions of dollars, companies will be tempted to follow this path, and consumers will continue to pay the price. A different approach is needed.

C THE ROAD AHEAD

As the results demonstrate, the citizen petition process has been hijacked by pharmaceutical companies as a route to frustrate generic approvals. We found evidence that many citizen petitions are not filed as soon as potentially worrisome information about a drug is discovered, but are instead filed near the later stages of the generic approval process. Nearly half of potentially delay-related citizen petitions between 2000 and 2012 were filed within a year and a half of approval, with numbers even higher when the data are restricted to the period after the 2007 Amendments. In fact, 46 percent of the post-2007 Amendment citizen petitions were filed within a year of final approval of the generic drug, and 24 percent were filed within six months. These findings suggest that the citizen petitions were some of the last barriers to approval for some generics.

Also troubling is that citizen petitions appear to be a significant catalyst and foundation for attempting a variety of other obstructionist delay strategies. Many of the delay tactics outlined in Chapter 4 operate through the citizen petition process. Thus, citizen petitions are now a key portal through which pharmaceutical companies attempt to make changes and raise concerns (often spurious ones) to obstruct or delay generic approval. At the moment, the FDA appears powerless to stop it, but what pathways would be more effective?

Looking at the nature of the problem, one could imagine three types of approaches to curb the behavior of filing citizen petitions to delay generic entry. These might include (1) a simple prohibition on competitors filing citizen petitions related to generic entry, if one were to conclude that most behavior represented by this type of petition is likely to be inappropriate; (2) procedural blocks to ensure that the behavior cannot create suboptimal results; or (3) punitive measures as a deterrent. The following sections describe each and set out mechanisms for accomplishing the goals. The details of the mechanism are less important, however, than choosing among the pathways and identifying the proper incentive structures and the optimal institutional actors.

1 A Simple Prohibition

The simplest approach for curbing abuse of the citizen petition process would be to prevent competitors from filing citizen petitions related to generic applications.

This would be analogous to the per se rules in antitrust. If one concludes that the vast majority of behavior within a certain category is likely to be improper, societal resources may be better served by declaring the category per se off limits, rather than weighing each instance.

This approach carries a certain cynicism regarding the likelihood that companies would have society's best interests in mind when commenting on whether the FDA should trust their competitors to enter the market. The approach implies that in these circumstances, one should consider competitors to be somewhat like the fox offering to guard the henhouse.[45] The incentives are not well aligned with the desired outcome.

Although banning competitors from filing citizen petitions is a simple approach, it is also simplistic. Pharmaceutical companies are likely to argue that, as the actors in the field most familiar with a drug, they are best positioned to sound the alarm when problems are on the horizon. Nor would this approach necessarily be fully effective. Companies could still submit generalized citizen petitions before any generic applications. They could also file petitions that have the effect of delaying entry – for example, by asking the FDA to reconsider all labeling related to the drug – without specifically requesting a delay.

2 *Procedural Blocks*

An alternative approach would involve enacting procedural blocks to channel the behavior into positive, rather than suboptimal, results. In other words, one might preserve the citizen petition process for all – including competitors – while ensuring that citizen petitions filed by competitors do not delay generic entry.

For example, one might direct that citizen petitions filed by competitors must be filed within a year of when the generic company files for approval.[46] Given that the average length of time for a generic application to move from filing to approval is roughly four years, citizen petitions filed within a year of when the generic application was filed are less likely to delay final approval.

Similarly, when competitors raise an issue related to the drug in general, the rule could be that the generic application goes forward on a timeline unrelated to the citizen petition. In other words, the generic can receive approval if the FDA determines that the drug meets the Agency's standards, and whatever issue is raised

---

[45] See *The CREATES ACT: Ending Regulatory Abuse, Protecting Consumers, and Ensuring Drug Price Competition: Hearing Before the S. Comm. On the Judiciary Subcomm. on Antitrust, Competition Policy and Consumer Rights*, 114th Cong. 58 (2016) (transcript of statement of Robin Feldman, using fox analogy in response to a senator's question) (transcript on file with author).

[46] This would require that the FDA make all generic applications public and easily searchable when they are filed.

can be resolved after that approval, if necessary. After all, the branded drug remains on the market under the current requirements for the drug, which suggests that the issues raised in the citizen petition, at least in some cases, are not of such magnitude that the drug cannot be offered to the public. Thus, whatever issues must be resolved would be resolved as to all forms of the drug – generic and brand-name – on a timeline unrelated to the generic's approval. One could refer to this as the "band plays on" rule. Even for issues related to whether the generic is bioequivalent or satisfies the FDA's requirements, one could once again conclude that the Agency is generally the best judge of that – at least with issues so serious that approval must be denied.

One concern is that although most citizen petitions are denied, some are granted. This suggests that occasionally, legitimate issues are at stake, and safety must remain the FDA's primary focus. Looking at concerns from the other direction, a "band plays on rule" still may squander some societal resources. The FDA must spend time responding to each concern raised. Similarly, branded companies could still use the tactic of filing citizen petitions to raise their rivals' costs.[47] In other words, generic competitors conceivably could be forced to spend time and money responding to spurious issues raised. Nevertheless, with the prospect of delayed entry off the table, such a procedural block could substantially reduce a brand-name company's incentives to engage in this behavior. Of the choices discussed here, this may, indeed, be the most effective.

3 Punitive Deterrents

The third approach would be to adopt some form of punitive measure designed to deter abuse of the citizen petition process, through either the courts or the FDA. Thus, parties that engage in behavior to try to block or delay generic entry through citizen petitions could be subject to a penalty calibrated to deter all but the hardiest of souls from engaging in the behavior in the first place.

In contemplating this approach, the initial question would involve determining the proper adjudicatory body to task with deciding whether the behavior falls beyond bounds. In theory, one might suggest that the FDA is the proper adjudicatory body. After all, the FDA has the greatest expertise for evaluating whether the issues raised in a citizen petition are spurious or well-founded.

The FDA, however, has proven more effective at evaluating patient safety than party behavior. Since 2007, the Agency has had the power to summarily deny any petition

---

[47] *See, generally,* Thomas G. Krattenmaker & Steven C. Salop, *Anticompetitive Exclusion: Raising Rivals' Costs to Achieve Power over Price,* 96 YALE L.J. 209 (1986) (seminal work identifying ability of competitors to impose costs on rivals without similarly incurring such costs).

filed with the primary purpose of delaying generic approval if the petition does not also raise valid scientific or regulatory issues.[48] As noted, the FDA had not used the provision even once through fiscal year 2014. It is certainly possible that a differently worded authority would prompt greater activity from the Agency, but one could argue that the FDA may not be the right fit for such a role. The FDA may be better suited to evaluate science-related bad behavior than competition-related bad behavior.

An alternative would be to provide greater power for competition authorities (such as the Federal Trade Commission (FTC) or the Department of Justice (DOJ)) or third-party actors (such as the competitors who suffer harm) to act against anti-competitive behavior involving citizen petitions. Antitrust actions, however, are slow and expensive.[49] Moreover, if the experience with pay-for-delay settlements is a guide, by the time the courts slowly begin choking off the behavior, pharmaceutical companies will have altered their tactics. Antitrust law simply may not be sufficiently nimble.

Most important, providing an effective antitrust pathway for challenging citizen petitions may require substantial shifts in doctrines related to antitrust and regulatory agencies. As described in Chapter 4, the *Noerr-Pennington* line of cases, dating back to the 1960s, establishes the general principle that one has the right to petition the government without fear of antitrust liability. Although antitrust liability may still attach if one's petition to the government is judged to be a "sham," the bar for establishing a sham petition, at the moment, is extremely high.[50]

Certain types of citizen petition actions could be even more difficult to attack under antitrust law. For example, if citizen petitions are used to prevent a generic hopeful from obtaining samples of the branded product – which the generic needs in order to demonstrate that its drug is bioequivalent – antitrust actors trying to challenge the behavior would also run up against *Trinko*.[51] In the *Trinko* opinion, the Supreme Court all but shut the door on antitrust actions that claim a party's competitor has improperly refused to sell to it. In general, competitors are not required to sell to each other, and as the Department of Justice has argued, refusals to deal or "forced sharing" rarely helps consumers in the long run.[52] Although providing

---

[48] *See* 21 U.S.C. §355(q)(1)(E) (2012).

[49] *See generally* Robin Feldman, *Ending Patent Exceptionalism and Structuring the Rule of Reason: The Supreme Court Opens the Door for Both*, 15 MINN. J.L. SCI. & TECH 61 (2014).

[50] For a detailed discussion of the history of the *Noerr-Pennington* doctrine and its operation in practice, see Robin Feldman, *Federalism, First Amendment & Patents: The Fraud Fallacy*, 17 COLUM. SCI. & TECH. L. REV. 30 (2015).

[51] *See Verizon Comm. Inc. v. Law Offices of Curtis V. Trinko LLP.*, 540 U.S. 398 (2004).

[52] *See* U.S. Dep't of Justice, *Competition and Monopoly: Single-Firm Conduct Under Section 2 of the Sherman Act*, Ch. 7, Unilateral, Unconditional Refusals to Deal with Rivals (2008), www.justice .gov/atr/competition-and-monopoly-single-firm-conduct-under-section-2-sherman-act-chapter-7; *see also* Geoffrey Manne, *Senator Lee's Prescription for Regulatory Failure in the Generic Drug Market*

samples for generic approval may be the rare exception to the rule, getting past *Trinko* would be difficult.

In short, Congress or the Supreme Court would have to be willing to alter anti-trust doctrines in a manner sufficient to allow antitrust actors to bring successful litigation – without, of course, breaking the bank in the process. A punitive measure that costs exorbitant amounts to activate will have very little deterrent effect.

4 Transparency

No approach is a perfect or permanent solution. Fixing abuse of the citizen petition pathway may require a combination of these approaches. Moreover, this book shows that when the legal system closes off one pathway, pharmaceutical companies will search for others. Thus, whatever paths and approaches are chosen to curb citizen petition abuse, it will be critical to ensure that regulators, legislators, and courts can see new techniques as they emerge. A little sunshine goes a long way.

In particular, greater transparency from the FDA could be tremendously effective in exposing new drug pricing schemes early on. Although the FDA makes a wealth of information publicly available, there are significant gaps in the system. For example, as described in Section A, there is no systematic way to find the date on which a generic application was filed. Perhaps all generic applications should be posted when filed, along with the date of their filing, and the public should not have to wait until the generic is approved to find that information, if it even appears in the approval letter. As it stands now, the more effective a drug company is at blocking generic competition, the longer that company has before anyone outside of the FDA can see what is being done.

At the very least, however, once a generic application has been approved, the public should be able to tell easily when the application was filed. Specifically, all approval letters should be posted on the FDA website, and the FDA website should always list filing and approval dates for every generic, and not just in these letters.

Unfortunately, the FDA appears to be moving in the opposite direction and lessening transparency. For our study, we were able to extract filing dates from some of the approval letters that the FDA posted and back fill many others through our estimation technique when the FDA approval letters did not mention the filing date. The FDA recently changed its protocols, however, so that the public will no longer be able to do even that. According to one report, the FDA has initiated a new

(June 14, 2016), https://truthonthemarket.com/2016/06/14/senator-lees-prescription-for-regulatory-failure-in-the-generic-drug-market (describing *Trinko* as an impediment to antitrust cases regarding refusals to provide samples to generic applicants).

protocol in which it will omit from approval letters any mention of the filing date of the original generic application.[53]

Other basic information could improve transparency as well, including more complete labeling of citizen petitions themselves, and full information on generic application numbers and how they are assigned. Finally, the massive Freedom of Information Act (FOIA) backlog at the FDA also operates to mask improper behavior. When we inquired for our research, Agency personnel were wonderfully helpful but noted that FOIA requests would require approximately two years for a response.

Making full data on generic applications quickly and clearly available to the public is essential for curbing inappropriate behavior. Particularly if the FDA is not assigned the full task of policing competition, other actors – including state and federal regulators, legislators, academic researchers, public interest groups, and generics companies themselves – must have easy access to the relevant information. Transparency efforts such as these, along with the types of approaches described here for curbing attempts to delay generic competition through citizen petitions, are essential for addressing the problems. Without such endeavors, we will continue to see a citizen's process diverted to the service of pharmaceutical companies playing games to hold off generic entry as long as possible. Consumers, of course, pay the price. In our Conclusion, we will scale some of our specific citizen petition recommendations to address the larger problem of pharmaceutical delay in general. In other words, where do we go from here?

---

[53] Pollock, *Do You Notice Something Missing? supra* note 11.

Conclusion

A Call for Systematic Reform

Thirty years of the Hatch-Waxman regime have produced an extraordinary revolution in the introduction of generic drugs. The progress, however, has not been without resistance. As detailed throughout the book, pharmaceutical companies have engaged in three waves of behaviors to stave off generic competition as long as possible. The first generation involves paying generic companies to delay their entry into the market – that is, sharing a portion of monopoly profits with a generic in exchange for an agreement to delay competition. With antitrust scrutiny of such behaviors on the horizon, pharmaceutical companies developed a further generation of behaviors centered on multiple side deals, in which the companies settle many cases at once or agree to provide overvalued or undervalued services to each other as a way to camouflage the value of the transfers occurring in exchange for delayed entry. Each of these approaches is a clever way to try to obfuscate the nature of the behavior. Finally, Generation 3.0 games no longer focus on colluding with generic competitors; instead, the games rely on microobstructions against generic companies. These include using administrative processes, regulatory schemes with connections to Hatch-Waxman, and drug modifications to obstruct generics from getting to market. Further, they often combine a number of these tactics to create a multiplicity effect. Of course, Generations 2.0 and 3.0 can be combined by developing obstructive behaviors and then promising not to engage in them, using what we call boy scout clauses.

Of all of the approaches, the boy scout clauses are perhaps the most cynical. Here, a brand-name company engages in collusive behavior to prevent competition while trying to insulate itself from attack by claiming that it is behaving honorably. While boy scout clauses may be particularly cynical, all of the Generation 3.0 approaches threaten a new wave of behaviors that will be difficult for Congress, the courts, and regulatory agencies to control.

A SOCIETAL HARMS

The strategic behaviors in the Hatch-Waxman arena are troubling from the perspective of the theoretical underpinnings of both patent and antitrust law. The patent concern traces back to the constitutional provision that frames all of patent law. From the activities that should be free to all and reserved to none, the patent system chooses to dedicate to some, for a limited period, the exclusive use of an innovation, based on the theory that this exclusion will redound to the benefit of society.[1] The bargain, however, is not unlimited. When the patent expires, everyone should be free to engage in those activities, returning to a competitive environment. Hatch-Waxman is intended to ensure the prompt return to a competitive environment at the end of the patent term, as well as to create incentives to weed out weak patent claims that are improperly keeping competitors out of the particular innovative space. Pharmaceutical company behavior that extends the period in which the company can hold off competition runs contrary to the patent bargain in general and to Hatch-Waxman in particular.

The behaviors described in this book also raise antitrust concerns, although those concerns are framed at a slightly different angle.[2] As a general matter in antitrust doctrine, big is not necessarily bad; it is what you do with your size that matters.[3] Thus, brand-name companies that have earned a monopoly in the market with their blockbuster drugs are targets of antitrust concern only when they attempt to extend their monopoly improperly by colluding with competitors or inappropriately suppressing competition. As scholarly works by one of the authors and others have noted, agreements not to compete and activities that abuse the regulatory process to block competitors raise antitrust concerns.[4] Thus, when pharmaceutical companies improperly delay or impede the entry of generic competition, that behavior runs contrary to the open, competitive market environment for which antitrust law yearns.

The theoretical concerns translate into tangible damage to society as well. With patents, the legal system chooses to tolerate certain societal losses for the innovation effects that may result. When brand-name companies extend their monopoly power

---

[1]   *See* U.S. CONST., art. I, § 8, cl. 8 ("To promote the Progress of [the] useful Arts, by securing for limited Times to … Inventors the exclusive Right to their respective … Discoveries."); *see also* Robin Feldman, *Intellectual Property Wrongs*, 18 STAN. J.L. BUS. & FIN. 250, 318 (2013).

[2]   For a discussion of the differing perspectives of patent law and antitrust law regarding inappropriate behavior by patent holders, see generally Robin Feldman, *Patent and Antitrust: Differing Shades of Meaning*, 13 VA. J.L. & TECH. 5 (2008).

[3]   Tom Ewing & Robin Feldman, *The Giants Among Us*, 2012 STAN. TECH. L. REV. 1, 26 (2012).

[4]   *See, e.g., ibid.* at 26–33; Michael A. Carrier, Nicole L. Levidow & Aaron S. Kesselheim, *Using Antitrust Law to Challenge Turing's Daraprim Price Increase*, 31 BERKELEY TECH. L.J., at *31 (2016), http://ssrn.com/abstract=2724604; C. Scott Hemphill, *An Aggregate Approach to Antitrust: Using New Data and Rulemaking to Preserve Drug Competition*, 109 COLUM. L. REV. 629 (2009).

beyond the expiration of the patents, however, there are unanticipated deadweight losses to society in the form of higher prices. Whether Congress has chosen the optimal parameters for the patent system is a separate question. Once those parameters are set, behaviors that cause additional deadweight losses for society are contrary to the system's incentive structure, and the damage to society should not be tolerated.

The Hatch-Waxman manipulations also are damaging to society in the form of activities that are wasteful for companies and institutions alike. Hide-and-seek games that the courts, the FDA, the FTC, and the Patent and Trademark Office are forced to play are wasteful to all. The games are particularly burdensome on the court system, with pharmaceutical litigation regarding generic competition now joining patent troll litigation as a major component of new patent lawsuit filings.[5] Sadly, given the amount of money at stake, the behaviors are likely to continue unless the legal system finds a way to change the incentives or to create sufficient disincentives. This is not to suggest that progress has been negligible. The shift from simple pay-for-delay agreements to side deals and then to microobstructions reflects the progress that regulatory agencies have begun to achieve in the courts. In addition, although microobstructions can create a valuable delay in competition, they are more difficult to achieve and often less lengthy than pay-for-delay.

Nevertheless, although the form of the behavior may have shifted, the behavior remains. Moreover, although changes such as the Supreme Court decision in *Actavis* and various congressional amendments have been important, by the time the changes are implemented, the market has moved beyond. The question is, what should happen next.

The following discussion explores new directions for the legal system in its continuing efforts to alleviate the gamesmanship that the Hatch-Waxman system has wrought. The discussion is not intended to provide a blueprint for legislation or a description of specific doctrinal provisions. Rather, it is an attempt to suggest the contours of how new approaches could be structured, and to generate discussion of a shift in approach.

B SYSTEMS, SIMPLIFICATION, SUNSHINE, AND STANDARDS-BASED DOCTRINES

In addition to the approaches that have been undertaken so far, managing the evolution of the Hatch-Waxman games will require a systems approach. One could use an

---

[5] *See* Jacqueline Bell, *Smartphone, Pharma Giants Dominate List of Top IP Targets*, Law360 (Feb. 10, 2016), www.law360.com/articles/756254/smartphone-pharma-giants-dominate-list-of-top-ip-targets (noting that the number of new patent lawsuits filed in 2015 increased by 15 percent over the prior year and that generic pharmaceutical companies were frequent targets of those lawsuits, along with technology companies); *2015 Patent Dispute Report*, UNIFIED PATS. http://unifiedpatents.com/2015-year-end-report/ (showing the prevalence of lawsuits filed by nonpracticing entities in 2015).

analogy from the medical field itself.[6] Under the old approach to cancer treatment, physicians would attack a tumor by trying to reduce its size or deny substances that seemed to be feeding it. Modern medical research has suggested, however, that cancer treatment can be far more effective when using a systems approach. Specifically, tumors seem to operate in a networked or systems fashion. Cutting off one approach may simply lead the tumor to develop work-around approaches, and the new approaches may be even more dangerous and damaging than the original pathway. Thus, attacking the problem by trying to mitigate it when it emerges may be as outdated an approach for the patenting and approval of medicines as it is for treatments in which those medicines will be involved.[7]

Taking a systems approach may allow us to move away from what one of the authors has called death by tinkering – a problem endemic throughout the patent system.[8] In this problematic approach, legal actors address difficult questions by adjusting the doctrines a little here and a little there without developing a comprehensive logic for the full breadth of the legal area. Eventually, the entire doctrinal base threatens to collapse under its own weight.

One can see a classic example of death by tinkering in the Federal Circuit's failed attempts to create a workable rule for determining what types of inventions should qualify as patentable subject matter. For years, the court clung to its infamous "machine-or-transformation" test,[9] making ever-finer distinctions to try to prevent uncomfortable results. In the end, the test required considerable hand waving, and one had to suspend a certain amount of disbelief to overlook the logical discrepancies.[10] After a series of three cases gently encouraging the Federal Circuit to develop a workable test, the Supreme Court eventually gave up and supplied its own test.[11]

---

[6] This system theory example is taken from Robin Feldman, *Cultural Property and Human Cells*, 21 INT'L J. CULTURAL PROP. 1, 6 (2014).

[7] *Cf.* Feldman, *Intellectual Property Wrongs, supra* note 1, at 255 (noting that when a comprehensive problem exists, the answer lies in attacking its roots, in addition to trimming the tendrils as they emerge in various places).

[8] *See* Robin Feldman, *A Conversation on Judicial Decision-Making*, 5 HASTINGS SCI. & TECH. L.J. 1, 2 (2013) (introducing the concept in the context of Federal Circuit attempts to fix problems in patent doctrines such as patentable subject matter without taking into account the doctrinal area as a whole).

[9] The machine-or-transformation test suggested that the Holy Grail for patentability of certain types of inventions would be to determine whether the invention was tied to a machine or resulted in a transformation. *See Bilski v. Kappos*, 130 S. Ct. 3218, 3227 (2010) (rejecting the Federal Circuit's machine-or-transformation test as the sole test for patentability of process inventions).

[10] *See* Robin Feldman, *Coming of Age for the Federal Circuit*, 18 GREEN BAG 2D 27, 32–33 (2014). For a detailed discussion of the problems with the Federal Circuit's machine-or-transformation test, see Feldman, *A Conversation on Judicial Decision-Making, supra* note 8, at 15–20, 23–25. *See also* ROBIN FELDMAN, RETHINKING PATENT LAW 113–24 (2012) (describing various failed tests the Federal Circuit has tried for patentable subject matter).

[11] Feldman, *Coming of Age, supra* note 10, at 7 (describing the final opinion in the Supreme Court's quartet, *Alice Corp. Pty. Ltd. v. CLS Bank Int'l*, 134 S. Ct. 2347 (2014), along with the justices' three

In the pharmaceutical context, the first step in a systems approach would involve focusing on the extent to which various systems interact in the process. These include not only the patent approval system, but also the patent litigation system,[12] FDA approval systems – including the Orange Book, REMS, citizens' petitions, and other FDA processes – and antitrust doctrines as they apply to this arena. It will also require thinking about how the patent-based aspects of the generic approval system interact with more than a dozen nonpatent exclusivities available to pharmaceutical companies for things such as pediatric trials, new chemical entities, orphan drugs, and many more.[13] Effective progress will require working with all of these systems at the same time, lest adjustments to one area lead to counteraction in another. With 30 years of Hatch-Waxman experience, it is time to consider a comprehensive overhaul of the system for generic approval, one that looks more broadly at the interaction of all of the systems.

The second step is to simplify ruthlessly. For those who value complexity, the Hatch-Waxman system is a garden of delights. Complexity breeds opportunity, however, and, in the case of Hatch-Waxman, the act's complexity has spawned opportunities for manipulation. An overhaul of the Hatch-Waxman system that resulted in equivalent or even greater complexity would serve little purpose, other than as a full employment act for lawyers. In contrast, a simplified, slimmed-down system would provide fewer opportunities for clever gamesmanship, as well as absorbing fewer resources for the system as a whole.

From this perspective, the 2009 Biologics Price Competition and Innovation Act ("BPCIA," also commonly known as the "Biosimilars Act") is not encouraging. The legislation was intended to provide a pathway for swift approval of biosimilars, or what could be called generic biologic drugs, in the same way that Hatch-Waxman provided a speedier pathway for ordinary generic drugs. Biologics are complex cell-derived drugs. They differ from the more familiar chemical drugs, such as aspirin, and include antibodies that fight autoimmune diseases and proteins that boost white

---

prior attempts to prompt the Federal Circuit in *Bilski v. Kappos*, 561 U.S. 593, 659 (2010), *Mayo Collaborative Services v. Prometheus Laboratories, Inc.*, 132 S. Ct. 1289 (2012), and *Association for Molecular Pathology v. Myriad Genetics, Inc.*, 133 S. Ct. 2107 (2013)); *see also* Robin Feldman, *Rethinking Rights in Biospace*, 79 So. Cal. L. Rev. 1, 8–12 (2006) (describing a similar phenomenon that plagues the various doctrines related to whether the definition of an invention reaches beyond the state of the art at the time of the invention).

[12] In light of the introduction of more robust forms of postgrant review in the 2011 patent reform America Invents Act, a comprehensive approach would also need to consider how those systems interact with Hatch-Waxman and how they could be used for gamesmanship.

[13] For a discussion of the 13 different nonpatent exclusivities, see Robin Feldman, *Regulatory Property: The New IP* 40 Columbia J.L & Arts 53 (2016) (arguing that these powerful exclusionary forces must be considered as a coherent whole to make sense of how they interact with each other and with other IP rights systems such as patent and trade secret).

blood cell counts during chemotherapy. Biologics such as Humira and Sovaldi are already among the world's top-selling prescription drugs. The Biosimilars Act, however, is even more complex and convoluted than Hatch-Waxman and seems designed on entirely the wrong template.[14] It was not until September 2015 – six years after the act's passage – that the first biosimilar reached the market.[15]

Already, new games and disputes are bubbling up to the courts. A case on the biosimilar approval process, *Amgen v. Sandoz*, was heard by the Federal Circuit in 2015,[16] and a core section of the dispute focused on the definition of the word "shall" in a BPCIA statute related to information disclosure[17] – a disclosure process already called the "patent dance" by many commentators. The battlegrounds of biosimilar game playing already have names! From the start, the brave new biosimilar era seems unable to escape the ghosts of its small-molecule cousins, such as intentionally obtuse citizen petitions or the confusing questions of statutory interpretation that led to the Abilify dispute in Chapter 4. Within the first page of the Federal Circuit opinion, the circuit judge cites Winston Churchill, calling the BPCIA "a riddle wrapped in a mystery inside an enigma."[18] Overall, not a great start for biologics.

Leaving biologics out of any solution calculus, however, would be a grave mistake. A third of the new drugs approved in 2015 were biologics, and it would make little sense to fix a regulatory problem, but leave out a third of the new drugs. Biologics represent the future of pharmaceuticals and will be the source of revolutionary new patient treatments.

Simplification is not the instinct of lawyers in general nor of patent lawyers in particular. Lawyers are trained to see the nuances in any circumstance and may wish to keep options open for whatever their clients need. Moreover, the patent bar has never been accused of an attraction to exorbitant simplicity. Overcoming these instincts, which are deeply embedded in the habits of patent stakeholders, will be an essential component of designing a more effective system.

The third step is to let the sun shine in. Both markets and regulators work best when information is fully available – information that invites competition where competition is needed and exposes behavior that regulators can challenge. Moreover, in a world of instant communication, information plays a powerful role

---

[14] *See generally* Jason Kanter & Robin Feldman, *Understanding and Incentivizing Biosimilars*, 64 HASTINGS L.J. 57 (2012) (analyzing and identifying issues with the Biosimilars Act).

[15] *See* Ben Hirschler & Michael Shields, *Novartis Launches First U.S. 'Biosimilar' Drug at 15 Percent Discount*, REUTERS (Sept. 3, 2015), www.reuters.com/article/us-novartis-drug-idUSKCN0R30C220 150903 (reporting on the release of a biosimilar version of Amgen's Neupogen).

[16] *Amgen Inc. v. Sandoz Inc.*, No. 2015-1499 (Fed. Cir. 2015), slip op. available at www.cafc.uscourts.gov/sites/default/files/15-1499.pdf.

[17] *Ibid.* at *10–15.

[18] *Ibid.* at *3 n.1.

in disciplining behavior. Information in pharmaceutical deals and pricing is increasingly segmented, however, and hidden from key players in the industry – whether those players are competitors, regulators, or consumers.

What we have discussed in this book about generic competition is only the tip of the pharmaceutical pricing iceberg. In particular, pricing is not necessarily drug-specific anymore. Rather, "pharmaceutical benefit managers," known as PBMs, negotiate the prices for the vast majority of commercially insured drug purchases.[19] In other words, PBMs are third-party intermediaries that negotiate drug prices between payers and others. This frequently results in bundled drug pricing, tucked into which may be pricing that reaps supracompetitive rewards or blocks generic competition. For example, a drug company could offer attractive discounts on one drug in exchange for pricing or listing practices that block competition where prices are elevated or competition would be a greater threat.

None of this information is available, either to the market or to regulators. The pharmaceutical ecosystem would benefit tremendously from sunshine rules that require disclosure of PBM pricing deals and rebates, some of which are now being considered. This is not to suggest regulation of pricing, but rather to provide the information that markets and regulators need for efficient functioning.

A fourth step would be to move away from the Supreme Court's rule of reason analysis for pharmaceutical deals that involve generics. Despite the opening that the Supreme Court created in *Actavis*, the lower courts largely have been unable or unwilling to walk through it very far. The burden remains too great for anyone to bear. Rather, with deals involving generic entry, Congress should place the burden on those who are making the deals to show that the deals are proper.[20] The taint of anticompetitive behavior is too strong throughout these arrangements, and the extent to which these deals undermine Hatch-Waxman's intent to introduce generics early and often is too great. One who creates complexity, and the resultant capacity to hide behind that complexity, should have the burden to demonstrate that the effects are justifiable.

The most important step, however, is to make more liberal use of standards-based legal doctrines. The Hatch-Waxman system and its various amendments have tended to focus on precise and particularized legal rules. A typical example is the rule that brand-name drug companies are forbidden to receive more than one 30-month stay; the FDA must take final action on a citizen petition in 150 days.

---

[19] 149 Cong. Rec. 15,570 (2003).

[20] At least two bills have been introduced that would begin to shift the burden for some pay-for-delay settlements. *See* Preserve Access to Affordable Generics Act, S. 2019, 114th Cong. (2015); Prescription Drug Affordability Act of 2015, S. 2023, 114th Cong. (2015).

Some fixes have leaned toward the standards approach. For example, the FDA's ability to deny a citizen petition at any time if it believes a petition was "submitted with the primary purpose of delaying the approval of an application" is an excellent example of a standards-based approach. The amendment granting that power, however, goes on to require that the "petition does not on its face raise valid scientific or regulatory issues,"[21] a provision that moves back toward the realm of rule-based approaches. Plus, as we have described, the rule has been interpreted in such a way that it has never been used to deny a citizen petition.

A classic standards-based approach can be found in the tax code's "step transaction doctrine." The doctrine allows tax authorities to collapse all the steps of a transaction together if the authority deems that they are part of an overall plan by the taxpayer to avoid taxation by taking a circuitous route.[22] Thus, the doctrine looks at the result and intent of the overall plan, rather than focusing on whether each detail technically passes muster. A more liberal use of this type of standards-based approach could give courts and regulators the latitude to shut down strategic behavior, as opposed to playing cat and mouse across the regulatory provisions.

One should not be overly optimistic. From a political economy perspective, the pressure on members of Congress to avoid an overhaul of the system – let alone a simplified approach that will close off strategic behavior – will be great. When Congress tried to block Hatch-Waxman strategic behaviors in the 2003 amendments to the act, Congressman Henry Waxman, one of the original authors of the act, addressed the pharmaceutical industry:

> I call upon the brand-name industry to cease and desist from inventing new games, and that they return to the scientific research that they are good at and that has been their real contribution.[23]

The congressman's comments appear to have been in vain. Nevertheless, a comprehensive overhaul of Hatch-Waxman, that takes a systems perspective, focuses on simplification, and includes a healthy dose of standards-based authority, could go a long way toward placing these drug wars under control. After 30 years of experience with Hatch-Waxman, it is time for the next phase. Otherwise, we will all keep paying the price.

---

[21]   21 U.S.C. § 355(q)(1)(E) (2012).

[22]   *See* Feldman, *Intellectual Property Wrongs, supra* note 1, at 310 (describing the value of using this type of doctrine in the patent context).

[23]   FELDMAN, *Intellectual Property Wrongs, supra* note 1, at 160 (citing Press Release, Henry A. Waxman, Representative Henry A. Waxman on the Delay of Approval of Generic Drugs (Nov. 20, 2001), www .citizen.org/congress/article_redirect.cfm?ID=6496).

Index

Abbreviated New Drug Application (ANDA), 21, 118. *See also* generic drug application; Hatch-Waxman Act (U.S., 1984)

AbbVie, 6

Abilify (antipsychotic, Otsuka), 110–12

acceleration clauses, 57–59

Accupril (hypertension drug), 53–56

Actavis (drug company)
- *FTC v. Actavis* and, 24, 43–45, 49–50, 65
- product hopping of Namenda to Namenda XR, 76–78

Actelion (drug company), 82–83

active ingredient
- defined, 27
- strength of, 27

Actos (antidiabetic drug, Takeda), 58–59

Aleve (naproxen), 4

Alice line of cases, 84

Alnylam, 6

antitrust cases, 24. *See also FTC v. Actavis*
- as curb of citizen petitions as delay tactic, 133–35
- *In re Cipro* (California Supreme Court), 46–47
- *In re Loestrin*, 61, 64
- *Noerr-Pennington* cases, 99–100, 134
- rule of reason test in, 45–46
- Teva over provigil (narcolepsy drug), 47–48
- *Trinko* opinion, 134

Approved Drug Products with Therapeutic Equivalence Evaluations. *See* Orange Book

Argatroban (drug to prevent blood clotting), 117

Asacol (chronic ulcerative colitis drug, Warner Chilcott), 74–76

AstraZeneca
- product hopping of Prilosec to Nexium by, 71–74

authorized generics, 59–60

automatic substitution laws, 20

Bayer, 46

Best Pharmaceuticals for Children Act (2002), 110

bioequivalency of generics, 22

Biogen, 6

biotech stocks
- concern over drop in at J.P. Morgan Healthcare Conference (2016), 1–2

Bloomberg, 1, 16

boy scout contract clauses, 59–61, 137
- defined, 24
- Product hopping by Endo and, 78–79

brand-name drug companies
- costs to society of unscrupulous monopoly extensions and patent abuse by, 23
- efforts of to block generic competition, 9
- loss of market share after generic drug entry, 7
- use of clinical trial data of by generic competitors, 22

business method patents, 83

carve-out requests, 103–04
- carve-outs defined, 103
- for generic Abilify (antipsychotic, Otsuka), 110–12
- for generic Crestor (AstraZeneca), 108–10, 111–12
- for generic Skelaxin (King Pharmaceuticals), 105–08

Celgene (pharmaceutical company), 83–84

Cipro (antibiotic, Bayer)
- *In re Cipro* antitrust case, 46–47